O9-CFS-945

Directing for Television

Conversations with American TV Directors

Brian G. Rose

The Scarecrow Press, Inc.
Lanham, Maryland, and London
1999

SCARECROW PRESS, INC.

Published in the United States of America
by Scarecrow Press, Inc.
4720 Boston Way
Lanham, Maryland 20706

4 Pleydell Gardens, Folkestone
Kent CT20 2DN, England

British Library Cataloguing in Publication Information Available

Library of Congress Cataloging-in-Publication Data

Rose, Brian Geoffrey.
Directing for television : conversations with American TV directors / Brian G. Rose.
p. cm.
Includes index.
ISBN 0-8108-3591-6 (cloth : alk. paper)
1. Television—Production and direction—United States.
2. Television producers and directors—United States—Interviews.
I. Title.
PN1992.75.R59 1999
791.45'0233—dc21 98-39159
CIP

™ The paper used in this publication meets the minimum requirements of American National Standard for Information Sciences—Permanence of Paper for Printed Library Materials, ANSI Z39.48–1984.
Manufactured in the United States of America.

for my mother

CONTENTS

PREFACE

I first became intrigued by the craft and techniques of TV directing fifteen years ago, when I began researching my book *Television and the Performing Arts* (Greenwood Press, 1986). As I traced the history of televised opera, dance, theater, and music, I viewed hundreds of programs of extraordinary quality. What struck me about these broadcasts was not only the high level of performances, but also the unusually responsive directing. Fortunately, I was able to meet many of the directors who had worked on these shows and to discuss with them in detail how they approached their material and essentially recreated large-scale theatrical works for the limits and possibilities of the small screen. My interest in examining the specific methods and artistry of cultural programming's most prominent directors led to my next book, *Televising the Performing Arts* (Greenwood Press, 1992), which collected my interviews with Merrill Brockway, Kirk Browning, and Roger Englander.

The achievements of televised opera and ballet directors might seem easy to celebrate—after all, these directors have bravely dedicated themselves to the rarefied and always perilous world of television and the fine arts—but I began to wonder about the challenges of other forms of TV directing. What was involved in directing sports or news or prime-time entertainment? What skills needed to be mastered and how did TV directors go about acquiring them? I also wanted to find out what made TV directing different than directing theater or film and why its practitioners were accorded so little attention and respect compared to their more illustrious stage and motion picture counterparts.

To answer these questions I spent a great deal of time in television control rooms and studios, watching directors in action and talking with them about what they do and how they do it. I was immediately struck by the fact that TV directing is as diverse as TV programming itself, with each format having its own distinctive strategies and tempos. I wanted to explore the varying methods directors use in coming to terms with the major television genres and to do so in a way that would capture the energy and enthusiasm I invariably saw them bring to their work. A series of interviews seemed to be the best approach and this book is the result of five years of conversations with directors representing virtually every part of the TV schedule. I am extraordinarily grateful for their cooperation and kindness and their willingness to patiently explore the intricate aspects of their craft.

I am also grateful for the support I received from the Directors Guild of America, which has a long tradition of encouraging critical studies of film and television directors. The DGA provided a crucial entree to most of the directors I met, and several of my interviews originally appeared in the pages of the *DGA Magazine*. I would like to thank the DGA for their permission to reprint them in this book. I would also like to thank the DGA's Executive Director Jay D. Roth, and the staff of its New York office, including Eastern Executive Director Alan Gordon, Paul Erbach, John D'Angelo, and Gerry Angel, who were so gracious in their assistance during the many years I worked on this project.

My investigation into the broader world of directing for television received its initial impetus from Dick Pack, the editor of *Television Quarterly*. My interviews with TV directors first began appearing in his magazine in the early 1990s and Dick continued to support my research at every opportunity. I am grateful for his inspiration, and for his kind permission to allow me to reprint the many articles I wrote for him in this book. Another vital source of encouragement was Ron Simon, curator of the Museum of Television and Radio, who once again provided me with many important leads and helped me keep this latest project on track.

My colleagues at Fordham University's Department of Communication and Media Studies offered an intellectually challenging environment in which to test my ideas, and I would like to thank the University for awarding me a Faculty Research grant to underwrite my field work.

Many friends also sustained me throughout my writing, including Michael Barson, Jean Behrend, Alexandra Isles, Serena Leigh, and Elisa Shokoff.

For more than two decades, Kassie Schwan and I have shared just about everything, including thousands of happy hours critically and not-so-critically watching the small screen. I simply couldn't have done this book without her.

Introduction

While it's no longer in critical favor, there's no question that the *auteur* theory (the 1950s French doctrine extolling the director as the true "author" of a film) helped elevate the role and the power of American motion picture directors. Movies are now routinely identified as being "by" Spielberg or Tarantino, for example, and film directors often share marquee status with Hollywood's biggest stars.

But in American television, the *politique des auteurs* has never really caught on (despite a few earnest academic efforts). It's easy to understand why. Unlike their glamorous Hollywood counterparts, television directors tend to toil in relative, though fairly well-paid, obscurity. There are no TV shows in which the director's name comes above the title, nor are TV directors the subject of retrospectives or categorized according to prevailing styles and themes. Their careers are not studied in college courses; their work is rarely profiled and little understood.

One reason for this comparative neglect is the simple fact that in contrast to film, the television industry operates as a producer-based system. The power clearly lies with producers or producer/writers like Steven Bochco or David E. Kelley who maintain a large degree of control over a program's story, cast, and overall approach. This is equally true of nonfictional formats such as news and sports, with its legendary producers like Don Hewitt and Roone Arledge. As a result, TV directors perform in a somewhat different capacity. Rather than function as a "lone visionary" (a common misperception in film promoted by *auteurism*), directors in television usually work as a part of a highly integrated team, with final authority resting with the producer.

Yet these structural differences do not inherently preclude directorial creativity. TV directors are the ones responsible for how things *appear* on the screen, which includes everything from pacing to framing, from shot selection to graphic superimpositions, from instant editing to the blending of several layers of visual and audio material. To this is added the distinctive pressures of an electronic medium—immediacy and speed. Unlike directing theater or film, a good portion of television is done live or live-on-tape; even prime-time fictional programming is produced at a dizzyingly fast rate. TV directors must be able to react quickly, often to a vast amount of information, while also being alert to the dynamics of composition and emotional content (whether through performance or live action).

Far more than their counterparts working on the stage or screen, television directors tend to specialize, concentrating their energies on one particular format. News directors, for example, may occasionally try their hands at other forms of nonfiction programming, but they rarely, if ever, venture into fiction. So too with directors of sports broadcasts, talk shows, and entertainment specials. Comedy directors usually remain in comedy, though prime-time drama directors may sometimes make the leap to feature films (or more likely to movies-of-the-week). On the other hand, music video directors never seem to move to conventional television of any sort, but will often be picked up by Hollywood in its relentless quest for the youth market and flavors-of-the-month.

A primary reason for such directorial specialization is that each type of TV programming demands its own individual skills and techniques. Live formats, like news and sports, are very different enterprises than fictional formats (normally shot on film) like dramas and sitcoms. These generic boundaries have their roots back in the medium's earliest days, when television's unique ability to broadcast performances and events "as they happened" was promoted as its major asset. To this end, directors were trained using a model developed in live network radio. Rather than work exclusively on the studio floor, as was common in theater and film, broadcast directors were based in the control room. Though it might be only be a few feet down the hall (or later as distant as several thousand miles), the control room became the centerpiece of production, with all material flowing into its myriad monitors, speakers, and switchers. Directors were now connected to the studio stage largely through electronic means, such as cameras, microphones, and headphones, and they shaped the final product as it occurred, editing live for immediate transmission.

Interestingly, this method of production was employed regardless of format during the late 1940s through the mid-1950s, when the TV industry was centered in New York City. Drama, commercials, newscasts, quiz shows, and variety shows all utilized two or three cameras arranged within a generally cramped studio setting. What made this type of directing so challenging was its reliance on multiple control-room monitors and instant editing. The varying perspectives provided by the studio cameras (and their rotating assortment of lenses) permitted a new type of flexibility in shot selection. At the same time, it made the director's job far more demanding, since attention needed to be paid not only to the changing views from the monitors but also to instructing the cameras where to go next. Adding to the pressure were the strict time constraints and the finality of the editing process—once the shot was chosen, there was no going back for retakes.

While these live production practices were evolving in New York, an alternative filmed-TV approach was developing on the West Coast. *I Love Lucy* led the way by adapting the three-camera studio system of live television to motion pictures. The sitcom's proscenium-stage performances were photographed from the unconventional (for Hollywood) perspective of the audience, with 35 mm cameras replacing electronic ones. Rather than light, block, rehearse, and shoot one shot/setup at a time (the traditional film technique), the director now could plan scene by scene, filming the action in continuous takes that would later be assembled in post-production. The chief difference of the *Lucy* method from live TV was the absence of both the control room and the tension of instant cutting. Shooting on film permitted the director to remain on the studio floor, with the performers and technicians, and the luxury of choosing which shots to use during the final editing process.

As the popularity of this approach grew, particularly as prime-time episodic TV abandoned New York for Hollywood in the late 1950s, not all fictional TV programs embraced the multi-camera, stage-bound style. Many sitcoms and all one-hour dramas continued to employ standard film production techniques, opting for the greater control and versatility of shooting with one camera. Though it was somewhat more expensive, directors could make their programs at least resemble the look of the big screen, with detailed lighting, flexible camera angles, and, on special occasions, remote locations.

Gradually, electronic TV cameras and separate control rooms found their way to Hollywood as well, where they were used for some half-hour comedies (though the majority would continue to be shot using the multi-camera film approach) and entertainment specials. These video productions resembled their earlier East Coast counterparts, except for one crucial distinction—they weren't broadcast live. Thanks to the introduction of videotape in 1956, the pressures of instant editing were no longer an overriding concern; mistakes could now be corrected with retakes or with footage captured by another camera and substituted in post-production. For directors, not having to worry about getting things perfect on the first take made it easier to concentrate on non-technical aspects, such as performances and pacing, which were sometimes neglected in the stress of live television.

As Hollywood became the center for fictional television programming, whether shot on film or tape, New York remained the home of live TV, which now meant reality-based formats such as news, sports, and talk. However, with the introduction of new technologies, the task of directing these formats became much more complicated. Each advance, whether lightweight ENG[electronic newsgathering] cameras, microwave antennas, remote trucks capable of carrying an entire engineering complex, communication satellites, or computerized graphics, brought new possibilities and new problems. News directors were now able to quite literally bring the world into the control room; sports directors could go anywhere to cover an event and think nothing of setting up dozens of cameras. But this dramatic increase in scope and versatility also meant far greater directorial responsibilities and pressures. The more cameras being used, the more images to monitor; the more satellite remotes employed, the more need for the most precise technical coordination (and the larger the chance for something to go wrong). If the pace of live TV had been relentless before, the continuing addition of new television technologies now made live TV directing seem like supervising Mission Control.

While it's true that most live TV operates out of the major networks' headquarters in Manhattan, the division of East vs. West Coast directing is not a precise one—there are a few fictional series (both on film and tape) shot in New York, just as there are various live events (awards shows, newscasts, and celebrity trials) broadcast from Hollywood. But regardless of where they work or in what format, TV directors rarely receive the respect or prestige of their counterparts in other arts. Their achievements tend to go unrecognized, I suspect, largely because of the nature of the medium in which they toil. Not only is the visual frame much smaller than motion pictures or theater (thereby discouraging flashy directorial "signatures"), but there are rarely single works to contemplate, since most TV is series based, with multiple directors (once again removing the stamp of the autonomous "author"). Television's very ubiquity and its blatant commercialism and industrial structure have also helped to minimize the director's role. In the eyes of the industry, they are frequently viewed as replaceable technicians; in the eyes of the public, they're simply part of the crawl of names at the beginning or the end of the show.

To change these perceptions requires a reappraisal of what TV directors do and how they do it. Working in a hybrid medium like television, which enthusiastically incorporates elements from its fictional and nonfictional predecessors, makes the director's position somewhat confusing. Are they stagers of small thirty- or sixty-minute playlets? Directors of serialized mini-movies? Instant editors of live journalism? Electronic choreographers combining vast arrays of images, graphics, and sound? The answer depends on the format and on recognizing that TV directors utilize an arsenal of skills gleaned from theater, film, newsreels, and radio. Sports coverage, for example, often resembles epic drama, with its grand battles and emotional close-ups. Talk shows are often staged like small drawing-room comedies or intense character studies. Directing live news events requires the ability to shape a "story" and give it a form and style as it happens (often for hours at a stretch).

Ironically, the sheer variety of challenges facing TV directors—economic, logistical, technical—contributes to their comparatively understated status. Even within their own specialties, they must be adept at so many different crafts and procedures that their creative roles are often overlooked. Few people consider the tremendous expertise involved in directing live news and sports or in maintaining the performance style and dramatic energy of episodic television. Working with greater speed and urgency than any of their counterparts, TV directors still manage to produce an extraordinary amount of programming that is compelling to watch and of surprisingly high quality.

While it's doubtful that the *auteur* theory will ever find a home in television—such a romantic celebration of individualism is much more suited to the glamour of film—it's time to reevaluate the nature of TV directing and the talents of its practitioners. Much as we tend to take the medium for granted, the skills and artistry TV directors employ in shaping what we see deserve to be recognized.

Early Morning News and Talk

Joe Michaels

Directors of network morning news programs have one of the toughest jobs in television—they're responsible for directing ten hours of live programming per week, fifty-two weeks a year. It's a formidable challenge, not only because of the sheer quantity of material, but also because of its variety. The 7-9 a.m. morning programs are a grab bag of formats, combining news, interviews, cooking and lifestyle segments, live remotes, and musical performances.

The demands are particularly intense at NBC's *Today Show*. With the move to spacious ground-floor, glass-windowed studios at Rockefeller Center in 1995, the program quite literally transformed itself. The confined, traditional studio space of "30 Rock" and its confining atmosphere were blown apart and replaced by the energetic environment of midtown Manhattan. The *Today Show* now takes full advantage of what lies outside its windows, utilizing the crowds and street activities as often as it can. This has helped lead to a surge in the program's ratings and to a more interesting workday for the show's director, Joe Michaels. Interviews, weather reports, and even news segments can now take place outdoors, and extravaganzas employing up to nine cameras are not uncommon (in warm weather).

As the director of the *Today Show* since 1994, Joe Michaels must also deal with the fact that there's no such thing as a routine day. Because the program is news driven, the schedule may instantly shift in reaction to breaking stories, sometimes devoting the entire two hours to one event. Even on less momentous days, executive producer Jeff Zucker frequently juggles the segment lineup in response to new developments or in an effort to improve pacing and flow.

While the control room of the *Today Show* is often a hectic, pressure-filled environment for Joe Michaels and his technical crew, it's also an environment of camaraderie and good cheer, united by the massive effort of daily live TV production. The same easy-going professionalism that viewers find so attractive when watching the *Today Show* is clearly mirrored behind the cameras as well.

How did you get into directing?

Around 1977 I became a utility assistant director at NBC, where I basically got to work on every type of program. That continued for two wonderful years, and then in 1979, Mike Weisman, who was executive producer at NBC Sports, hired me and John LiBretto to work for him. We went through the ranks, and by the time we left we were directing football games and tennis. After twelve years on the road, I was tired, and I came back to work on *Sunrise* as an associate director, and moved up to backup director. I then moved to the *Today Show* in 1989 as an A.D. [associate director], then in 1991 became the director for about eight months. When Steve Friedman became executive producer of the show, he hired Bob McKinnon from ABC as director, which was fine with me. He was there for about a year and a half; Friedman left and was replaced by Jeff Zucker, and I returned as director of the show in 1994.

What do you think are your biggest challenges as director of Today*?*

Besides the hours and besides ten hours a week of live television? Basically, it's the amazing range of the show, where you can go from some celebrity dying, where everything has to be treated with great care and seriousness, to circus clowns performing outside on the street. The toughest part of the show is that you can do anything on it—in one day.

How do you gear yourself as a director to be responsive to such changes in tone?

Let's take an example. Sonny Bono died a few days ago, and so the first half hour of the show was very sensitive and emotional in tone. You have to get in that mode, which primarily means great attentiveness to the guests that are being interviewed. Everything is much slower paced, with far greater use of dissolves and pushing in cameras closer to the subjects, who may be crying, as a way to convey as much emotion as possible. Still, you're not looking for a tabloid approach as much as a serious news approach where you're as careful as possible in how you treat the material.

Then, in the next half hour, you may continue the Sonny Bono story a bit, but you also have a cooking segment, which is designed to be more fun. Here, as a director, you try to be quicker and use more reaction shots. Then, at 8 o'clock, you may open with a football player kicking a field goal out on the street. Three different kinds of things, all in the same show.

What about when breaking news occurs, and the pre-planned format of the show has to be abandoned?

At this point it ceases to be as much a director's call. For example, when we're using satellites to bring the story we have tech managers and production managers and unit managers. If something happens, and Jeff Zucker, the executive producer, decides to go with it, you hear a whirlwind behind you—satellites being ordered, reporters and producers getting in place, and eyewitnesses being set up. I sit there and wait until they get what they need, and then I follow what Jeff orders, in terms of when we cut to location, when we come back to the studio, who we're interviewing next, and so forth.

A good portion of the Today Show *is made up of interviews. What do you think is the key to good interview directing?*

You've got to listen. When I've been unhappy with what I've done, it's usually because I didn't listen. That's one of the great things about our show is that everybody listens—camera people listen, producers listen, the technical director listens. And if I'm not paying attention at any given spot, they let me know. Everything is a gigantic team effort—you simply couldn't do a show like this without a crew that really cares about the show.

One of the signatures of the program, beginning in its early years, and then picking up again three years ago, is its street-level studio, with an eager crowd outside. What has the move to this open-type studio meant for you as a director?

It's made the show twenty times harder. Now, you're no longer restricted to the studio with four sets or six sets or whatever the program is configured for that day. You now have windows, which makes it extremely difficult to shoot technically in terms of changing lighting. Plus you have whatever is going on outside, which you can't ignore. We're lucky to be in Rockefeller Center, so there are always tourists, and I mean always. Even in the worst blizzard we've had in years, we had a crowd outside big enough to fill the window.

How many cameras do you have stationed outside?

On a regular day when we have no outside production I have one camera for Al Roker. We have a wide cover shot from a remote camera stationed above Rockefeller Center. When we have any kind of interview situation outside, I'll add another camera. It can grow from there. Once we had an extravaganza concert in the summer with musicians and an artist and we used nine cameras, plus a helicopter and the remote camera.

How much planning is involved for these outside remotes?

Obviously there is a great deal of technical planning in terms of the logistics of camera equipment and so on. I'll block it out in my head and in the morning we may have a chance to rehearse each segment. But when you're actually on the air, the talent begin to ad-lib, and the planning goes out the window. That's what makes it the kind of show it is—you don't know what's going to happen next. On the other hand, all of your advance planning may shift if the executive producer looks at the scene and says, "I don't like it, let's do this instead" and all of a sudden, at the last minute, you're moving your cameras from where you thought you were going to do it. You can pull your hair out, but it's still a lot of fun. It's like a big jigsaw puzzle—when you get to it, you try to put all the pieces together and make it look good on the air.

I guess if you had to make a defining statement about the show it would be that nothing is stable and fixed.

That's right, nothing. Even if you have a plan, and you decide yes, this is definitely what we're going to do—bam, a plane crashes. It's tough to stay on your feet, two hours a day, five days a week, but when something happens, everybody gets on their toes. Our executive producer at that point turns into a coach—he's constantly up on the show, and rarely, if ever, laid back. That's a big help to have a guy pushing you onwards.

It's funny, we all make mistakes. But on a two-hour, primetime special, if a camera person, or technical director, or director makes a mistake, that might be the last time you'll do that show. On our show, you've got to go with the flow, and recognize that sometimes people are going to have a bad day, particularly when you're doing ten hours of live production a week, early in the morning. Still, there are not a lot of mistakes on *Today*.

Plus you do have the option, at least for West Coast viewers, of redoing segments.

We can even redo a segment at 9 a.m. for central or mountain time viewers, and if it's a breaking story, we do a fair amount of updating for these time zones. We particularly like to localize a story for the west coast, and do more on it at 10 a.m. for them.

Discuss your relationship as a director with the cast.

I've been really fortunate in having a wonderful group of talent to work with. I was lucky when I first came on the show because I had worked with Bryant Gumbel before in sports, and knew him for about fifteen years, and adored him. He's a consummate professional, and it's impossible to throw him, ever. The only time he was ever caught was his last day, when he still knew what was going on, but just couldn't handle it emotionally. It was the only time he didn't know what was going to happen next, and didn't know what to do or say. I could make all the mistakes I wanted and he would cover them up for me. That's the kind of talent he was. If we were juggling and changing the show around at the last minute, it would look like he had had days to rehearse it. And that makes you look great.

Katie Couric was just starting out when I joined up, and is an incredibly fast learner. She's been a pleasure to work with, and just gets better and better.

Matt Lauer took over as co-host about a year ago, and I felt it was important for me as a director to protect him while he got his feet wet. With Bryant, for example, I could go out of my way to make him look bad and he still came off great. Once Stevie Wonder was performing live, and one of my camera people broke away and gave me a shot showing Bryant standing up, pretending he was singing. I cut to him, and everybody laughed. When Matt first started, I would never think of doing that. I didn't want to do anything to hurt his credibility. My job was to make him look good, and he's grown tremendously in the role.

Another example—in interview situations, when Bryant was getting tough with somebody, you'd go for Bryant. He may make a face—Bryant was good at that. If he disagreed with somebody, he'd be fair, but he'd let the person know he didn't quite agree with them. I wouldn't hesitate to cut to Bryant to show his reaction. With Matt, you might not have done that right away, only because you didn't want the press to start jumping on him, and you didn't want viewers to dislike him.

You're doing ten hours a week of very strenuous, live TV directing. What's it like for you at the end of the day?

If it's been a very complicated show, with remotes and helicopters, etc., you're definitely a little frazzled. Obviously, with any show, there are set routines you fall into, and we definitely have a certain look for the way we do each thing. But it's often hard to remember the ways we've handled everything in the past, so it comes out a little bit different each time.

When we were shooting at 30 Rockefeller Center in a confined studio, you knew you could only shoot the interview area maybe three different ways. But now we're shooting Katie and Matt inside and outside, with all sorts of variations.

I've been warned about burn-out, but it hasn't happened yet.

This interview took place at the Today Show *offices in New York in February 1998.*

Daytime Dramas

Larry Auerbach, David Pressman

Directors of TV soap operas may be the hardest working directors in the entertainment industry. Unlike their counterparts in film or theater, their activities are not limited to one or two projects a year, with lots of long planning and down time in between. Even the directors of prime-time television, who they most closely resemble, still lead a life of comparative ease, with a schedule measured by, at most, a little more than a dozen hours of actual on-air production per season, mixed with repeats and months off for summer vacation.

Until recently, soap opera directors rarely heard of long vacations or extended periods for reflection. They were simply too busy, staging up to a dozen hours per month of programs that never take off for the summer or end up as repeats half the year. Their working schedule alone, with days often running from 7 a.m. to late at night, in addition to extensive pre-production meetings and hours of preparatory script-reading and blocking, would be enough to defeat all but the heartiest veterans of stage or screen.

Yet, for all the demands of directing daytime drama, its practitioners are probably accorded the least respect of any comparable directors in New York or Hollywood. Part of this undoubtedly has to do with the genre they serve. Disparaged for decades as the respite of bored housewives, soap operas continue to be regarded as the low-rent district of television drama. Despite the increase in production values, its growing prominence and appeal (witness the large prime-time viewership which comes out of the woodwork for the annual Daytime Emmy Awards), and the renewed interest of academics (who now hold the genre in surprisingly high esteem), those who toil behind the scenes still tend to be viewed, in the words of Larry Auerbach, as "hacks."

Directors of daytime drama are also relegated to a different level of consideration because of the sheer quantity and profusion of their work. By being part of the regular daily TV schedule, new installments of their programs must be produced Monday through Friday, fifty-two weeks a year—a feat of abundance unequaled by any other dramatic format in history. As a result, the often factory-like methods required of soap opera production make it difficult to look at daytime directors in the same way we evaluate the individualistic efforts of *auteurs* in film or some prime-time TV.

Still, there is an artistry to soap opera direction that merits serious attention. As the following interview with Larry Auerbach and David Pressman reveals, staging a daytime drama calls for a tremendous variety of skills and talents. The primary qualification is the ability to shape and guide performances under the fiercest of time constraints. Because of the genre's extended storylines and long-term character relationships, soap opera directors play a vital role in helping the actors understand and develop their roles while maintaining an essential character stability that is often forgotten by ever-changing regimes of writers and producers.

Daytime directors must also be well-schooled in all the technical aspects of television production, since so much of the program is filtered through their eyes. Soap operas have no director of photography; instead, the lighting and camera work are guided by the director's feelings about the scene. So too is the editing and blocking, which is usually fashioned by the directors as they read the script for a given episode a few weeks in advance.

Though it is true that soap opera directors are rarely distinguished by a unique style or visual approach—keeping the show uniform from day-to-day and director-to-director generally precludes such overt signatures—their craftsmanship comes across more in creating dynamic performances and sustaining a high level of dramatic energy. It is here, in the struggle to produce an hour of lively and compelling new drama every weekday, that skilled daytime directors can truly make a difference.

With a combined seventy years of soap opera experience between them, the two men interviewed for this article have helped define the standards of resourceful daytime directing. Both Larry Auerbach and David Pressman came to soap operas with backgrounds in theater and live television—two environments that provided invaluable training for their work in daytime TV. Larry Auerbach studied drama at Northwestern University and after graduation moved to directing positions at NBC's network radio operations in Chicago. In 1949, he switched to television, where he worked on a number of the innovative live shows originating from Chicago. A few years later he moved to New York and quickly found a job as the first director of one of the earliest television soap operas, CBS's *Love of Life*. Originally broadcast live for fifteen minutes a day, Auerbach was the program's sole director for more than fifteen years, and he remained with the show until it went off the air in 1980. After directing *All My Children* from 1980-83, he spent the next nine years at *One Life to Live*. Since 1991, he has directed episodes of *As the World Turns* and *Another World*, as well as a new soap opera, *Family Passions*, produced in Toronto and scheduled for broadcast in both Germany and Canada.

David Pressman started out an actor, graduating from the Neighborhood Playhouse before directing plays in Toronto from 1936-38. After serving in World War II, he became a charter member of the Actors Studio in 1947, and one of the directors of their live TV program, in addition to directing several other New York-based live dramatic shows. Unable to work in television for more than a decade due to blacklisting, he directed several plays on Broadway as well as serving as the chairman of the Acting Department at Boston University and heading the Neighborhood Playhouse for five years. He returned to television in 1964, directing cultural programs for David Susskind. *The Nurses* was his first soap opera, which he began directing in 1966. After the show's cancellation in 1967, he spent two years on *Another World*, before moving to *One Life to Live*, where he has been a staff director since 1970. He has also directed prime-time episodes of *The Defenders*, *The Nurses*, *NYPD*, and *The Hallmark Hall of Fame*, as well as continuing his theatrical work in New York and regional theater.

In this interview, Larry Auerbach and David Pressman discuss the changes in soap opera production over the last four decades and the challenges of directing daytime drama.

Larry, you started out directing radio programs in Chicago and then made the switch to TV directing. What were some of the changes you encountered?

LARRY AUERBACH: It was certainly a learning experience. Now, of course, you had to think about the visual elements, rather than just the oral elements. I think it was certainly very helpful to have had the radio experience, because now when I go into a television control room I'm very much aware of the audio and sound effects. The audio guys I work with are grateful, since unlike a lot of directors I pay attention to them and don't find them a nuisance.

Obviously, TV directing was much more complicated and difficult, with many more things to consider. I learned all about timing from radio which was so important in the early days of television because you couldn't cut, there was no editing. You had to get on and get off.

What was it like to learn to direct three cameras live?

AUERBACH: The first couple of months I was in the control room I didn't see anything. It was just panic time. It was either sink or swim. They just threw you in, and nobody knew any better, thank God. I didn't see any boom shadows back then, though today they call me "eagle eye. "

Working in live television was tremendous preparation for working with taped television. Directors who started with live TV, like David and I did, do all the editing in our heads before we ever get in the control room. You had to know what you were doing, I think even more so than today.

Of course, back then you didn't have the kind of supervision that you have today. You didn't have three people sitting in the control room behind you, coming in there with the idea that "whatever I see I have to change."

So directors back then had much more creative power?

AUERBACH: Much more power and much more creative power. There was never a producer in the control room in TV back in the days of live TV in Chicago, much less an executive producer and a line producer.

How did you move to directing TV soap operas?

AUERBACH: I came to New York in the summer of 1951, taking a leave of absence to look after my father, who was very ill. I began looking for work in the city without much success. After about six weeks, Chicago called and said either you have to come back or quit. At that time, Danny Petrie suggested that I contact a guy I had worked with back in Chicago, Roy Windsor, who was now head of radio and TV for the BIOW advertising agency and was planning to do a couple of soap operas.

What was your knowledge of soap operas at this point?

AUERBACH: Except for sitting in the control room on the radio side and listening to all those soaps, zilch. There weren't any on TV to be found, or if there were, they were ill-fated and weren't really soap operas, but more continuing family stories. Not what I call soap operas.

I went to see Roy and he thought maybe I could do the pilot on his new CBS show *Love of Life*. The producer Carl Green interviewed me, but decided not to use me. Instead he hired Marcella Cisney, who worked as a staff director at CBS and was one of the first women directors. She ended up teaching at Michigan, I think. She did the pilot, but they weren't happy with it. They went through two more directors, but Roy still wasn't satisfied. Finally he called me up and said, "Can you start Monday?" and this was Thursday. I said sure, closed up my apartment in Chicago, got my car shipped here, and was ready to start.

I reported to the BIOW Company at 51st and Madison, which at that time was a very important advertising agency, with accounts from Procter & Gamble, Seagrams, and American Home Products. BIOW was producing it for American Home, which owned the show, and was its sole sponsor—a situation which doesn't exist anymore except for Procter and Gamble. I met my assistant director, who sat there with a feather boa around her neck and a pile of cigarettes in the ashtray in front of her—and it was Gloria Monty. She worked with me for three years, until Roy got *The Secret Storm* started, and he hired her to direct it.

What were your first impressions of this completely new environment?

AUERBACH: The casting had already been done for the most part, but in those days directors used to do the casting, along with the executive producer, who was Roy Windsor. We had a line producer, but there were no producers in the control room. The producers stayed, for the most part, in the office and watched the show on the air. We were live, for fifteen minutes a day, in black and white. The producer's job was to work with the writer, primarily on continuity issues.

What was your day like?

AUERBACH: In the morning, starting about 7:30, we had an hour of dry rehearsal, in a rehearsal hall, which allowed us to block organically, directly from what the actors were saying. Then at 9:30 we brought the cameras in to follow what we had created with the actors. A dress rehearsal followed, and then a take. After the show went off the air at 12:30, we would go have lunch for a half hour. We then had three hours of rehearsal in the afternoon. Then you would do your camera blocking on your script. It was in a rehearsal hall, with chairs marking out the sets. You maybe had a P.A. [production assistant] there, though I usually didn't since I timed everything myself. Then I would go to the office for an hour or so. Then I would go home and block my script for the next day. I directed all five episodes a week for a long time.

The three hours of rehearsal in the afternoon was a luxury, giving us as much time to plan next day's half-hour show as we're now given today to do a one-hour program.

What new challenges did you face as a director doing live daytime drama?

AUERBACH: It really wasn't that dramatic. It was somewhat different in having to work with the same group of actors day after day and establish the relationships with them that were required, but that's a situation that continues even up to this day.

My experience in live TV certainly helped, but so did my work in live radio, where we got on and got off in a finite period of time. Both of these experiences were important to have at this point—to know how to be able to start a show and finish a show and do it in fourteen minutes and thirty seconds. And to know that the cameras had to go from here to there to the other place, and that the cables had to come from here and not get crossed. There was a good deal of mechanics that I already had under my belt.

Like live TV and radio, there was no editing back then on *Love of Life*. If there was an error, you had to live with the error.

And were there any?

AUERBACH: Oh, sure, and plenty of close calls. American Home Products was the penny-pinching outfit of all time. We had a very low budget and we were limited to twenty-five appearances a week, which included principals and extras and everything else. So, for example, if you had six people on today, you could only have four people on tomorrow, and so forth.

One day I was doing a show with Peggy McKay, Dick Coogan, and Hildy Parks. Hildy was single at the time and she said to me after rehearsal one afternoon "I'm going down to Washington to have dinner with Justice Douglas." She was quite the lady about town. I said to her, "For God's sake, if the weather's bad, take the last train back, will you please?"

Well, in the evening, the weather was fine, but next morning when she got up, it was terrible fog. A friend of hers called me from Washington and said "The golden girl will not be there on time. She'll be there in time for dress." Then I got another call, "She won't be there for dress, but she'll be there for air." She never showed up, so we just had to fake it. There was nothing else I could do.

So I sat the cast down at a coffee table, and we wrote new lines to explain what she was going to be talking about. There were no teleprompters back then, so the script was written on little cards hidden by plates on a coffee table.

What was it like to direct a soap under the time pressures of live TV? Were you monitoring the time or was it an assistant director?

AUERBACH: No, we had a script girl, who would tell me, and then I would send word out to the stage manager to signal to the cast to either speed up or slow down. Plus you had credits at the end so that you had a little flexibility.

And you've got to remember that we had four live commercials to do, two thirty-second spots and two one-minute, which I also had to direct. Plus, I was the only director on staff for years, up until the time they started shooting *Love of Life* in color.

Roy Windsor, who was producing the show, wanted to give me a raise, and he went to American Home Products, saying color was much more difficult to do, and he'd need to hire an additional director. They agreed to let someone come in to work one day a week, but they refused to give me an increase. So I began doing a four-day a week schedule. A few years later, Daryll Hickman became the producer, and he felt four days a week was too much, so I went down to a three-a-week schedule, which I continued until the show went off the air in 1980.

When I went to *All My Children*, there were three directors on staff, and we averaged about one-and-a-half shows a week. Now on *As the World Turns*, there are five directors on contract.

Since you were the sole director on Love of Life *for close to fifteen years, did you try to develop a distinctive style so that when someone turned on the program they would say, "That's definitely Auerbach's work?"*

AUERBACH: The medium itself, for the most part, requires a certain way of doing things, particularly in terms of soap operas. It's shot with a lot of close-ups, at least it was back then because the sets were so much smaller. We wanted to concentrate attention to the characters, plus the fact we didn't have a lot of scenery in those days. We were limited in the amount of movement we could do, the equipment wasn't as flexible, the studios were smaller.

So technical factors had as much to do with shaping what you did as a director as anything else?

AUERBACH: They had a lot to do with it, and they still do.

David, you'd been a director of live prime-time drama for a decade before you moved to soaps. What lessons were you able to bring from that experience?

DAVID PRESSMAN: I never worked with live soap operas, but my first soap opera *The Nurses* in 1966, was done very much like a live show. We were given access to the videotape recorders at the network's engineering center at 2 or 3 p.m. and were given only a half hour. That was it. We did the show directly to tape, with no edits or retakes.

Sometimes, for special occasions, like a dream sequence, we would have pre-tapes. We would get the machines at a special time at twelve noon, say, and that would be rolled into the show.

What special challenges did soaps present to you as a director?

PRESSMAN: There was the pressure of having to do it rapidly and get it done in one day. It was a hard adaptation for me at the beginning, especially since I was directing all five episodes a week. There was also the challenge of getting the acting up to par.

Did you find there was a difference in directing soap opera actors compared to actors in other formats and media?

PRESSMAN: Most of the actors working on soaps were people who came from the theater or from film. The technologies might be different, but acting is acting. There's no such thing as special soap opera actors.

For both of you, was acting always your priority as a director?

AUERBACH: It always was and always should be.

PRESSMAN: What's missing now is that you really should be able to do a show with only two or three very good performers, a good script, and just black velour for the backdrop.

AUERBACH: Which was exactly the way we originally did it back in the 1950s. We had black velour and wainscoting about two feet high to delineate one area from another. We would put a desk or couch in front of it, and we would hang pictures from the air on trick wire.

PRESSMAN: And it would look exactly like it was walls. Sets for a long time were minimal. It wasn't a big deal.

AUERBACH: Mike Chase was my stage manager on *Love of Life* and he used to joke that the world's greatest salesman of black wallpaper went through Rose Hill, which was the name of the show's community.

PRESSMAN: Sam Leve was a wonderful stage designer on the CBS staff for many years, and he designed a circular cyclorama [a bent, blank wall made of sheetrock] that went around the entire studio, and that's what we hung pictures, and mirrors, and whatever. The color of that cyclorama for black-and-white TV was perfect and looked just like a wall.

AUERBACH: We didn't use a cyc; we used actual black velour flats. The basic reason was they were too cheap; they didn't want to spend the money for sets. They put up gray wainscoting, and a black flat, and then all you needed was set decoration.

PRESSMAN: One of the things that needs to be mentioned as well is the demanding technical nature of soap opera directing. During camera blocking, which followed the dry rehearsal in the morning, and usually took about an hour-and-a-half or two hours, we would have to concentrate all of our energies on the technical side. You have to solve all the problems of where the camera goes, is it a one-shot, a two-shot, a dolly, or a pan. The cameras have to be placed to avoid the boom microphones and their shadows. The actors are there only to verify their position, as they run their lines.

After the taping, we went over to the Hotel Empire to rehearse next day's show from about 3 to 5 p.m. We would stage and block everything, then I would mark my camera shots on the script. I would leave my script for my assistant director, Kenny Rockefeller, who by the way was a real Rockefeller, and he would come in early the next morning to get to work lining up the shots. The cast also had time for another rehearsal the day of the taping as well.

In essence, your job was split in two. You had to work creatively with the actors, and then suddenly shift gears to work with the cameras.

AUERBACH: And you can't separate the two. It's like movies.

PRESSMAN: You're staging in relation to the camera, and how the actor fits in. As you're blocking the show at home, you look at each scene in terms of its emotion and what you're going to do with the actors. Will you have them go to the phone or walk to the door? When will she act upset or happy? This is usually all our invention.

AUERBACH: Then you have an actor come in and say, "But I don't think I should sit down here." So then you have to figure out how are you going to deal with that mechanically, technically, or what reason can I give him or her for sitting at that point.

PRESSMAN: If it's an emotional reason, they'll generally accept it. Or you'll explain that you'll have to change all the shots. You are staging, you are acting teacher, you are acting coach, and you are an editor. When the show is being taped, the director has edited 98 percent of the show in his or her head, usually on paper the day before. Of course you make changes as you go along, as you see the set in the morning and discover that something just may not work, the furniture has to be moved, etc.

What did you feel your reputation was like as a director of soap operas? Were you regarded as low director on the totem pole?

AUERBACH: Absolutely. No question about it, and it still exists. It's still an elitist thing in the way other directors look down on us.

PRESSMAN: When I think of the way sitcom directors work and the hours they work and the salaries they're paid, and compare it to ours, it's ridiculous.

And this was true right from the beginning—you were slighted because you were working in daytime and what you did was for women?

AUERBACH: Yes, we were seen as hacks.

PRESSMAN: I've always felt that any daytime director who has been on a show at least a year can go and do a film tomorrow. Any guy who's only been doing film could not come in and do a soap.

AUERBACH: It would be impossible for me to do film because I wouldn't have the patience. I'd go nuts.

What skills did you have to have as a soap opera director that are different than directing other formats?

AUERBACH: The ability to deal with problems without bull. Just get it done.

PRESSMAN: Plus the special relationship one has with actors.

How do you approach acting for soap operas?

AUERBACH: That depends on the actor. With some, you have to approach everything as organic and as part of the method. With others you just have just to tell them where to stand and what to say and which way to turn. You can't generalize about it. The generalization is you have to know who you're dealing with.

PRESSMAN: I come mainly from the theater, and was a teacher of acting for years. It's my primary emphasis. Forget the special effects, and fires and floods they ask us to do. Acting is the focus.

Do you think you're given enough time to shape performances?

PRESSMAN: Never enough time, and we often have to deal with actors cruelly.

AUERBACH: And we often have producers that don't understand the first thing about acting so all of their emphasis goes on to the mechanics of things, or they ask for performance aspects that simply can't be done.

Such as?

AUERBACH: They want emotional transitions that aren't possible for a performer to achieve without just doing it arbitrarily. That's not the way you deal with most actors. Or you can't deal with an actor after a dress rehearsal and say "No, that's not what we want. *That's* what we want."

Acting is a tapestry and if you pull one thread out, the whole thing goes to pieces.

In what ways do these conditions force you to treat actors cruelly?

PRESSMAN: One of the problems is that producers often cast improperly, because they look for the body and not necessarily for the talent. Very often we'll do the auditions as requested by the producer, and we'll have four or five people. We'll select one, and say "there's your actor." And they'll respond, "Yeah, but we want the hunk." And they'll get the hunk, and a month into the show, they'll find out the guy can't act.

One time we hired an actress, and she was forced to do an incredible amount of emotional stuff, discovering she wasn't dead and so forth. Scene after scene she had to be crying, but she just wasn't up to it. I had to go out and say, "It's your job on the line, come on and do it." And I scared her, using the tactics of my position, to almost force it out of her. She was now crying all the time, scared of her job—but now the performance came out very well. Then the producer watched the take and said, "Why didn't you do it like you did the first day?" They simply don't understand. They think a performance is just something an actor can crank out because it's their job. An actor is not a machine.

You don't know how much the actors depend on the director to help them out in terms of creative guidance.

What happened to your schedule when soaps went from a half hour to an hour?

PRESSMAN: To me it was like working nine times harder.

AUERBACH: First of all, you don't have to be through at any particular time, so you can go forever—eight, nine, ten, or eleven o'clock at night.

PRESSMAN: This came about as well because of the technology and the new editing systems.

AUERBACH: Rather than the old system where we would have the videotape machines for only a half hour or an hour, we now have dedicated tape machines, assigned exclusively to us. The equipment was smaller, and cheaper, and the network could afford to give them to us.

Our day now basically goes as follows. You go in and block the actors. There are no dry rehearsals. You come in in the morning and your dry rehearsals and camera blocking are on the set at the same time. The actors go on the set and the cameramen are there, and the actors are acting, and the cameras are moving. And this is what I hate—you don't have a chance to sit down and work with the actors. I absolutely hate it.

What do producers now expect to happen in terms of the quality of performances?

AUERBACH: Quicker, they just want it quicker. You've got to follow a much tighter schedule.

PRESSMAN: The schedule for us actually begins much earlier than just coming in in the morning. I get the script for a show two weeks before. Blocking it out takes about six hours. There's a production meeting the following Wednesday. We talk over the floor plans for the six or seven sets in our large studio, and I might ask for a little bit more room here or there. Then I keep the floor plan, and get a mimeographed script. Then I sit down at home and block the show, which will usually be about 500 shots. Everything is there in the script—two-shots, close-ups, etc. Then a few days before the show I stop at the studio and talk to the lighting director. I show him the floor plan, where everything goes, where it will be moved, what the sets will look like, where the booms will go.

On the day of taping, I get in at 6:30 in the morning, look over the sets and the props, tell the prop guys what else I need, where the furniture should be moved (we change the position of furniture a lot to accommodate action we've invented that can't quite fit in to the design of the sets). At 7:15 I start rehearsing with the actors till about 9:30 or 9:45. Then I take a short break. From 10 to 12:30, we block actors and the cameras—we need that much time since I have a full one-hour show to do, plus usually a few extra scenes. Then it's time to break for lunch. I bring mine with me, go to the director's room and take a twenty-minute nap. At 1 we used to have a full dress rehearsal and then tape. No more. Now we dress/tape. Before, we would take a bunch of scenes, dress them, there are notes from the producer, discussion, fights, I deal with the actors and the crew, then we would tape. It's now a combined process, and we shoot a little bit out of sequence, doing all the scenes that take place in one set together, then move to the next set.

AUERBACH: It's a little bit different on *As the World Turns*. The director on that show is on his feet all day long, from the time you come in in the morning till sometimes late at night. During the blocking, for example, you go on the floor and block three scenes. Then because they don't have any floor monitors, you run from camera to camera to check the shots. Then you run into the control room and dress three scenes, talk to the producer, then go out and talk to the actors, then back to the control room to tape the three scenes. After that, you do the next three scenes, and so on. This goes on all day long, since they have a morning and an afternoon session. The morning session has got to be done by 2:15, then you immediately go into dry rehearsal for the afternoon session. The director doesn't get a lunch break—they bring you a sandwich. Then you go off to the other studio and do the same thing, until 7, 8, or even 11 o'clock at night.

PRESSMAN: I would really not like to lose the morning dry rehearsal, because that's where you really lay out how the scene is to be played. Plus you get a chance then to check your shots.

Do you think performances have suffered as a result of this incredibly pressured schedule?

AUERBACH: It depends on the actor. They're adaptable too, just like we have to be.

PRESSMAN: The people who come from the theater are the most

disciplined and the best to work with. They come in, they know their lines, they're there ahead of time.

AUERBACH: The older actors are frequently much better as well.

Soap opera actors must memorize an enormous quantity of material, far more than actors in any other field. What problems does this present for them and for you?

PRESSMAN: Some actors, particularly the veterans like Erika Slezak, Susan Lucci, and Robin Strasser are magnificent at it. They may not have all their lines memorized before they get in, but they're so expert they can pick them up during the day.

AUERBACH: For actors who are on four or five times a week, line memorization is a big issue, but as David said, they're experienced enough to pick up their lines in the morning, perhaps hold the script in their hands during dry rehearsal, and by the time we go to camera blocking, they know it. The ones who aren't so experienced may continue to hold the script during camera blocking, but then they've got it down.

There was a period during the early 1980s when many soap operas began to use teleprompters to help the actors with their lines. How did you feel this worked out?

PRESSMAN: Unfortunately, actors began to depend on them, they wouldn't really know the words comfortably, and very few knew how to use the prompters without making it look obvious. I remember one of the actors was nearsighted so she was constantly squinting to make out her lines. They eventually got magnifiers for them, but it didn't help. We only used the prompters for about five years up until about the mid-1980s.

AUERBACH: I would love to go back to live where the show simply had to get done at a set time, with no fuss.

PRESSMAN: I would love it too, particularly for the actors. Some of the young actors I work with today come in and don't even have their lines down. I'd say to them, "come on, you make $600, $700 a day to learn your craft. How dare you come into work and not know your lines cold?" They'd protest, but in the bottom of their hearts, not having been on the stage and working hard for their career, they know they can do it over again.

AUERBACH: It's a discipline problem. If we had to do it live, they'd have to know their parts. I hate it when an actor, right in the middle of taping, says "can I do it over again?" What can you do, you have to do it over.

You mentioned that in the past when a mistake occurred during taping, it was very difficult to do anything about it because you only had the network's VTRs for a very limited, set period of time. What happens now?

PRESSMAN: You stop and do a pick-up, since the editing and technology permits you to do it.

AUERBACH: The terrible problem with that is if you have a very emotional scene, and one of the actors makes a mistake and you have to do a pick-up, you have to stop and find the place to do the pick-up—well, by then, all of the emotion goes out of the scene. You're better off to just go back to the start of the scene and let them play it from there.

A dramatic change occurred in daytime drama when you were able to get out of the studio and shoot a few scenes or even an entire show on location. How did this come about?

PRESSMAN: The technology permitted it. Smaller cameras, simplified editing—all of these things made it much more feasible to leave the studio.

What was it like for you as a director shooting remotes, where previously you were confined to the studio?

PRESSMAN: It was fun. We were shooting with two cameras, sometimes three, unlike film production. In 1980, I did a week in Southampton, Long Island, where we rented a villa, all the major characters came out. We used two hand-held cameras, plus a Steadicam. There were fifty extras, as well as an elaborate horse race. The sequences were ultimately used in the next twenty shows.

AUERBACH: Even at that, you had to take the sequence of the remote and break it down, much like a film continuity script. You had to keep in mind what followed what, where the characters were at the end of the closing shot, even if the scenes were shot with a few days in between. It could get very complicated.

PRESSMAN: I think if a strictly movie guy came in to do these remote shots, with a single camera, it would have taken two weeks at least. We had to keep in mind how the scenes were built, how the conflicts developed.

So in essence you were shooting multi-camera, studio-style, while on location?

AUERBACH: Yes. I did a big remote on *All My Children* up in Canada for ten days. We shot two-camera material, for the most part, but with each camera on a separate tape machine. Then we had to go into the editing room, to put together what we shot on the isolated cameras. But you still had to do the editing in your head, so you knew that when this piece came up, and you might have done two or three takes, you wanted, for example, the second take only.

The assistant director would sit out in the remote truck, which was a quarter mile away, and I would be out by the cameras. The A.D. would keep a log, and I would be watching the separate monitors, which would be hooked up to each camera. We laid it out this way in advance, with the A.D. taking notes in the script so she could cue the cameras. You had to do the editing beforehand. We would be out in the field all day long, and I would go back to the hotel at night to get the next day's script ready.

PRESSMAN: I was talking to my son Michael Pressman, who's a director on *Picket Fences* and they're now starting to use two cameras more on prime-time film production. They find that it's better for editing, they can do the show quicker. But working in film, as opposed to video, is so different anyway.

AUERBACH: Take lighting, for instance. They've got a director of photography to help in so many areas. Our lighting director is hardly the same thing. We've got to place the cameras, worry where the booms are, watch for shadows. We've got to be our own director of photography.

The lighting director in television works for you. I go in to meet with him the day before with the floor plan and I say "here's where the actors are, here's where the cameras are, here's what angle I'm shooting from, here's where the booms going to be." And he lights from what I tell him. He doesn't tell me where the lights are going to go.

PRESSMAN: In the daytime situation, if the director is not prepared when he comes in the early morning for the first rehearsal with the actors, if he's not 102 percent prepared, it's a disaster. You can't come in, like a film director can, and say, I'm going to try this, and then we'll do a master shot, and then we'll cover it, and put it all together in the editing room.

AUERBACH: Plus, they'll do six takes.

When did you first begin to encounter the problem of soap opera producers making the kind of creative decisions formerly reserved for the director?

AUERBACH: For me it was when CBS took over *Love of Life* from Roy Windsor. There it was primarily network interference. They began a very active presence in the control room. They would come in and talk about the performance, without understanding that the performers can't be told to develop a particular emotional response just because the producers want them to have it at that point. They never comprehended that responses need to be organic and develop from the material and the emotional situation at the time.

This started a precedent and after that point, producers then routinely came into the control room, and a great deal of interference with the director's job began.

Producers who weren't very good would attempt to impose their desires on a framework which is very tightly constructed. The minute you attempt to do something like that, the whole thing begins to unravel. Far too often in the old days, you had producers come in and anything the director chose to do, it should be changed, or else you weren't earning your salary. You had a lot of second guessing, just because they were there.

If you have a good producer, they understand what's going on, realize how it works, and can make succinct notes that deal with the overall emotional level and the overall shooting scheme of a particular show.

PRESSMAN: I worked with Doris Quinlan for two years on *The Nurses* and seven years on *One Life to Live* and she was an ideal producer. She came from radio and had respect for directors. She never interfered. She might say, "David, I think the scene should be played so and so," and I would usually agree. The casting was done strictly between her and me, together. I wouldn't hesitate to go to her with script problems or anything else.

Paul Rausch, who was a producer of *Another World*, and later became head of CBS daytime, also did his job very well. I wasn't at work every day, but he was there in the control room, making sure the story and show went OK. Sometimes I would disagree with him about a scene and how it should be, but he would say, "But David, I'm here every day, and what we're doing today is a little too much compared with yesterday, so we should temper certain performances."

This brings up the issue of consistency—do you watch the show on the days you're not working?

AUERBACH: Sometimes, but you can't watch the stuff that's in sequence with yours, because it's being done too far in advance.

PRESSMAN: If I want to watch anything, I'll record it, and then watch it later.

AUERBACH: I read every script.

PRESSMAN: You have to, you have to know what's going on. Even now when I'm only doing one or two shows a month, it's essential. You have to keep up, and know where the actors are emotionally.

AUERBACH: You don't want to be in a rehearsal situation where the actor says, "Gee, but we changed that last week." You have to know when you read the script how it differs from what happened the week before and be prepared to deal with it in the studio. Often, it's a problem with the writers, who didn't read last week's script before they wrote this week's script. So you have to know how you're going to work around that kind of problem. Or you have to go to the producer and say "we have to change this."

PRESSMAN: I think the hardest part of daytime is the writing, because that's where it falls down very often, where you have writers who don't know what happened three weeks ago, or suddenly change characterization.

Will you be there when lines are changed to correct these problems?

AUERBACH: We may change them ourselves, or the actors may change them.

Is the producer involved?

AUERBACH: We try to avoid that. We have to turn in a script the day before, and the producer may take a look at the revised script, since I always put my changes on the cover, primarily for the sake of my production assistant. I'm always very careful not to change the author's intent, but I might change the way it's said to fit a particular performer's style.

PRESSMAN: Sometimes I feel the writers as they're writing don't try to stand up and speak their lines. They'll write alliterations and so forth that are impossible to say clearly.

You've both been associated with numerous daytime dramas in your career; did you find it difficult to move from one soap opera to another?

PRESSMAN: The basic technique is the same, inherited from live television. This is important to understand. In the days of live TV, we all developed the procedure and technology and techniques of doing half-hour or hour dramatic programs, using three or four cameras.

AUERBACH: Still, there are differences in the way some shows are shot. Some shows demand a lot more physical action, some demand that the pace be faster. As new man on the totem pole I want to fit in, unlike some directors who go to a new show and try to impose their way of working on the control room, for instance.

As a matter of fact, when I come in to a new soap, I'll go into the studio and spend at least several days there just to get the feel of the studio and the feel of the crew—see what cameramen are doing what kind of work, see how the A.D. works—just to get a feel of how the show gets put together and what the intangible feeling is around the studio and around the control room.

Over the last ten years, what other changes have you seen in soaps, other than the stronger role of post-production?

AUERBACH: The casts have gotten bigger, the stories have become more complicated, and I think there's been a growth in the medium.

And that's presented new directorial challenges?

AUERBACH: Any time you're dealing with fifteen people instead of eight, you have more challenges. When you're dealing with a story that's more complicated, it requires more of you in terms of what you know about what's going on and what the show's emotional structure is.

After working in soap operas for decades, did the work ever become routine? Do you ever get bored?

AUERBACH: No, because every day presents a different problem. You have a different mix of actors, you may have a different mix of crew, and certainly a different script. The days may be generally the same, but specifically different.

On the whole, it's a challenging, demanding type of job that requires something different every day.

Where do you see soap opera production moving in the future?

PRESSMAN: The only thing I can see is that maybe we'll shoot more and more out of sequence. Technology permits you to do extraordinarily sophisticated editing in assembling pieces together.

So you feel it might move more to a style of film shooting, with everything out of sequence?

PRESSMAN: We do everything out of sequence now. We shoot everything that takes place on one set for each show, then move to another set. All this requires a high degree of preparation, including more pre-editing.

AUERBACH: You may even do Friday's show before you do Wednesday's show, depending on the availability of actors. Still, I think the overriding issue will always be the need to save money, and soaps are going to have to be made cheaper.

How can that be achieved?

AUERBACH: You can have fewer actors, you can have fewer extravaganzas, you can have fewer remotes and fewer sets.

PRESSMAN: I'd like to see them move back to half-hour soaps. You can tell a better story. With an hour you sometimes feel they're filling in. It's a lot to do to create that much drama every day, five days a week.

I should note that I've always really enjoyed doing daytime, because you're dealing with your profession—actors—which is really what it's all about. The technology works hand-in-hand with this.

AUERBACH: Beginning directors get more concerned with the mechanics of directing than the performance, but the performance is the heart of the matter. I can tell somebody about how to shoot a show, where the cameras have to go, etc., but that's just mechanics.

PRESSMAN: Anybody can learn that.

AUERBACH: But you either know how to deal with actors or you don't.

And that can't be taught?

PRESSMAN: Yes and no, but certainly by example. I've taught directing workshops up in Maine and I tend to take the directors and break them up into groups and make them direct each other. Turn them into actors.

The rest is technology.

AUERBACH: And that's what you find the producers talking about. "There's a boom shadow there," and I'd say "how about a brain there, it will cut out at home [studio monitors reveal more of the frame than home viewers can see on their consumer TV sets]. " They don't even know what that means—cut out at home.

PRESSMAN: Technical mistakes just aren't important. Technology does permit us to do anything if we want to, but that's not the heart of the matter. You can do the show without it. All you need is a good story.

This interview was conducted at the Directors Guild offices in New York City in August 1994. It originally appeared in Television Quarterly, Vol. XXVI, No. 3, 1995.

Afternoon Talk Shows

Bryan Russo, Duke Struck, Joe Terry

Talk shows might seem like a fairly easy directing assignment. There's no complicated script to follow, the cast is small (a host and a few guests), the production demands modest (a couple of chairs and a wireless mike).

But inside the often cramped confines of the studio, the talk show is an explosive arena of emotions and energy that many directors compare with the excitement and unpredictability of televising sports. The structure of the program may appear routine—host-guest-audience—but the conversations and interactions can shift gears instantly, with no one quite sure how a segment or program will turn out.

Probably more than any TV format, directing a talk show depends on listening. Directors in the control room pay as much attention to audio as they do video, carefully monitoring what is being said as the surest guide to planning their next shots. How things are being said also plays a role as well, shaping the pace and overall feel of the program.

As talk show directors readily admit, the format's most important element is the host. Unlike an anchorperson or M.C., hosts like Oprah Winfrey, Phil Donahue, or Maury Povich are charismatic points of identification for the audience at home and in the studio. They act as valuable filters for the show's churning range of emotions and the true centerpiece of the daily drama. But it's more than simply keeping the camera on the star at all times. Talk show directors must skillfully weave the host into the fabric of the events, selecting just the right moment to cut to a reaction shot, or when to close in as the questioning takes a particularly intense turn.

Integrating the studio audience is another important resource, not just for the host, but also for the director. Faces in the crowd serve as useful punctuation, quick accents to underscore a point or shift the mood. Confined to the control room, talk show directors are particularly dependent on the abilities of their crew to act as their electronic nervous system, sensing the temperature of the audience and finding the telling shots without being asked.

There's no rule book to follow in talk show directing. Each program has its own unique personality and each episode its own rhythm. But, the format does depend on directors who are unusually alert to the dynamics of live television, even if most of the shows are done live-to-tape. The three directors interviewed for this article all have strong backgrounds in live programming, which they bring to the fore in their current assignments. Arthur "Duke" Struck worked for more than twenty-five years as a sports and news director at CBS and ABC, including Super Bowl telecasts and *Good Morning America*, before he joined the *Oprah Winfrey Show* in 1995, which he directed until 1997. Joe Terry had two decades of experience in network and local news, covering events such as the Challenger disaster and the royal wedding of Prince Andrew and Sarah Ferguson, before he began working on the *Maury Povich Show* when it premiered in 1991. He directed the program until 1997, when he moved to the *Oprah Winfrey Show*. Bryan Russo was a staff technical director at NBC working on every type of program originating in New York before joining the *Phil Donahue Show* in 1985 and becoming its director in 1987 (in June 1996, the program shut down production after a record-breaking 29 years).

As their interviews reveal, the talk show has clearly stimulated and challenged all three directors. Though they often face brutal production schedules (with two or sometimes three or even four tapings a day), they share a common enthusiasm for their work and its distinctive demands. Talk shows may seem the same day after day, week after week, but to directors in the control booth, every program is a special event.

Bryan Russo

You'd been the technical director of the Phil Donahue Show *since its move to New York in January 1985. How did you make the rather unusual transition to director two years later?*

David McGrail resigned as the show's director in the fall of 1986. I was approached by the show's executive staff to audition for the slot by directing three shows. Our schedule at the time was four live programs a week, with the fifth taped later on Thursday. I can't recall if any of the ones I directed were live, but I know the first was on tape, and after my three-show audition, they asked me if I wanted the job. I instantly said yes.

It's quite a shift going from technical director to director. How did you initially approach the position?

The transition was not all that difficult, because I was going into a very known entity—after all, I'd been switching the show for two years. I certainly became much more aware of audio cues. Remember, my experience had been largely video, first as a cameraman and then as a technical director, and I now had to concentrate on a whole new range of factors.

Of course, you had an advantage in having worked your way up with a supportive crew around you, colleagues who you knew well and who knew your strengths.

Absolutely. They couldn't have been more cooperative or positive. It was like "local boy makes good." They were very, very willing to let this happen. But this good feeling all around was very short-lived, since I now had an entire new range of issues to deal with. Quickly, I had to start dealing on a very real level with the personalities of the production staff. I think most directors will be willing to admit that the actual calling of the shots is only part of the job. The other part of the job is understanding the people around you, and learning how to translate their ideas into a working television show.

At the start I was so gung ho and anxious I would track down the producers a week ahead of time and try to get an understanding of everything they thought was going to happen on their particular program seven days later. We'd not only talk about the topic, but each of the guests, how they might relate to one another, what tape clips they plan to use, etc. Then I'd start planning from what they told me. However, what often happened is that as the day of the program came around, things would completely change—guests would drop out, the format would get shifted. I began to discover that it simply didn't pay to plan that far ahead—I was chasing my tail. I started arranging basic panel shows the morning they were to be aired.

How do you help the producer in creating their "vision" for that particular program?

I have them tell me what the story is—outline each guest, where the sparks of confrontation may lie, if they plan to have full-screen chiron quotes [electronically produced text, created on a Chiron character generator] from newspapers, if they have news clips, if they have a list of statistics. I wanted as much information as they could give me, primarily because I was shooting a live program and I didn't know where it was going. It's not like doing a ball game, which live as it is, at least has some parameters.

I also wanted to know how they envisioned the action taking place—when the guests would come out, who would be on stage with whom, who would likely be arguing with whom. I would then take this information back to my crew, and impart as much of it as I could. Because once the thing gets launched, it doesn't do me any good at that point to try to tell the camera people where the blow-ups might be. They've got to know as much as possible in advance so that they could go look for it. Since I'm in the control room I often can't see it.

So preparing this structure in advance is the crucial aspect of live talk directing?

For this style of show, letting the people in the crew know what *might* happen is a large part of directing. So that they can go into it with some forethought about what to look for.

You've worked in various kinds of live TV situations. What do you feel are the advantages of live talk directing?

Personally, I love live TV. My particular kind of personality lent itself to this approach, where if you made a mistake, you just kept on chugging. You simply didn't have the luxury to get caught up in an error, or else four more would quickly follow. Even when we did our tape shows, we kept it "live" by maintaining the same energy, and not stopping for anything but major technical problems. Phil was a "live" animal, and he never looked at tape shows that we used to do once a week as any different.

Live TV relies on the skills of the camera operators, who I have always thought of as very creative people. The joy for me as a director was to sit back and to orchestrate the shots these artists offer.

The key word is "offer." You give them their freedom to shoot what they think will work.

Absolutely. In this show there are certain parameters, certain cameras have to have the cover shot, or the single talking head of whoever's talking. But my instructions to the camera crew repeatedly are that if they see something happen, go for it. I'm stuck in the control booth, and the only way I'm going to know what's going on out there is if they show me. My favorite type of camera operators when we would travel on remotes (and unfortunately were unable to take our own local crew) were sports crews. They know how to react—they do live television, and they can follow the action.

The Phil Donahue Show is more like a ball game than any other television program. Sure, you have parameters—you have guests, you have certain things certain guests are probably going to say, Phil has a certain number of tape bits he may use—but after that, you really don't know. I can't tell you the number of times after a show I've come up to a producer and found out that guests did exactly the opposite of what they said they were going to do, that all the pre-production interviews had gone right out the window. And that's the genius of Phil, because he can then take what's now happening and do with it the special things only he can do.

One of the instructions I always give my crews is that I'd rather catch you in a swish pan [a rapid camera movement from left to right or vice-versa] going for the right thing than have you lay back and not get it. They're the ones who've got to make the decision, as they look out of the corner of their eyes, if they see a guest getting emotional, or something happening in the audience. Better to try and hope for that magic moment, than to just stand back, cut to a safe cover shot and never know that something special had happened. I'd rather be aggressive than safe, occasionally getting an ugly shot for the sake of what we might end up with.

Where does Donahue *fit into this equation?*

I directed the *Donahue Show* the way Phil wanted the show to be directed. He would tell me to give him more audience, to not forget them since that was how he got to where he is today. It's an unusual program, and I think what makes it unusual, and what I had to learn after so many years of working at NBC, was its emphasis on the studio audience. There were many times we would compromise in terms of television in favor of the studio audience. The reason behind that was that if it didn't happen in the studio audience, it simply didn't happen on the show. It's the only television program I've ever worked on where if someone in the audience said "I've got my flash camera, can I take a picture," they would say yes. The conventional wisdom was that the flash would damage the camera tubes, but on *Donahue* there was no question that the audience came first. There was never anything placed to impede the natural response of people in the audience. We never told them to clap or laugh or planted questions or screened questions.

Phil was a unique host in that you gave him the information on any given show, he absorbed it like a sponge, and then you put him out in the audience and watched what happened. You just let him go, and you followed his lead. He produced the show as he went along. He knew what tapes were available, what statistics were available, and then he weaved it together brilliantly.

As the size of our panels increased as the years went along—we sometimes had eight people out there—I would try to give him stage directions in order to get a clean shot. He would simply say, "You have to work around me."

If you look through the history of the show, certainly my history there as a director, you'll see Phil walking through shots, blocking shots, leaning into shots. And it was my challenge to anticipate where he was going to go and then reconfigure the cameras to get a different angle, not to work around him but work with him.

How did this impact on what you shot as a director? Was getting him on camera your number one priority?

There were very few moments when Phil wasn't on one of the monitors in the control room. I always knew where he was, whether I chose to show him or not. Still, when something happened on the program, my first response was often to go to the audience reaction, rather than Phil's. But someone paid me a compliment once by saying that they always knew what Phil was thinking. This tells me that to my way of thinking, you just don't take the host when the host is speaking. But there are times when I want to see the person listening to Phil ask the question. There was also great value in seeing him listening to the guest's response, whether it was the raising of an eyebrow or a small chuckle.

Some of the best work I did was showing people thinking about what's going on. Straight coverage is easy—you just show whoever's talking, and I'm sure if you go back and look at my early shows, that's what I did. But now that's not what's it about for me. What it's about is taking the viewer and putting the viewer in the studio audience. They can't see what's going on in the corner of the audience or the guy shaking his head saying, "I can't believe what's going on."

Did you as a director try to vary your approach depending on the topic of the day?

My goal was always to get the audience at home to feel what was happening in the studio. But that doesn't mean that things were the same day in and day out. For example, when I would go into the producer's meeting each morning and ask what was on tap, I might hear "Oh, it's no big deal. It's just your basic panel show approach." But I never treated it that way. There was no such thing as ordinary on Donahue. You could have a panel of four people talking about some social issue one day, and have four people the next on a social issue, and it would have no resemblance to the program the day before. You could never phone the show in. People would drop bombs on us all the time; we never knew what was going to happen. That's why a guy like me, who's pretty intense, could do the show every day for ten years and never get burned out. Monotony was never the problem, not with a host like Phil and the range of topics we explored.

Duke Struck

You'd worked in local and network news, as well as a long career at

CBS Sports. What was it like to make the transition to a talk show?

It was totally different. I'd never worked on a show so dominated by a single talent, let alone a talent like Oprah who also owns the building we work in. Her ownership extends to a tremendous care over not just the product, but over everybody here at Harpo Productions. I've worked in television a long time, and she's one of the few people left who still has an enormous sense of responsibility for what she's doing, and why she's doing it.

What did you notice as a director that was different now that you were doing a daily talk show?

I'd done daily shows before, and it's a tough process. The light at the end of the tunnel is always another locomotive coming at you. But a talk show is a much more complicated thing to produce than people realize, certainly than I initially realized. In some ways, it's like doing sports—it's a new event, happening every day. There may be scripted elements, but the show itself is constantly changing.

How much preparation do you feel is necessary in terms of capturing this "event" quality?

It calls for a lot of preparation. We use a lot of tapes and a lot of graphics. I meet with the producers extensively before each show to talk about how they want to present something and what resources they want to use. We meet every morning, and then I meet with the crew to discuss what we're looking for and what we want. I try to share the editorial content with the crew so they'll understand the show and be interested in the show.

In many ways it's like being a good football director. On any given play, you know where your cameras are, set up by what's happening in the game. It's the same with the *Oprah Winfrey Show*—in any given situation, we know where we're going. It's not quite as unstructured as it may appear. This comes from knowing where the show may go, based on talking with the producers, and, most importantly, watching Oprah very carefully. She's a fantastic listener—the best I've ever worked with—and she can take the show to different levels based on her reactions. Basically, we know which of the guests feels which way and where things might go, so we're as prepared as we can be. Still, guests may answer questions completely differently than they did in pre-interviews, and you have to listen to her and watch her body language to see how she'll react and where she will take the show.

You utilize seven cameras for the show, including a hand-held and a crane on a track circling behind the audience bleachers. How would you characterize the way you deploy your crew?

I inherited most of my crew when I came aboard two years ago, and most of them have a strong background in sports. They're freelancers, and usually still work sports on the weekend. They're quick, and they know how to react promptly, which is important for this type of program.

Do you give them the freedom to search for shots?

To a degree, but we do have certain patterns set up, depending on the type of show, whether it's a message show, or a musical act, or so forth. Plus, our set is in the round, which makes things harder. You're always crossing the angle, or trying not to cross the angle. It's important to give Oprah the freedom she needs—she's definitely not on any mark. If she sees someone she wants to talk to, she just goes. Lighting is also very crucial on the show, given the amount of movement that goes on.

How would you characterize the way you utilize the audience? Are they a key factor?

The editorial content of the show always comes first. Then, you want to capture the excitement or sadness that results from that content in the audience, because it's part of the event too. But we don't use the audience above everything else. Unlike some shows, we don't use an applause sign. We pretty much let whatever happens happen, and let the show generate the response from the audience. It's similar to doing a basketball game or any kinds of sports event. Reaction is important but it's secondary to the action on the field.

We have an audience in the studio of about 300, and some 20 million viewers at home. So even though the live audience generates the energy, we're also interested in how the audience at home reacts to the show as well.

As you noted, one of the distinctive qualities of the Oprah Winfrey Show *is its variety. Probably more than any other talk show, it features everything from serious conversation to music to dance to extravagant remotes. How does this affect your work as a director?*

Well, it certainly makes it fun, and keeps you on your toes as well. Probably the biggest changes we make, depending on what we're showing, is in terms of lighting. We really can't vary the camera positions that much, since the studio is relatively small at 100 x 100, and we have a 300-person audience to work around.

The key really is to just follow the show. I know when I started out I fell into the trap many young directors do—you tend to get in the way of the show. You want to show off your shot skills instead of just showing what's in front of you. If someone is sitting at home watching us and saying "Gee, that show's really directed" then I know I'm not doing my job. But if they say "that's a really good show, and I saw everything that happened" then I'm doing my job. As you get older and more experienced, you tend to get a bit more conservative, particularly on a show like this. The style should never get in the way of the message that is usually being delivered on most of Oprah's shows.

You tend to cut fairly rapidly. Is that a result of your years of working on sports?

Not really. I think it's more a matter of reacting to what's going on on the show. Listening is really the whole key in determining what to show and when to show it.

What about the issue of showing the host? Do you feel it's important to show Oprah as much as possible?

She's part of the event. I don't necessarily take a shot because it's Oprah sitting there doing nothing. But she's an incredible listener herself, and will react instantly, and it's important to follow her lead. Her instincts are very, very good. Plus we pay a great deal of attention to her body language and you can tell basically what she's thinking or where she's going. There's always at least one camera on her at all times.

The Oprah Winfrey Show *has a tremendously demanding production schedule of six shows in three days.*

Sometimes we'll tape four shows a day, ranging from serious talk to music acts from the 1970s. Still, working on this show is a lot like going back to school. You've got summers off, there's a Christmas break, a spring break. I've never had such luxury in television. As Marv Albert once said about his life, "I'd love to, but I've got a game," and that's what it's like working news and sports—no weekends off, no holidays. Here we even get Memorial Day off.

Often, the show will go live. Given your background in live sports and news, do you prefer this approach?

I like live. There's much more energy in a live show. I prefer it, and I think Oprah does as well. Last year, we were going live for the first show every day, but it was changed this year, primarily for convenience. But we will still go live if the situation deems it. I try to maintain the live energy even when we're on tape, since there's no question there's a feeling of excitement and a little more attention to detail.

What elements do you think you've added to the show in the two years you've been here?

I'd like to think I've given Oprah more production freedom to do what she wants to do. We've eliminated her reliance on the hand mike when she's out in the audience, using RF mikes [wireless microphones] on guests in the audience that we know we're going to call on. Hopefully, this has helped make the program more of an event than just a television show, letting her do what she feels, with as little restrictions as possible.

Joe Terry

How did you get involved with the Maury Povich Show*?*

After four years of freelancing in L.A., Maury called and said "I'm going to have a talk show, and I've been speaking to David Corvo [now of NBC News] who had some good things to say about you. Let's talk when you're in New York next." So when I was there next, we talked and had a good conversation, and he said maybe we can do business.

It's rare that a director is right there from the start of a show and remains with it as long as you have. Tell us about what these early stages for you were like.

It's fair to say that in the beginning, I survived. It's difficult for any show to just start off a hit, particularly in talk and news. And when they don't go well, and most don't at the start, it's the director who's the first to go. So my objective in the beginning was just to survive; to be here and give myself enough time so my technique would take hold.

How would you characterize that technique?

I mold a team and mold the personalities, and that takes time, particularly when, like me, you don't yell and scream. But the result is that when it takes hold, it works very, very well.

How much of your team is still here, four years later?

All of it, the entire crew, except for the production assistant, who left for Nashville with his wife who wanted to be a country music star. My A.D. Paul Casey left to direct, because I encourage people in that position to step up and learn. So when I'm not here, rather than go to someone outside, I want it to be inside. Plus it also provides an incentive for people to be here, knowing that if they work for me, there's a chance they can move over one chair. It's an incentive I believe in.

That's the basic teamwork technique I use, but it doesn't happen instantly. I strongly believe that directors who impress everyone that they're getting it done by yelling and shouting don't really produce a better product than what I'm trying to get done as I'm trying to mold my team.

Let's talk about that process of molding the team. What is it you're trying to impart?

I want people to feel that I trust them. I don't give "readys" [the spoken cue a director gives to initiate an action, such as "ready to take camera one"] as cues to the technical director. I just gently signal what shot I want. *Maury*, remember, is a taped show; if it were live I would take a more conservative approach. But since it's on tape, we can always fix it. So therefore I want my camera crew, for example, to be very aggressive in what they choose to shoot. I'm not out there, and if they had to depend on my "readys" the moment may be gone. In talk shows the moment can disappear in a second. All five of my camera people are extremely aggressive and I rely on that.

You're kind of an orchestrator/director?

Yeah, orchestrator is something that I use in the way that I am. Also a coach, particularly a football coach. I'm like a player/coach—I call the plays and I'm involved in running the plays. So it's a team concept; I don't pound people. I like them to feel involved and feel good about what they contribute. You can make mistakes and I won't come down on you, but if there's a pattern of mistakes I will nail you. The anger and the sternness are in my arsenal but they're not up front.

What did you find was the biggest difference in moving from news to the talk show format?

I think it's the fact that in talk you're reacting to what's happening out in the studio. I'm interpreting in my mind what's going on out there, changing my style on the mood and the emotion of the show's topic. I may cut more energetically sometimes or more steady, or lean on Maury or on the audience. It depends on my interpretation of the feeling of what the show gives me—it's not a cut-and-dried formula that I apply every day.

How soon did it take for you to discover that, as a talk show director, you're an accompanist to the mood of the show?

I always felt that way from the very beginning, although I couldn't express that early on because we were so involved in just getting this show off and running. I always felt that my interpretation was a good, solid interpretation of what was going on out there, as opposed to my just listening to the orders of various producers and so on. It's difficult for me to please everybody—I'm the director, I just please myself.

While news is formatted, and your sense of what's going to take place is very ordered, on a talk show nobody knows what's going to happen. People break down and cry, people get up and walk off. Maury gets emotional, Maury laughs at something that just tickles him to death. Maury is the show's most important element, and Maury should never be off camera. He's the franchise, and a camera should always be covering him.

Was that made clear to you from the first?

Yes, but I also made it clear to them that I wanted him on. He is never to be off camera; I may whip off and do an audience reaction shot, but 100 percent of the time he's on someone's camera. I choose when he's on, obviously, but I always want to see him. I want to see what he's doing, because he can express the mood of the show so clearly, and react so expressively. If someone says something, I want to see *his* reaction. I like to let people know how he's feeling about things. This is the *Maury Povich Show* and this is how he feels about what's going on here. I like to show what he's doing, even when he's not talking.

How long did it take after you arrived to realize that you now had a certain degree of freedom that you never had with news?

During the first year of the show I was somewhat boxed in as a director, but this changed as soon as new management came in, and I wasn't constantly being told what to do and what I missed. Still, there's not a show ever in which there's not something I wish I had gotten but didn't. It's impossible to get everything you want unless you bring in ten cameras and start ISO-ing [isolating a camera, by dedicating a separate video recorder to taping its individual feed], and even then you're going to sometimes miss something. But I like to feel I get a pretty high ercentage of the good things going on in the audience and throughout the show.

In a sense, as a director you've got five eyes—one for each camera, and you kind of play them like a pianist, choosing which one has got the right note for the mood you're trying to capture.

Exactly. For example, when I meet with the crew each morning, I try to set the mood for what the show might be like that day. If it's an emotional show, they'll be prepared for more close-ups and the audience reaction cameras know to look for criers. Or if it's going to be a fun show, the cameras are going to lean a lot more towards the audience, and that there will be a lot more energetic cutting. It's not always the same. Sometimes I may lean on somebody's face, and I go tight—I make them eat the camera, I will fill the entire screen with a face, which is something I didn't do earlier on.

And your crew is like your tentacles in the sense that they know what you want.

Absolutely. If somebody's talking, I don't have to say anything—they know I'm going to go right in. I'm not the kind of director who says you don't do anything unless I say do it. I'm a coach, I'm a conductor. My camera people know what to do, and my job is to just keep picking off the shots they've given me.

Of course one of the new elements for you as you shift from news to talk is the presence of the audience. How do you fit them into the equation?

It's basically the same thing. The camera people are constantly searching, constantly looking. They know certain things that I like to see and don't want to see. I don't want to see weird-looking people, not because of any prejudice, but because it's distracting and takes away from what's going on. They know that I like ethnically diverse shots. If there's one African-American out there, we got to get him in there at some point. But, to be fair, our audiences have come a long way from the beginning when we started, when we were almost 100 percent white. Now, it's more culturally diverse—Asians, Hispanics, African-Americans, and I like to reflect that because that's the world out there.

Another aspect of talk show direction is its unpredictability—you never know what's going to happen.

That's the juice for me. Even though this is live-on-tape, you still only have one shot at it, and I get tremendously pumped up about it. Often we'll do two shows a day, which means you have to keep focused even more. I feed off of the show, and even when a show isn't meeting our expectations, I'm still keeping it at a high level of production values. That's my deal here, regardless of how I feel about a particular program.

Has the show ever gone live?

Occasionally, and when it does I become a bit more conservative in the way I cut the show. There's also a lot more "readys" to the technical director.

So live-to-tape has freed you?

Absolutely, my attitude now is "let's take a chance." We also have a switchable ISO machine controlled by the A.D. I want him to get what's going on if he sees something, plus it's good training when they move on. A lot of times I may see a shot that I want to ISO and ask the

A.D. if he's got that in ISO. Or when I'm cutting a show live I may say "take that shot out, I don't like it" and we'll use the ISO in post-production. I'll give notes as I go along, and when we're touching shows up later because they've run heavy, the ISO comes in handy. Still, I dare you to look at a show and say "oh, there's an edit." We have a full-time editor, Russ Siberini, and he does a great job. He's very conscientious. I used to edit with my A.D. and stay all the time, figuring out what to do. But, now that my method has taken flight more, I'm willing to sit back and say, "You know how to do it, you know what I want." I let people do what they're here to do; why do I want to do everybody's job. Take audio, for example. Sometimes I may feel strongly about some aspect on a performance show, where I may suggest one type of arrangement over another. But in most cases I'll simply say "make me hear them. However you want to do that is up to you." The reason why I do things this way is that it frees me up to do what I have to do. I also don't dwell on mistakes, they're gone. If I get angry about one screw up, I'll just screw up the next thing. I don't get distracted, I just keep on going.

The interview with Bryan Russo was conducted in the offices of the Phil Donahue Show *in New York in February 1996. The interview with Duke Struck took place in the studios of the* Oprah Winfrey Show *in Chicago in May 1996. The interview with Joe Terry was conducted in the control room of the* Maury Povich Show *in New York in May 1996. This article originally appeared in the DGA Magazine, Vol. 21, No. 4, September-October 1996.*

Local Newscasts

Dan Berg, Mark Fetner, Steve Grymes, Jon Keller

TV newsrooms are congested, frantic environments. Reporters dash from their computers to the editing rooms, assignment editors try to juggle three or four phones at the same time, producers scramble from desk to desk preparing for their rundowns, all to the accompaniment of shrieking police radios, blaring TV sets, and telephones that never stop ringing.

Unlike network news, where on most days there's an orderly progression of activity leading to the climax of the 6:30 newscast, local TV news is far more turbulent and chaotic. One reason is the insistence on "live" television, which means crews are sent to cover any event which moves, often right up until show time. Another is the expanded nature of "show time" itself, which now means predawn newscasts, noon newscasts, early afternoon newscasts, as well as the perennial 6, 10, and 11 o'clock reports.

In the midst of this whirlwind sits the director, who must ultimately process all of the incoming information, guide the anchors and technical crew, and get it on the air. Though not responsible for the editorial product (that's the job of the producer), the director must skillfully weave the prepackaged stories, live remotes, graphics, and studio personnel into a seamless whole.

It's a demanding and stressful job, whose pressures and responsibilities have significantly increased over the last decade. New technologies and equipment, ranging from satellite remotes to helicopters to powerful computer graphics systems have made local newscasts every bit as sophisticated and slick as their network counterparts. But they've also added an extra technical burden, and, as in the case of robotic cameras, even reduced a measure of creative flexibility.

The reigning mantra of downsizing observed by TV station managements has also affected directors not only through the replacement of their camera operators by robots, but through a growing pressure to do more with less. As the following interviews reveal, the stability and bounty which used to be the hallmark of local news operations, at least in New York City, have largely disappeared. New batches of reporters and producers (and even anchors) seem to move in and out of newsrooms every few years, leaving the director and his reduced technical crew to hold onto the reins.

Nevertheless, the directors interviewed for this article are, as they freely admit, "adrenaline junkies," who love local news for the continuing excitement and thrill of the unexpected it provides. They're clearly energized by their work, especially during breaking news when the script is thrown out and they're left to pilot the ship on their own skill and resources. Directing a newscast in the number-one market provides them with ample opportunities to test their mettle, as New York City regularly careens from one crisis to the next every few weeks.

Between them, the four directors for the city's owned-and-operated stations bring nearly forty years of experience to their assignments. Dan Berg of Fox's WNYW started out directing commercials at KKTV in Colorado Springs in the late 1970s then moved to KOA and KUSA in Denver; in 1982 he began work at WHDH in Boston, staying there until 1991 when he came to WNYW. Mark Fetner has worked at ABC's WABC-TV throughout his entire career, starting out as a clerk in 1969, then associate director in 1972, a weekend news and public affairs director in 1975, and then finally moving to the weekdays, taking on the 11 o'clock news in 1977 and becoming permanent director of the 6 o'clock in 1979. He's still at both tasks. Steve Grymes came to General Electric's WNBC after working as a director for WJXT in Jacksonville, Florida from 1972-76, and then shifting to WBAL in Baltimore for seven more years. He's been directing a variety of weekday newscasts at WNBC since 1983. Jon Keller has been at Westinghouse's WCBS since 1976, working at a number of positions before becoming the director of their 5 o'clock and 11 o'clock newscasts starting in 1990.

Though these four directors work in the largest TV market, their insights on the changes and operations of local news tell us a great deal about the state of news broadcasting around the country.

What changes do you think have had the most impact over the last ten years in local news?

JON KELLER: I think robotic cameras were probably the most major change in my career as a director. You can't be spontaneous anymore, at least in terms of shots. You can't say, "Quick, get that" now. With one guy operating five cameras, you just don't have the flexibility we once had.

STEVE GRYMES: And you can only be moving one camera at one time. When we went over to robotics, I was still doing a very spontaneous show called *Live at 5* and part of the charm of the show was the wild interplay between the anchors and weathermen. It was one of the most frustrating times for me as director because I could no longer capture that feeling without four camera operators searching for reactions. All I can do now is to use a master four-shot, instead of relying on quick reaction cuts.

DAN BERG: I actually like certain aspects of robotics. They can do more than is humanly possible. I can have a camera truck, pan, tilt, and zoom, all at the same time. Be smooth and stay in focus. It's a little tougher to be spontaneous and this makes the director work harder in anticipation of what is going to happen next. You also need a good operator to get things quickly when called for.

KELLER: I remember when Brian Williams was an anchor for us, and once he and Tyler Mathieson were sitting in what we called the pit—a round, circular part of our set. The robotic cameras have bumpers so they will stop when they bump into each other, but we didn't count on the fact that the teleprompters' mirrors stick out further than the bumpers do. As we're on the air, one of the cameras begins moving and its prompter mirror hits the set and started moving it and kept moving it. The anchors were hysterical.

Another big change that needs to be mentioned has been the influx of new people. For years and years and years we had the same people—the same producers, the same writers, the same directors, the same news management. Once we started losing this old guard, the way we covered news changed, the way our news sounded changed. The way I direct the show started to change.

With the old-timers, we would have the show set fifteen minutes before the newscast. Now it's much more fly by the seat of your pants. Things have changed drastically for us.

MARK FETNER: One problem with this influx is that we now have a lot of non-New Yorkers who, for example, don't know the layout of the town.

GRYMES: We've gone through periods like that, but I've found the inexperienced people tend to get weeded out pretty fast, especially once they end up on the assignment desk or become a producer.

BERG: This situation also happens with the quick turnover of reporters, who come into town and don't know the history of the city, or how to pronounce Houston Street.

GRYMES: Among the biggest changes for me over the last decade has been the volume of personnel changes. You have to deal with new situations every day. Producers come and go very rapidly, and that's extremely difficult.

Yet as I look around this room, I'm struck by the fact that there seems to be great stability among directors. How do you account for that?

BERG: I'd say the reason for this is each station only has one or two directors, compared to the ranks of reporters, producers, and writers. I think it's also when ratings are a problem it's usually the on-air personalities that seem to change.

GRYMES: You need a few old-timers around for some sort of continuity and to be the glue. I've gone through a hellish four or five years recently as new management has taken over, and you have to sit back and say, why did I survive when so many others didn't? And the answer is there has to be some glue in the middle of things to keep it all together, especially when they're throwing new producers and reporters into the mix every few months. You need somebody in the storm to keep it together.

Local news seems to be far more driven by live events than network news. Is that your impression as well?

BERG: I would say so. We all have our four or five remote trucks, and our helicopters, and even though they may be used for gratuitous live shots, especially at night, they're all out there and they're being used. I think it's become a breaking news medium. You want to be the first guy out there with a breaking story, no matter what it takes.

FETNER: Even though we may be the only ones out there who really care who's got the story first. We're all watching each other.

GRYMES: But it's also important to note that there are times when a story comes up that if you're there first, you own it, and viewers will stay with you. This was certainly true for the two big stories for us this year—the "Blizzard of 1996" (as it was dubbed) and the tragedy of TWA Flight 800.

Those are two interesting examples, because in both cases your stations were all on the air almost continuously for hour after hour. What's the pressure like on you as directors in those kinds of situations?

FETNER: Actually, it sometimes lessens the pressure on us, at least in terms of what we get from management. The news director will simply be happy that we got the situation on the air, and isn't as concerned with misspelled chirons [electronically produced text, created on a Chiron character generator]. Whereas if it's a lead story that they've been working on all day, they are insistent that it have high quality and high production values.

BERG: I'm often asked why I'm so calm if it's a breaking news situation, and I say it's because we have a built-in excuse if something goes wrong. You get to throw out the scripts, you sit in a chair for four hours or more, and everything is going crazy. So if something does go wrong there's a certain acceptability about it, and time goes by like that. The next day when you're back to doing straight news packages it seems like a boring job.

GRYMES: I'll be frank about it, I'm an adrenaline junkie. I find I thrive in the control room when the heat goes up.

KELLER: I find I'm also planning next day's coverage while I'm going live, figuring out how we're going to package what we're showing, what kind of graphics and animation to add.

And this is all going on at the same time while you're on the air with it?

FETNER: In the case of the TWA crash, we had to also concern ourselves with how long our helicopters could stay up there without refueling. How long it would take to find gas at midnight, and what we would do on the air in between?

BERG: There's something extraordinarily exciting about the live element. Going in there knowing you're not completely prepared because you can't be. You've got to stay on your toes. It also has a lot to do with working with crews. You've got to watch everybody else and make sure you set them up two steps ahead of time, and yet you still have to stay in the present. It's like a conductor who has to stay two beats ahead of time.

FETNER: Not only that, but you have to worry about whether the person you're setting up two steps ahead can do it, and if not, what can you fall back on.

You contrast live directing with your typical days, which involve a great deal of production packaging—putting the best face on the stories in the newscast for that day. Has the degree of packaging changed over the last decade?

KELLER: I think there's more production in the packages now, with less time to do it. We used to have an hour more during the day to get them done.

GRYMES: Ten or so years ago, we as directors had a lot more aesthetic control over what the stories looked like. Everything used to come through the control room because we had all the fancy bells and whistles to make news stories more attractive. Now with the way technology has evolved, there are separate graphics rooms that can do a tremendous amount of manipulation. Plus the editing rooms themselves have a lot of technical flexibility. At one point we had so many different graphic styles in our stories that we were simply all over the place. Now we have a lead director who maintains the look of the station and tries to make the "wipes" [electronically created transition effect, in which one image is replaced by another in manner resembling a "wiping away"] and graphics observe some unity.

BERG: At my station, the graphic look of the newscasts is now pretty much the responsibility of the graphics department, and I think it's better this way. They have the advantage of spending their whole day in a postproduction room, developing and working on a graphic look, whereas the director would not have the time to do that. Then the director is usually brought in for a consultation to see how the graphic package can be applied to the newscast.

FETNER: There's not really a power struggle, it's usually a consensus between the art department, news management, and the three main directors of the newscasts to work things out.

KELLER: We work essentially the same way, by consensus. We try to keep the shows looking similar so people know they're watching our station.

Yet when it comes to graphic looks, there's no question in my mind that WNYW, as a Fox station, is the most edgy. Dan, how did this decision to be come about?

BERG: It was a consortium of opinion to be different and try different things in contrast to what's going on at other stations. Each of our shows makes a deliberate attempt to look different from one another. And each night we try to do things differently within each show, different wipes, etc., all to provide some kind of freshness and edge. This is done because we realize that our audience at Fox, or at least our intended audience, is younger.

Do you think that's a direction all stations will be following—to concentrate far more on graphic elements?

GRYMES: I think that's a philosophy that depends on the station. It can change with the general manager. Our last general manager, who's now with CNBC, deliberately wanted a more uniform look, as well as a less ostentatious look, in order to be more network like.

All of you work for owned-and-operated stations. Is there any kind of relationship between the networks and you at the local stations?

BERG: We don't really have a network look at Fox, since there's no national news which drives our graphics.

FETNER: Aside from using stories from the network feeds, we have very little to do with the network news. We do much more with the affiliate feed, but that would be the same relationship any ABC station would have. There's also an O&O feed [a transmission that goes only to the owned-and-operated stations of the network], but that often leans towards human interest stories.

KELLER: We don't have much to do with them either. We pick up packages off the network feeds; we don't share a graphic look, we don't even share a chiron look.

GRYMES: We have made an effort to marry our look to the network, so there isn't as much distinction when you look at them and look at us. There's certainly more of a give-and-take between the network and us in local now than there was when I first got there thirteen years ago. Back then local was clearly looked down upon, and that's changed to a degree.

KELLER: Three of the directors at CBS came out of our station, so we get a little more respect for what we do.

What do you think are the chief differences between what you do at local vs. your counterparts at network news?

FETNER: It seems to me at the network there's a very clear and sharp line between what the director does and any editorial decisions. We'll all discuss what to lead with on occasion, and since I've been in New York far longer than many producers have they'll often consider my input.

BERG: We also vote on leads and story selection sometimes, though the news director has four votes to our one.

KELLER: The director and the producer work so much closer in local news vs. network, both physically and emotionally. You learn to trust each other—you know how they think, and you trust their judgment. It works out very well. I worked at CBS as an A.D., and I know that at that level you get so much more time to plan your show. Your show is set by the middle of the afternoon. But at local, that's just not the case—the show blows up four times between two o'clock and five o'clock.

FETNER: And twice more after that.

BERG: I think local is willing to take more chances, while national is not. Maybe it's because the audience is so much larger at the network, and risk taking is far too dangerous. Our show may be constantly changing while it is on the air.

GRYMES: This is also because so many different things can take over the lead on a local show that wouldn't even be thought of on a national show. I think that's part of the reason. Just look at how many elements we put into our shows vs. the Nightly News. I've worked at the network and I know the atmosphere there is much more staid. Everything is preordained about what is done, and the show is set hours before airtime.

At the local level, we're liquid. That's what makes our job so hard, but it's also what makes us, I think, better equipped to handle any situation because we're tried in fire.

KELLER: Local stations are willing to go on the air and say, "There's been this car accident, we don't have much information, but we're going to try and get it for you and we'll get it on as soon as we can." The networks would never say that, unless they have video and a great deal of verifiable information. They won't go on the air with anything unless it's absolutely set, and we will.

BERG: Doing that on the local level also serves as a hook-and-tease, because it helps hold the audience throughout the newscast.

Over the years, there has been a tremendous expansion in local news—newscasts start at 5:30 a.m., pick up again at noon, then at 5:00. Has this changed the nature of your work?

FETNER: It's certainly changed mine. Until 1980 we only did an hour-long 6 o'clock news and then an 11 o'clock news and that was it. Then they decided to add an hour-long 5 o'clock news, and I volunteered to direct that. Then management asked who would direct the 11? And I said I would do that too.

KELLER: So you're the one responsible for our increased workload? *(laughter all around)*

GRYMES: Before I came to New York, I used to direct the two local newscasts at the stations I worked for. But when I was hired at WNBC, it was exclusively for the 6 o'clock news. Each newscast had its own director. But all that changed after the heady times of the mid-1980s went down the toilet.

The hard times didn't start immediately after GE took over NBC; it was really in the early 1990s. At that point new product was being created, while people were going out the door. So we were literally shouldering more and more responsibility with more and more shows. I'm doing more work now than I did at the start of my career in Jacksonville, Florida.

Do all of you agree with that?

FETNER: Yes, but I also want to add that the adrenaline of the experience makes it all bearable. When I stop feeling that rush, I'll know it's time to stop working. For example, last night our 11 o'clock newscast was delayed until 12:30 in the morning because of a football game. We were all dragging. But when it got close to airtime, not just me but the whole crew was chipper and alert.

KELLER: The down time is the rough time, the time between shows. The hour or so before the show is crucial to get everybody on the crew up and running.

Our job used to be one of finesse—make it look great so that people will remember it. Now it's just get it on the air. We used to be artistic, but that's changed in favor of just keeping it on the air.

When did this begin to happen?

GRYMES: There was a phrase that came into operation at our station during the early 1990s—risk management. Risk management is basically that we will take this risk lopping off this person, lopping off that person, and cutting here in terms of production costs. And we'll take that risk. What ends up happening to us is that we don't have enough key backups.

BERG: That's happens to us as well. For example, we may have a fill-in technical director who isn't up to speed, and they'll say to us, "Well, in that case, just simplify your show." That really bothers me because this means I have to scale back my show.

GRYMES: We don't get that attitude. Even though there's been cutbacks in every area, management still expects us to do business as usual and see the same things.

Describe your relationship with the anchors.

KELLER: You want them to look their best, you want them to feel comfortable, you don't want them to be left hanging. We talk to our anchors a lot, we're in their ears constantly, keeping them posted, letting them know about any changes.

GRYMES: I think the relationship between directors and anchors varies a lot, depending on the personalities of the individuals involved. I've been fortunate enough to deal with our anchors over a long period of time.

BERG: There's an important trust factor. The anchors who are the smartest generally have a good rapport with directors. My job is protecting them and making sure they look good.

Jon, you once said to me that working in local news is crazy—there's never enough time or enough people. Would you all agree?

FETNER: You always feel you could do better if you had a bit more time to get things preproduced. But I have a feeling that's one of those laws that no matter how much time you had, you always want more. You could probably keep tweaking the product forever.

GRYMES: I don't think it can ever be improved. We were as pressed for time ten to twelve years ago with twice the number of people as we are today.

This interview was conducted at the offices of the Directors Guild of America in New York in February 1996. It originally appeared in Television Quarterly, Vol. XXVIII, No. 4, 1997.

Network Newscasts

Julian Finkelstein, Charles Heinz, Richard Mutschler

Every weeknight at 6:29:50 p.m. in the heart of Manhattan, Control Rooms 3 at ABC Television, 47 at CBS, and 3B at NBC resemble Mission Control in Houston. A crowd of people are flanked in front of dozens of monitors, which silently beam in signals from around the world. There is an atmosphere of controlled edginess and whispered concentration. In these windowless rooms, illuminated by small, sharply focused spotlights, all eyes are glued to the flashing screens, as the ten-second countdown rolls. At exactly 6:30:00, the bright graphics and portentous theme music begin. Once again, another edition of the networks' evening news broadcasts is successfully launched.

The three directors who hold the controls of the network newscasts are, like their NASA counterparts, highly skilled and overly pressured individuals with decades of technical expertise to guide them. During the half hour they are on the air, they are the broadcast's unseen pilots, steering it smoothly along its prescribed course, while handling the sudden hazards and split-second changes of direction that invariably occur.

Directing the nightly news is not a profession for the indecisive. No matter how much advance planning and organization go into each night's program, situations arise—updated information from Washington, a breaking disaster, a report not ready until 6:40—that require immediate response. The director must be able to instantly shift gears to make the newly assembled pieces of script, voice-overs, graphics, and tape and live inserts fit together in a seamless flow.

Though they are not responsible for the editorial content or the overall look and pace of the show—that's the job of the executive producer—the directors of the network newscasts are, in many ways, the stabilizing technical engine. During their long tenure as directors, they have each weathered many storms, including changes in technologies, executive producers (a position typically lasting about two to three years), network news presidents, and even anchorpeople. Through it all, Julian Finkelstein (director of the *NBC Nightly News* since 1982), Charles Heinz (who's directed ABC's network newscast since 1970), and Richard Mutschler (director of the *CBS Evening News* from 1969 to 1996) have provided their broadcasts with an impressive sense of control and graceful coordination.

Network news directors have a particularly difficult job, since they must straddle the worlds of editorial (writers, producers, reporters, anchors) and production (computer graphic artists, tape editors, studio and remote crews). Their nine-to-ten-hour days are filled with meetings and planning sessions to address the concerns of both environments. The transformations wrought by technology have made their work even more demanding. While each new development may speed up the news gathering process, sometimes exponentially, it's usually accompanied by ever increasing pressures on time and resources. Satellite coverage may have opened the floodgates to instant worldwide reporting, but it has also allowed stories to pour into the control room right up to, and sometimes way long past, the broadcast deadline. Computer graphics now permit immediate changes in titles and artwork, but it's often a mad scramble to alter and rearrange all of these various elements at the same time the program is being sent out on the air.

Ensuring that every aspect of the newscast flows together smoothly is not a simple task. While the executive producer sets the agenda in terms of content, story order, and method of presentation (voice-overs, full-screen graphics, etc.), the final assembly and execution of the package is left to the program's director. Preparation may take hours, but the director's main work is largely performed live, culminating in thirty minutes of intense enterprise and concentration. During the broadcast, they become the technical nerve center of the entire news operation, directing and cueing the activities of the control room, the studio floor, network bureaus, and live remotes throughout the globe. In the midst of all this bustle, often enhanced by assorted exhortations from the executive producer, the director must also anticipate the next two or three things that lie ahead, while maintaining a firm control over each image and sound appearing on the screen at that moment. Skillfully weaving all of these elements into a tight ensemble is a challenge worthy of a Toscanini.

After a combined half century at the control room helm, Julian Finkelstein, Charles Heinz, and Richard Mutschler have each developed a flexible approach towards handling their high-wire half hours on the air. Stories may be delayed, equipment may go down, voices may rise, tensions may explode, but nevertheless, their deftness and expertise helps keep the broadcast aloft through every type of situation. Whether it's occasionally steering the anchor via the hidden earpiece, or quickly changing course when technology fails to cooperate, they are at the heart of the evening news broadcast, exercising a steady authority and a vital sense of direction.

Julian Finkelstein began his career in broadcasting in 1963 at KNBC-TV in Los Angeles, working his way up from the mailroom to stage manager and eventually director of the station's public affairs and local news programs—a position he held for eight years. In 1980, he was asked by Steve Friedman to come to New York to direct the *Today Show*. When Tom Brokaw left the program to assume the anchor role at *NBC Nightly News* two years later, Brokaw invited him to join the broadcast as its director. He has been there ever since.

Charles Heinz also began in the mailroom, at ABC, in the mid-1950s. Prior to being drafted in 1959 he had worked his way up to second in command of studio operations. After the service, he returned to the network, first in station clearance, then as an A.D. for programs varying from news to musicals. Promoted to director, he began working with Harry Reasoner on a weekly news report, then shifted to the nightly newscast in the early 1970s at then executive producer Av Westin's invitation. He has continued as director of the broadcast for more than two decades, participating in its transformation from the ill-fated Barbara Walters/Harry Reasoner pairing to the unwieldy three-anchor format of Frank Reynolds, Peter Jennings, and Max Robinson to *ABC World News Tonight*'s present configuration with Peter Jennings as solo anchorman.

Richard Mutschler started working for CBS in 1961 doing radio logs at WCBS-AM. After a few months he moved to Walter Cronkite's program *Eyewitness to History*, first as a gofer, then as a production assistant. When Cronkite moved to *The CBS Evening News*, replacing Douglas Edwards in 1963, Mutschler moved with him, rising to the rank of associate director. Five years later, he became director of the broadcast.

This interview took place in February 1995 and offered a unique opportunity for these three directors to get together and compare their experiences. Though they work within a square mile of one another, they rarely have a chance to meet, since their positions keep them securely tied to their control rooms (in contrast to the ever-traveling network anchors and correspondents). Yet, as this interview reveals, newscast directors share a common approach to their work, comprising equal parts skill, discipline, and extraordinarily steady nerves.

What was the CBS Evening News *like when you first started out?*

RICHARD MUTSCHLER: I started with the program in 1963, when things were very primitive. We'd wait for film to come out of the lab, there were limited visuals. It was basically an electronic radio show for a long time. Still, it was a group of wonderful people back then at all three networks, people who were true pioneers. Particularly people like Don Hewitt at CBS, who essentially invented television news production. You have to remember that back in the 1960s nobody knew how to approach TV news. Don, who possessed the greatest mind I ever worked with in television, came up with all kinds of new ways to present visuals, new kinds of lens shots. To my mind, he's the father of electronic news directing.

Today most of the producers and journalists are true technology kids, who have a strong appetite for glitz. When I started out, most of the people in network news were former newspaper men, or men and women who came from radio, so there was a real atmosphere of experimentation.

JULIAN FINKELSTEIN: As Richard mentioned, most of today's producers and whiz kids grew up on TV and its speed. But when we started, the pace was a lot slower. The technology wasn't there, and consequently the shows looked very different.

What were your roles back then as directors?

MUTSCHLER: For me it was rather good, because the journalists and radio people in news back then weren't too familiar with the technology, so they would always come to the director and say I would like to do this—this is my idea, I don't have time to do it, can you figure it out. It was an extremely challenging time, because you would meet with graphic artists, scenic artists, engineers, and take their ideas and translate it into television terms. It sure doesn't happen like that anymore.

CHARLES HEINZ: No, now you have young, young producers coming in saying I want this done. And you might say "really? We just did that yesterday. Why don't we try something different."

Was this same atmosphere of experimentation true for you at ABC?

HEINZ: Yes, certainly, because we were pioneers. Plus, it was a lot more fun back then because you were trying things that are now very easy to do, like getting a head shot of somebody. This may sound simple now, but I remember the awful times when we would get an artist down to the tape room—we finally had machines that could do an electronic freeze—and we'd put a piece of tracing paper on top of the monitor, the artist would trace the outline of the head, we'd rush it upstairs, put it on a chroma-key card and line it up with the same freeze frame to get the head shot. I'm surprised we made it out alive.

MUTSCHLER: In the early 1960s, CBS subscribed to the UPI Picture Service and they had in the newsroom not only the wire stories, but the fax service, and many times this was our only source of getting pictures. We'd take the fax, put it on an easel card, and shoot it with a live camera, and then project it into the Eidophor [a predecessor to the chroma-key, which permitted visuals to be electronically projected and inserted behind the talent]. If you were lucky, and had the time, you might call UPI who would drop off a photograph you'd need in the tel-op form—the television ratio. But just to get still pictures was a big problem.

Back in the 1960s you were still largely working with film. What kinds of problems did that present?

MUTSCHLER: We did three 16 mm projector pieces live on the air—one reel would have narration, one would have the main story, one would have cutaways. We'd go live on the air, and if they had to drop a story that was a big problem for the editor who had to take the reels off, cut the story out, and then put it back on. Every director's nightmare was if the splice of one of the edited pieces broke while you were on the air.

HEINZ: When we were using film, we used to have what you might call a quadruple chain, with two video sources and two audio sources. A film story might run four minutes long, for example. We would get the cue sheet and have a chance to rehearse it just once before we went on the air. We'd all be sitting in the control room, rolling the film down, making the crossovers between one projector and the next, as well as balancing the audio. When we'd reach the end of the piece, we'd tell the projectionist "OK, rerack it." Well sometimes the projectionists, instead of taking the film spools off and rewinding it on the film bench, cleaning the film as they went, would just hit the reverse switch on the projector. The film would rewind back to the top, but in doing that, it would open up all the splices, so you had film all over the place—and absolute panic. This didn't happen all the time, but it happened often enough that you had to bring a change of clothes to work by the time it was over.

How did the transition to videotape take place?

MUTSCHLER: My very first job at CBS was on a show called *Eyewitness to History*, which went on the air Friday nights from 10:30 to 11. It starred Walter Cronkite, way before his work on the *CBS Evening News*. The genesis of that show was based on videotape—they suddenly found out they could take a story, breaking anywhere, shoot it on videotape, edit it, and get it on the air fast, cutting down on lab costs and delays, giving that feeling of live. Videotape made its first big appearance in the news department with Khruschev's visit.

HEINZ: We began using videotape a bit later, but when it arrived, it was certainly welcome, even though it brought with it its own problems. It was the next best thing to live, and compared to film, it was instant. Now we figured we didn't have to go through a thousand deaths every day waiting for stories to come out of the film lab and out of the splicing room with seconds to go before airtime.

But videotape also seemed to move the deadlines closer and closer to air anyway. When we used to do a 6 p.m. feed, things would be ready right at 6 o'clock; when we moved to 6:30, we figured this would give us room to breathe. Nope, everybody took an extra half hour. I think if we did a 10:00 p.m. show, the stories would be ready at 9:59:14. Even now, some stories are so late, they're feeding them in as we're on the air.

MUTSCHLER: The advent of the ENG camera [electronic news gathering camera, permitting live transmission from outside the studio] in many ways stripped a director of a lot of directorial duties, which were an important aspect of our work. Prior to the ENG camera, there would be a director with the talent to set up the shots for the camera. Now that we're a worldwide news gathering organization, our anchors travel anywhere at the drop of a hat, while the director remains by necessity in New York. The anchor site is set up, but the sole responsibility for framing that for the camera belongs to the producer and/or camera person. The director has no say in lighting, location, or even the shot, since the anchors may not show up to that site until five minutes before air, giving us no time to reframe or recompose. So the downside of this new technology is that the director's role is very slowly being diminished, as is the creativity in news. I don't think any of us want to be reduced to the role of high-priced plumber, rolling a piece of tape.

HEINZ: I think the reason that we don't go out on location is that the money people have a louder voice than they ever did. We're looked upon as expendable, and certainly as something not worth the expense to be flown over. The situation is totally different on the prime-time news magazines where directors like George Paul on *20/20* go out with Barbara Walters to direct the shots, set up the lighting, etc. Roger Goodman when he started out on *20/20* would set up all the shots on the remote shoots, and lots of money was spent, and everything looked great. I think it makes a hell of a lot of difference.

So when you all are looking at the remote satellite feeds, there's no chance for you to recompose the shot or ask for changes if you don't like it?

MUTSCHLER: The director doesn't have the option. First of all, it's too late, it's preset already, and I don't know what the alternatives are because I'm not there. The executives all say we need you in New York because you can coordinate the control room better than if you were over there. And that's a very nice way of saying it's too expensive to bring you over.

I know at CBS News everybody wants to be a director; everybody feels that they're a director in news, particularly the young producers.

And if they find a shot, and I don't like it, very rarely do I have a chance to change it because of the time factor.

FINKELSTEIN: If Tom Brokaw goes on a planned remote, a week or so before he goes, a producer or associate producer will go out and shoot four or five different locations, which I then get to pore over and together with the executive producer we choose.

MUTSCHLER: I don't get that luxury anymore.

HEINZ: The other thing about ENG is that a lot of the camera people working the remote shots are not used to working with directors. I may be talking to them over the earpiece telling them to pan right, but they're used to talking to the producer ahead of time and setting up their shots that way. To have to react to us like that is tough for them.

MUTSCHLER: The same holds for us at CBS. When talent is on remote, we don't have studio camera people shooting them, but an ENG camera person. When you say move in or pull back slowly, it's a completely different language to them. They operate in totally different terms. You're talking to someone who only has a few minutes to set up, and the day before may have just flown in from Beirut covering a bombing.

HEINZ: We've gotten to know most of the cameramen out in the field who might be doing our live shots, but every once in a while a name will come up that you've never heard of before in a live context. So you might say to them a few minutes before air time, "Give me a medium zoom." Then after you see what they've done, you decide, well, maybe we better not do a zoom after all, and you tell the guy "uh, I haven't gotten the pages yet, I was just checking things out."

Did technology add more chaos in the sense that you could now go live, anywhere, on a moment's notice? Were scripts being thrown out more regularly right before airtime?

HEINZ: The potential for chaos was there, but because we grew with the technology as it came in, and learned how to use it, things came under control.

MUTSCHLER: Because technology is so damned fast these days, you can take a character generator, a chiron, and while you are on the air with one story, you can add things and take away from what's to come next on the preview monitor at the same time. In the old days, I remember typists hand set mat cards, and if there was a misspelling, there wasn't much you could do about it, except decide not to superimpose it.

FINKELSTEIN: The introduction of electronic paint boxes has been a revolution as well. In the early 1980s, artists used to sit there with pen and brush in hand. It was slow, and it was very difficult to change.

Now that satellite dishes are so compact and portable, has there been a growing pressure to add more live remotes?

FINKELSTEIN: It's more a decision by the executive producers. Some love that "live" element, for the sake of live and simply because there's late information to disseminate. Still, I'd say it's more a matter of personality as to how much live we include.

Other than higher blood pressure, has the revolution in new technologies and electronic news gathering changed your working conditions?

HEINZ: Ten years ago if I could have seen what I would be doing now and been told that I would have to work that way every broadcast, I would have said that nobody can ever do that. There aren't enough neurons in the brain to make that happen.

All of you have worked with the anchors of your programs over a long period of time, which is a rather unusual situation in television where directors may be moved from show to show every few months. What is the nature of this long-term relationship like, which survives the comings and goings of executive producers and news department presidents? Is it in some ways a creative bond?

HEINZ: In my case, I wouldn't characterize it as a particularly creative bond. You find yourself surrounded by so many advisors between you and the anchor. There's also the nature of the director's duties, which keep you away from the intimate construction of the program until the very last minute. So when Peter Jennings shows up to do the broadcast, he's like everyone—it's the last few seconds before airtime. He's casual, sits down, a total professional, plugs in, turns up his IFB [Interrupted Feedback System—the earpiece the anchor wears, which permits them to hear the program and to talk with the executive producer and the director], and just as I'm rolling the opening he says, "Hiya, Charlie."

FINKELSTEIN: It's a little bit different at NBC. We like to get Tom Brokaw in a little bit early, rehearse a couple elements of the show. Still, you've got to grab and you have to tug and pull, because he's got so many different requirements and things to do, from promotions and cross talks with local stations to cleaning up copy and so forth.

MUTSCHLER: It's the same thing at CBS, except I've got two anchors to deal with. You don't really see these people at all throughout the day.

So in a sense they're just images on the screen in the control room?

MUTSCHLER: Well, that's not really true. The anchors are certainly around sometimes, and we talk, but it's never really the kind of conversation where they say "Hey, Rich, I think we should be doing this."

I think the most important thing we do as directors for the anchors is to provide an element of trust. I believe if they know who's in the booth, if they know who the director is, that they feel very relaxed. If a screw-up occurs, they know the best people are out there trying to prevent it from happening.

If the news department started to institute rotating directors for the *Evening News*, I think you'd see the anchors out there a hell of a lot more for rehearsals, for sitting in and going over pages.

We've all been working on these broadcasts a long time and if there is any rapport built up through the years, it's that the anchors know they can trust us and we're on their side in that booth.

FINKELSTEIN:This is especially true for remotes where your anchor is out of the studio, and we provide them with a feeling of comfort and the familiar. We're their lifeline. I don't have my associate directors cue the anchor—I cue Tom. I talk to him personally on the IFB. I may be turning pages and hitting buttons, but he feels comfortable with knowing that I'm there for him. The only other person who's talking to him through the earpiece is the executive producer.

MUTSCHLER: There are many times during a broadcast that something does happen—maybe a tape is not available, and we have to sort of have to play 52 pickup and throw the script out. I'll just go in Dan's ear and say "I don't care what they're saying or what they're telling you, I'm going to this page next, followed by this." And you do this only because you have to continue this broadcast and only you know what's ready.

Going, at this point, right over the executive producer's head?

MUTSCHLER: You have to if you're live. It's that or having a lot of black on the air.

HEINZ: Especially if you have an executive producer who when a tape doesn't roll or something else happens goes ballistic and carries on. You then have to maintain control and a level of calm through all the noise.

In addition to the anchor, your key relationship is with the executive producer of the newscast, someone who generally stays on the job about two years before being fired or moving on. What is the nature of this relationship—do they want to meet with you when they first start out and ask for your input?

MUTSCHLER: Sometimes.

HEINZ: Usually, but it's been my experience that they know of you before they come on. They've done their research, or the person leaving has told them about you. Still, there is some degree of anxiety when there's change at the top and you wonder if they're going to bring in their whole entourage or something like that.

But of course, the miraculous thing is that you all don't change. In fact you're probably the most stable aspect of the evening news, lasting longer than anchors or any other editorial personnel.

MUTSCHLER: I was thinking about it just recently. The fact is that we three here have a unique job that nobody else has in TV news, and that is that there are only three directors on the three evening newscasts. Still, I've found that all executive producers want to make a "mark" on the broadcast.

FINKELSTEIN: It's in the fine print. Actually it's not so fine. It's in the bold print in the contract. *(laughter all around.)*

MUTSCHLER: That's right. They just have to put their mark on it, be it anything—a font change in graphics, a different light cue, a different hue of blue or green behind the anchor. But that's probably part of their job. I find the important thing for me as a director is to understand what he or she wants, and how easily they're able to communicate what they want. It's very important, I think we'll all agree, that while we're on air, we have to have somebody who has a plan and knows how to communicate that plan.

FINKELSTEIN: You have to know how to plan for what can't be planned as well, such as a live event or breaking story like a plane crash. This depends on the skill of the whole team, and knowing who to call on when something breaks live—for example, which correspondent has the most information on that subject.

MUTSCHLER: This is particularly true during our coverage of the O.J. Simpson trial, where the special events unit will be in the control room right up to the newscast, and then we have to suddenly take over with only a forty-second break in between.

FINKELSTEIN: We've gone from fade to black of the special events coverage to a two seconds fade up and we're back to the *Nightly News.*

HEINZ: We had an awful moment of switching over from Los Angeles one day early in the Simpson trial coverage, and wresting control from the special events group, who were off in their own control room, and who felt they were in charge, since Peter was anchoring their coverage. As we got closer to 6:30, we had to figure out how to take over from them and start *World News Tonight.* A bunch of senior executives, including news president Roone Arledge, were there, and in the heat of the moment, things got a little bit confused. There was a period of about a minute and a half or so where we had control of Peter's IFB, but it was so loud in our control room that nobody could hear what he was saying. Meanwhile the special events group is telling us that they don't want us to interrupt Peter's trial coverage. For a moment or two there, we left Peter kind of hanging out, which wasn't too good. Needless to say, it was an interesting evening, but you need those every now and then, to show you that normal bad days are really good days.

Has any executive producer ever come in and said, "I'm going to change the way you work and how you do things?"

FINKELSTEIN: No, it's never overtly said. You know you're going to have to change what they're asking or demanding, so it may change how you operate.

MUTSCHLER: I've learned that when they do come aboard, most of their changes are first on the editorial side, maybe analyzing the writing and the list of correspondents. But they'll eventually come down to the production area, and as I said, make their mark in some fashion.

ABC is a bit different than the other networks in that its news president, Roone Arledge, comes out of directing, as does Roger Goodman, who holds the title of senior director. Does this make your work easier there, Charlie?

HEINZ: It's certainly made it more interesting. Roone brought to our news division all sorts of things that helped make us a real news division—the drive, the money. Roger would be bored doing our kind of show—he's a very creative type of person who likes to set up new shows, but he has certainly influenced our show in virtually every area. He is often impatient that we can't do the things on our broadcast that he is able to do on his magazine shows and special events. One of the reasons we can't, aside from his own creativity, is that he gets the "A Team," often taking away our top people. When we need them, they're simply not available. It's a struggle for me keeping a good crew on the show—it seems to me that when people get real good, they're often yanked away to do something else.

Is this condition true at the other networks?

MUTSCHLER: My same crew has been working for me for a very long time.

HEINZ: I think a real important part of our job is the crew you work with. We have a damn good crew, as I'm sure they do at the other networks, and they go off and do other little tasks, which is good for the brain: the TV crew may go off and do the Indy 500 and the audio people are off doing other things. They've got to go off and learn some new stuff and then bring it back with them.

How about you as directors? Do you feel the need to shift gears?

FINKELSTEIN: I do so occasionally. I do a few other shows: one once a month for United Airlines and another once a week for the Superchannel over in Europe.

MUTSCHLER: I do one for United Air, and promos for visiting

dignitaries—affiliates and so forth. The biggest change is to go out on the road, which breaks it up a little bit.

Do you all get out on the road?

HEINZ: Not any more.

FINKELSTEIN: I used to, but not now.

What's a typical day like for you?

FINKELSTEIN: I come in about 9:30 or 10 in the morning and begin finding out what will be in the show that night. From my end, I need to find out what's in store graphically, what full screens, what over-the-shoulder shots. We're in the process of changing our look, little by little, and that's putting more of a burden on our graphics areas.

MUTSCHLER: I have a meeting with the art director, production assistants, and all the writers at 12 noon. It's held out in the newsroom and I talk with the writers about what stories are being worked on, and possible lead-ins they could write so we can coordinate appropriate graphics. We also want to know what nontape stories they're thinking of, again for selecting graphics.

One thing I think is a little different at CBS than the other networks is that the director is in charge of the total graphic look of the broadcast. Writers don't say "I need a map of" or indicate on the script what the visuals are. These are done in meetings, and it's the director's decision what headshot, what graphics, what generics, should come up, as well as the entire graphics package.

FINKELSTEIN: At NBC, it's more of a shared responsibility.

HEINZ: Same at ABC. We would have a graphics meeting at 11:30 a.m. where we would have the production assistants, artist, and the editors sit in and go over the show list. There's also a morning meeting that I don't attend where all the bureaus get together over the phone and discuss and commission stories. One of our senior producers will put out a list of the probable stories of the day, the potentials, and the "tells" [stories the anchor narrates with either full-screen or over-the-shoulder graphics].

As the day wears on, producers might come in and say "Well, I'm due on that World Trade Center spot" and we may not have any moving pictures and have to fill the thing. One of the things that our former executive producer Rick Kaplan brought to the show was the "mess room," which is a dark room containing an Abacus and a paint-box machine [electronic graphic effects equipment] where we can digitally enhance video. It's an expensive addition, and it takes time to use these damn devices. We often wind up doing stuff in our control room, putting together the story with the visual elements. We get our control room about 4 o'clock, unless special events is there. On really bad days we can get the studio a bit earlier.

One of the big changes now from what it used to be is that a lot more stories are commissioned and decisions about what will be used on the air are later than they've ever been. We may not get a real lineup until 6 o'clock, which is tough—tough on the folks in the field who are working their tails off, only to find out at the last minute that they're not in. It seems that for producers the process of making up their minds gets later and later.

FINKELSTEIN: We may get the rundown and the line-up by 5 or 5:30 but the final script is much, much later. But my biggest complaint is that with the increasing amount of on-camera tells, we may get another fifteen pages of copy trickling in after 6:30.

MUTSCHLER: I have an additional problem. Not only are the scripts usually light, meaning that they have to fill with extra stories, but because I have two anchors, and the visual presentation of my broadcast is chroma-keyed, I sometimes run out of positions of where to put the extra graphic they've added at the last minute.

Earlier we were talking about the priorities of the news departments. I think deep down each president and each division head knows that their most important broadcast is their nightly or evening news. They know that. But I think now that they find themselves in a prime-time ratings war to come up with magazine shows. As a result, more time and energy and creativity and money are spent in developing the look of these programs, at the expense of the 6:30 news. They'll take our best crew members—our best lighting designers, our best scenic designer. And this ripple effect affects our broadcast—when we want a specific person, we can't have them because they're off working on a newsmagazine show.

HEINZ: This kind of problem is also similar to what happened to us when we became number one, a position which felt like it took centuries for us to get to. I think it was a lot more fun when we weren't number one, because our executives at the time wanted you to take chances, wanted to try some stuff out. There was an energy there, with everybody pulling together. Finally, after a year of topping the ratings, they finally admit it—Roone says "yes, we're number one," and we shared a bottle of champagne in the newsroom. And then our budget was cut. It's like we reached the top, and off with our heads—you all don't need to spend any more of this money. Now it's reached the point that when we're asked to assimilate some of the staff from canceled shows like *Turning Point*, they look at our facilities and are surprised at how archaic things are, with no real office space, an outdated computer system, primitive editing rooms. We on the other hand are surprised at what they used to take for granted and ask "you mean there's another life out there?"

It's the old grunt syndrome. Here we are, putting it out five days a week—the flagship show. I'm proud of working on the show, I think it's great. I always did think it was a lot of fun, and hard work, that half hour on the air every day. But it's not the place to look for glory.

MUTSCHLER: I do want to expand on what Charlie was saying about being number one. At CBS, we were used to being number one for a very long time, since 1968. But once you start going down, it's not only the news department where you start facing difficulties, but also in the area of technical support. When you're number one, you can get practically anything you want; when you start slipping you can't get that person or that piece of equipment because they've given it to someone else.

Still, I agree with Charlie's premise about being number two or three, particularly if you're number three, because you then have the greatest advantage of experimenting with anything on the air. You have nothing to lose.

FINKELSTEIN: That's certainly what's happening at NBC. I've never been number one, and we're always there trying to do new things. Again, this is largely a matter for the executive producers who are coming in. There are little tweaks and big tweaks which can happen, such as the way scripts are written, the way shots are framed, the way sets are painted, the way the studio is lit.

You're all kind of hinting that your power as a director is diminishing year by year.

MUTSCHLER: Absolutely, no doubt in my mind.

FINKELSTEIN: You almost end up being a traffic cop in the highway of the control room.

And that's primarily due to management's interference?

MUTSCHLER: I don't know if it's all management, but it's also because we're too feckless to stop them. The real issue is that news departments have grown, the bureaus have grown, the power of individual producers in the field have grown. Management now relies more on the producers in the field than the director. These new whiz kids, and I say that respectfully, think they know the answers to everything. They've gotten a few courses here and there, they come from little local stations where they worked hands on with everything, and they think, "We can do it." I think in many cases, producers think that directors are a real pain, and they don't need them.

FINKELSTEIN: This is certainly true at NBC as well. It's all producer driven and writer driven.

One of things I discovered in interviewing soap opera directors is that they feel that despite the enormous energy and creative involvement they put into their work, they're still regarded as the low men and women on the totem pole, in terms of other directors. How do you all feel you're looked upon by management and the industry at large?

FINKELSTEIN: It's a personal thing, obviously, with Roger Goodman and Roone Arledge clearly feeling like the big guns. I think more of the producers now feel they know how to do everything. We're in the trenches and we've got to crank out the shows, five days a week. At 6:30, I don't care what they've done for the past eight hours—it's now in our laps, for that half hour or hour. You have to make it work. You don't have the luxury of getting the best crews or spending two or three hours creating that nice move on that shot, or so forth. Boom! You've got to crank it out.

HEINZ: It's something that comes with doing it over years. Doing a straightforward show, where everything is there where you want it, is almost boring. Because somewhere tucked away a little generator's waiting to go wrong or some big change is about to happen.

FINKELSTEIN: Charlie commented earlier that maybe Roger Goodman might be bored doing a nightly show and I can understand that, since he's a very creative guy. Maybe I'm not as creative as him, but you have to be able to coordinate and put that effort 100 percent to your 6:30 show, and we don't have time to be that creative type of director.

MUTSCHLER: I think it would be fair to say that our most immediate concern is to get a show on the air between 6:30 and 7 the cleanest we possibly can, the best way we can, without getting into any arty-fartsy thing. This is a grind to us; we do it every single day. We don't have the luxury of sitting around for six to eight weeks of planning spectacular shots, we simply don't. We're on the line every day. We're up on the front line. Just to get away with a clean show is a great blessing for all of us.

I don't think any of us walk in expecting anyone to say "nice job." For me, the satisfaction comes when I'm driving home on the West Side Highway and realize we did our best, despite whatever problems we encountered.

HEINZ: You feel good at 7 o'clock if you've come through unscathed.

Does the accelerated speed in which you now work sometimes make you feel that there's no room or time left to add a single new element?

HEINZ: I think it's exhilarating. At this point I'd go crazy if I suddenly had to do a show that was only on one day a week, and I had all week long to prepare for it—every day there might be a new idea or plan being tried out, then revised, until you finally end up coming back to your original concept. At least now, we have a solid day of fear and loathing, then the euphoria when you get on the air, and you're done with it. It's a great feeling.

MUTSCHLER: It's very ironic. All three of us get paid for what we do at the finale of our day, that last hour that we really perform. We can sit around, work on a few things those first six hours—it doesn't mean anything. Where it does count is 6:30 to 7:30, at a time when everybody else has either completely wound down or left for home. I have to pace my day accordingly, knowing that I have to be up starting at about 5:30, when the adrenaline begins to flow.

I agree with Charlie about how deadly it would be if they suddenly put me on a once-a-week show. There's no living on the edge that way, and I think all three of us enjoy that, flying by the seat of our pants. It's great, and if we didn't like it we wouldn't be doing it.

FINKELSTEIN: I have to buy a new set of rubber pants every week.

This interview was conducted at the Directors Guild of America in New York in January 1995. It originally appeared in Television Quarterly, Vol. XXVII, No. 4, 1995.

Prime-Time Comedy

Jim Drake

Directing situation comedies is probably the closest TV work to theater. Most shows take place on a modified proscenium stage, in front of a live audience, and are shaped in a play-like manner, with individual scenes and acts, divided by intermissions. However, unlike Broadway or regional theater, sitcoms don't have the luxury of a month or more of rehearsals. They're put together over the course of a single week, with frantic rewrites, only a day or two for read-throughs before blocking begins, a night for dress rehearsal, a night (or maybe two) for the production, and then it's on to the next script, with no chance to look back or even hold a cast party.

The demands on a situation comedy director can be fearsome. Scripts are in such a state of flux (with changes often occurring during the actual production) that there is little time to concentrate on dramatic motivation or the subtleties of performance. Cast blocking is complicated by the addition of four (or more) cameras. Technology also poses challenges. Shows shot on videotape permit the director to maintain tighter control over the show's technical resources from the vantage point of the control booth, while losing the immediacy of working with the actors from the stage. Shows shot on film permit the director to grapple with the theatrical issues of the show from the floor, while losing a certain degree of technical finesse in terms of live calling of the shots and switching from the booth.

For more than twenty-five years, Jim Drake has skillfully directed every type of television comedy, including daily satiric serials and farcical talk shows, as well as hour-long sketch comedy programs. His credits include breakthrough series like *Mary Hartman, Mary Hartman* and *Fernwood 2Night*, the late-night cult favorite *SCTV Network*, and such fondly remembered programs as *Buffalo Bill*, *Newhart*, and *It's Your Move*. He also directed dozens of episodes of *Golden Girls, Night Court,* and *Dave's World*, and is currently working on series as diverse as *Malcolm & Eddie*, *House Rules*, and *Jamie Foxx*.

What led you into directing?

I went to Stanford University, with the thought that I might major in psychology. In my freshman year, I took what I thought would be an easy class, but actually was the toughest though the one I did best in—a film class taught by Henry Breitrose. This opened new doors for me, and I continued in film, getting a masters at Columbia. After graduating I ended up at CBS News, but after looking around for a while, I realized what I was really interested in was production. I worked on several CBS shows, including *Camera Three*, where I encountered Merrill Brockway, the first of my many mentors. But the guy who really gave me my big break was Tom Donovan. He gave me a job as an associate director for a show he was producing called *Where the Heart Is* back in 1969. Tom encouraged me to chart out a few scenes each day, and after several months he asked me if I'd like the chance to direct. I said sure, and I ended up directing five episodes of the program while the regular director went on vacation.

After that show went off the air, Tom took me along to work as an A.D. on *Love of Life*, where I also directed about five episodes a month, filling in for the regular director Larry Auerbach. I was out on the West Coast visiting a friend, when I was given the chance to work on a comedy pilot directed by Mel Ferber. Like *Happy Days*, it was a spinoff of *Love American Style*, focusing on an older woman living with her parents in a trailer camp. Once again, I was the A.D., watching very carefully and examining what was going on. It was a good experience, though the pilot never sold. I ended up next on *The Young and the Restless*, brought on board as "the A.D. who also directed." I also worked on some episodes of *General Hospital*.

After working on these daytime dramas, I was given the chance in 1974 to be an A.D. on Norman Lear's *Good Times*, which I grabbed because I was eager to gain more experience in situation comedy. Working for Lear was a great opportunity, because three months later, I was loaned out to work on the pilot of his latest project, a syndicated soap opera/farce called *Mary Hartman, Mary Hartman*. I came in as an A.D., with Joan Darling and Art Wolf working as codirectors. Norman Lear looked at our first run-through, and said he was very displeased with what he saw. I'd gotten to know him a bit from *Good Times*, and he took me aside and said, "This isn't like the soaps at all. You and Art both come from soaps, so try to make it more like that."

I talked to Art, who said he wanted to make the show more filmic, with more wide shots, and views of the set. I explained to him that that wasn't what Norman had in mind, who was paying a lot of money primarily so he could see faces. He was adamant about his approach. When I told him Norman said we had until midnight to assure him that we'd get the show in shape the way he wanted it to look, he responded "well, I'll save him the time, I'm leaving now," and he walked out.

Joan had never directed cameras before and they asked me if I'd be willing to do it. I said OK, and so we worked for the next four days solid, and then taped the show. We ended up doing five episodes in all, but it took a year before we were picked up.

Did your experience in soap operas prove useful, even if you're now doing what was intended to be soap opera as farce?

Oh yes. I was constantly being asked about basic soap mechanics. For example, at the end of a week's episodes, they didn't know what to do, until I suggested that we run a recap on the following Monday, which led to their well-known gags summarizing the plot in a totally over-the-top fashion.

How did it work with two directors—you and Joan Darling?

Joan would work with the actors, and my job was to visualize what she did for the cameras. She'd ask me if something was working or not, and I might say it was too slow or fast. I'd seen a similar arrangement of co-directing on a project I'd worked on in New York called *Change at 125th Street*, where Michael Schultz would basically work with the actors and Bob LaHendro would take care of shooting for the cameras. Ultimately they'd end up arguing, as Joan and I later did, over how things played, and what was funny. It's a very tough situation, because you have to work very closely together. Joan ultimately ended up leaving to do *The Nurses* after our first five weeks of shooting.

As the success of Mary Hartman, Mary Hartman *grew, did you feel the freedom to be able to change your directorial style?*

I came to believe that its success depended on the close soap-opera style we'd developed right from the start. But part of the reason for this approach had to do with the very tight budget constraints we operated under. Originally Norman Lear had treated us as a weekly sitcom, which just happened to shoot daily—that meant lavish expenses, catered meals, etc. But we quickly ran through our funds.

Still, my soap opera experience proved very valuable, particularly in terms of dealing with the pressures of just getting a show produced every single day. I've often told people that the best place to start in the business is working on daytime dramas—you may not be able to cross over easily, but you'll certainly have the skills to handle just about everything. We were laying down images live on tape, without isolated cameras. Things are very different today, where isolated cameras give you four different views, permitting you to literally build the show afterwards in postproduction, similar to a feature film.

Without ISOs [an "isolated" camera, with its own videotape recorder recording its feed] we tried to shoot the show as simply as possible, using a lot of close-ups and master shots only if someone was moving. We also had very good camera people who could keep up with what was going on, especially with our cast of actors.

It was a very tough grind for me; I did seventy-five shows in a row, with only the weekends off.

After this schedule, you took a break by jumping to Alice, *which was a conventional, once-a-week situation comedy. This must have seemed like the lap of luxury.*

No question about it. But it was short-lived, since after four episodes, a new regime of producers came in and fired everyone affiliated with the old. Suddenly, I was looking for work again, and ended up back at *Mary Hartman*. The show, however, was different in its second season. Jerry Perenchio, who had helped Norman Lear create Tandem Productions, had come in and said, "Here's the deal, you start at 8 in the morning and you stop at 4. If you can't, we're going to pull the plug on the show." So

I became the director who was there to get the program back on this very tight track, after a number of other directors had been there and made things a bit lax.

Then I was offered the chance to direct *Fernwood 2Night*, which was a spinoff of *Mary Hartman*, and designed to be the ultimate talk show parody. I took a long look at late-night shows to see how they were done, realizing that you couldn't be script bound. You had to learn to direct by impulse, following the drama of what was unfolding in front of you. It's a matter of flying by the seat of your pants, and figuring out how to handle things when they frequently go awry.

Was this more fun for you now that there was a definite air of improvisation?

To a great extent it was. It was like a three-ring circus, with a real sense of joy in just getting through it. You could feel the live television aspect of it. Once again, we had no isolated cameras; we shot the show, and if it was long, they pared it down. We tried to keep everybody to time, giving hand signals as we went into commercials and running the actual time frame. But they still had to cut the shows down afterwards.

From being the head director of Lear's renegade comedy universe, you then embarked on a variety of different projects, from conventional sitcoms to some unusual experiments.

Yes, one was a comedy called *Year at the Top*. The program had gone through three variations already—one was shot on film in New York by a director at Joseph Papp's theater, another was shot on tape, then I was brought in and our version was shot and then scrapped. Finally, a fourth version evolved which was a pairing of Norman Lear and music impresario Don Kirshner. What they tried to do was to have a seventeen-minute sitcom, plus a guest star, plus three musical numbers. The cast was highly unusual—Robert Alda, Vivian Blaine, Mickey Rooney, and Paul Shaffer.

Then I did another Lear project called *The Baxters*, where they would do an eleven-minute drama about some current controversy, then throw it to the local station for round-table discussions. There was also a PBS project, also with Lear, involving Supreme Court cases.

Still, I didn't stray that far from sitcoms, working as well on *Sanford, Gimme a Break*, and *Who's the Boss*. I stayed about a year or two on these shows before moving on to something which interested me more.

How did your experiences with SCTV Network *come about?*

NBC had bought the show, after it had originally been launched in syndication. I was called by producer Barry Sand to ask if I wanted to come up to Edmonton and help get the show on track, since they were falling behind and NBC was driving them crazy. I agreed, but as I was heading out the door, I got a call that the program's director, John Blanchard, was upset that I might be infringing on his territory, so I said fine, unpacked, and went to work on some other projects. A year later, I was asked again, since *SCTV* was now moving to Toronto, and Blanchard didn't want to move. I said yes, and moved to Toronto for six months from February to June 1983. The pay was low, but I didn't mind, since I'd already fallen in love with the show and I knew I would be working with the next generation of comics.

Working there proved to be a delight. It was truly a collective, with everybody having a say. My expertise in "conventional" TV proved to be an asset, particularly in their send-ups. In addition, a lot of the people they were parodying, like Walter Cronkite or Beverly Sills, were people that I had worked with, so I was able to give them some tips on how to make the impersonation click.

What was it like to now direct quick, sketch comedy, as opposed to half-hour situation comedy?

The interesting thing was that it was anything but "quick." Surprisingly, we would spend much more time working on sketches than I had done working on entire shows like *Fernwood 2Night* or *Mary Hartman*. Production was often fairly elaborate, and we might work two or three days to get two or three minutes of tape.

After one season with SCTV, *you came back to Los Angeles to work on a pioneering sitcom,* Buffalo Bill, *which was also one of the first you shot on film. What challenges did this type of production pose for you?*

At that time in 1984, everybody was saying that comedy production was going to move entirely to videotape since it was cheaper and you could reuse the tape. Nevertheless, there were four shows being shot on film, and I ended up working on three of them: *Buffalo Bill, The Duck Factory*, and *Newhart*.

Working with film is strange, particularly if you've had a lot of experience shooting on tape. With film, you're actually working on the studio floor, which doesn't give you that "creative rush," in John Frankenheimer's phrase, that you do get when you're in the booth and doing a great show. When I first began shooting film, I still walked in with a completely prepared script, with all of my shooting instructions and camera cuts. Everyone was surprised, since the camera people were used to doing it themselves. When I asked if they wanted to keep doing it that way, they said no, they'd rather not have the burden because nobody could now yell at them if they did it wrong.

The way film production typically works is that the director works with the performers and blocks the movements, and they would let somebody else, usually the technical coordinator, step in and do the cameras. To a certain extent, I'd say that's why there's so much film done today. It allows the director to primarily focus on the cast, while not having to worry as much about the visualization. Now there are lots of directors who do do both, like Jamie Widdowes and James Burrows. But there are people who literally say, "I don't want to know about the cameras, let somebody else do it." I always feel that's kind of violating half your job, because how it appears on screen—whether you're on a close-up or wide shot, for example—is going to have some impact on how an audience responds.

The way I approach a filmed production is to block the action out with the actors, as if it were a little play. Jimmy Burrows always turns off the video taps [a small video camera placed in the lens of a film camera, permitting live viewing of the scene being filmed] from his film cameras so the audience in the studio is forced to watch the action as if it were a play. He says, "I'm going to do it this way because that's the way my dad, Abe Burrows, did it. It's going to be played like it's a theater piece."

Was it different directing filmed shows in the mid-1980s, before the days of video taps, which now permit the audience to actually watch what the film cameras are shooting?

What I discovered was that as much as I loved working with the performers on the studio floor, when you finally got to shooting in front of the audience, you were just as much a viewer as the audience was. I would try to compensate for this by aligning myself with the perspective and angle of the camera in order to get some feel for the visual. Still, it was a very difficult approach to do.

Take us through the typical production schedule of a situation comedy.

The normal way is to come in and read on Monday, and then, in the old days, we'd actually rehearse those scenes which might stay fairly close to what's in the script. That's changed drastically now—I haven't done a show in five years where you actually stay on Monday, because they have such a major rewrite to accomplish. What you wind up doing then is talking to the guest cast, explaining the nuances of the show and how to relate to the star performers. Then you come in on Tuesday, and now you have a new script (or a new rewrite). You work very hard during that day, culminating in a run-through in the afternoon, not for the cameras, but for yourself and the producers. Then they do another rewrite, and you start fresh again Wednesday morning. Now you have a little more under your belt; your goal is to try to stay true to what they've written, and you now refine and shape and find some new things. By Wednesday afternoon, you give a run-through for the network, or the producers, depending on who comes in. Then they get together and change things.

If it's a video show, you do your camera blocking and prepare the script for the associate director to call. If it's a film show, I still tend to go over the blocking and mark my script, because I become more my own guy. This becomes very interesting on Thursdays, which is a long day if it's a film show and a short day if it's done on tape. With film you have to walk around with all of the four cameras and give detailed directions; distances have to be measured, they have to put marks on the floors for the actors and marks for the cameras. You start at 9 in the morning and finish at 7 or 8 at night. With video, if you've planned it well and know where people are going to move and don't have to worry that much about focal lengths (as you do in film), you can basically sit in the control room, direct the show, and be out of there in three hours. It moves that quickly.

Which approach do you find the most comfortable—film or tape?

I like them both for their own reasons. I feel tape moves faster and, in the old days, used to provide a more accurate picture of what the viewer is going to see. You were able to get bigger laughs from your audience because they could watch the monitors and actually see what was happening. Correspondingly, in the old days, film was broader and bigger because of the lack of true visual representation. Now with video taps, you've got that visual accuracy as well. One advantage to film is that it certainly makes your performers look better, especially performers who are beginning to age. Lighting can be handled much more subtly.

Jim Drake was interviewed by phone from his home in Los Angeles in October 1997.

Prime-Time Comedy and Drama

Gene Reynolds, Oz Scott

One of the greatest challenges of prime-time production is the relentless pace—half-hour programs are rehearsed, rewritten, and shot in just four to five days; hour-long programs are done in seven to eight. It's a demanding schedule, which forces directors to operate on overdrive, rushing from run-throughs to camera and cast blocking to the actual taping/filming of the show. Added to this is the pressure of entering an established series to direct an episode or two. The cast and crew have generally been with the show for a long period of time, and are intimately acquainted with their characters and the production routine. Directors usually come into this closed "theatrical" world with little time for creative authority or the chance to do more than keep the show running along familiar tracks.

Perhaps the easiest way to overcome these directorial restrictions is to also work as the series' producer. The most powerful person on the set, the producer in television supervises the shooting schedule, the budget, the casting, the writing, and just about everything in between. When that role is combined with directing, the combination is the closest to total control the medium affords. In the following interview, Gene Reynolds, who served as producer-director for shows like *Room 222*, *M*A*S*H*, and *Lou Grant*, examines the special problems directorhyphenates encounter in their dual positions.

Even without the luxury of being a producer, directing prime-time series, or at least one-hour dramas, has become a bit more creative in recent times, thanks to an increased emphasis on "style." In order to give their programs a "stand out from the crowd" quality, some producers now seek directors who can provide a distinctive feel. Among those who have welcomed this development is Oz Scott, who originally began in theater directing the landmark Broadway show *For Colored Girls Who Have Considered Suicide/When the Rainbow Is Enuf.* For nearly two decades, Scott has stressed skillful performances and a clear visual sense in his TV work—an approach which lends itself especially well to the artfully-written ensemble series of Steven Bochco (*L.A. Law*) and David E. Kelley (*Picket Fences, The Practice*). His interview in the second part of this chapter reveals the value of being an "actor's director," especially in the more showy environment of contemporary prime-time dramas.

Gene Reynolds

You've been in show business most of your life, starting out as a child actor. How did you make the move from being in front of the camera to working behind it?

I had worked as an actor since the age of ten, mostly in film but also in theater, radio, and television in New York and on the coast. I had been acting for around twenty-five years and for a number of personal reasons it was clear I would be better off going to work every day and not remaining in a profession where I was so vulnerable to the whims of others. I attempted unsuccessfully to get a job as a floor manager in live TV or as a script supervisor in film. Both these avenues were too tough to crack.

As an actor, I often supplemented an unpredictable income with work outside the business, for example, I sold Muntz TV sets of out my car from time to time. Late in the 1950s, I was working in a men's clothing store when in walked June Leff, an executive at NBC, whom I had approached for a casting director job weeks earlier. June decided that if I had the energy and enterprise to sell suits, added to my years of experience as an actor, perhaps I should be considered as a casting director on *NBC Matinee Theatre.* I worked there for about a year and a half, casting this daily one-hour live anthology series. We did classics, westerns, shows with an all-Irish cast, or plays with all character women. It was great experience and quite creative. After *Matinee Theatre* I cast *Peter Gunn* at Universal and early episodes of *Bonanza* for NBC. While I was at NBC, Don MacGuire and Jackie Cooper asked me to play a small part on the pilot of a new show called *Hennesey*. The show made the schedule and they offered me a chance to direct. Bob Butler and I started directing a week apart.

After *Hennesey*, I started doing a number of half-hour comedy shows, which in those days were one-camera.

What was it like for you to be behind the camera?

Extremely exciting and exhilarating. I was eager and energetic, which was helpful given the pace of production. My experience as an actor gave men an understanding of much of the process.

But in reality this was practically the first time I had directed anything. I had been tossed, willingly, into the deep end. I went to USC Cinema School nights and took courses in camera and editing. I formed a Cine Club with a group of directors, writers, actors and every Saturday morning we studied classic films. In the group was Bob Butler, Al Ruben, Werner Klemperer, Gene Nelson, Ivan Dixon. We would sometimes ensnare the directors or cameramen of the films and we were graced by John Ford and Bill Wellman, among others. It was an enriching experience and I wish I had kept it going up to today.

We often chose European films because we found we learned more from the technique of European directors whose style differed from our own.

How did cinema education translate into work in the factory method of sitcom production?

I was constantly employing the storytelling concepts I was learning into these one-camera film shows. They were not always appreciated by the companies who wanted a more simple, faster way of shooting but I was always trying to create a piece of film and not just photograph some action. I always tried to do something different, something new. When I produced we always tried to come up with a story concept, a kind of show we had never done before. You don't often succeed but when you do you have enriched your show.

In studying other directors I was doing what all directors do, consciously or not, and that is to build on the techniques that have gone on before them. But eventually you will find your own style.

At any rate, I did almost all the one-camera, half-hour comedies in town, with two years on *My Three Sons* and thirty-six episodes of *Hogan's Heroes*. I had actually directed several hundred shows when Bill Self at Fox asked me to produce and direct the pilot of *The Ghost and Mrs. Muir*. I worked with the writers Jean Holloway and Artie Julian who did a splendid rewrite. I cast the actors, found the captain's house in Santa Barbara, and shot the show. It worked well and NBC put it on the air. I still wanted to direct and declined the chance to produce the series.

After that, Fox offered me a contract and I was asked to develop a show. I wanted to do something with an African-American lead, a well-rounded hero, a teacher in an integrated high school. I needed a special writer and Bill Persky recommended Jim Brooks, who liked the idea. We realized we had both been out of high school too long so we went to Los Angeles High and did research. Jim wrote a brilliant script. The program was *Room 222* and I worked on it for two years, directing four or five episodes each year. Our stories reflected the youth revolution of the sixties, the black fight for civil rights and the experimentation in educational techniques. We won the Writers Guild Award each year but after the second year ABC asked me off the show because they wanted something funnier.

What was it like to direct shows for which you were also the producer?

Well, for some reason, there's a much warmer greeting when you walk on the set as the producer-director than when you come in, as I do these days as Joe Freelance. But I cannot complain as I am usually treated well in most of my current work.

Did your background as a director alter the way you worked with the directors you were now hiring?

I was certainly aware and appreciative of good work because I knew what directors were up against. I was also probably harder on directors who I felt were not doing their best work. When directors did not come in to edit their films after wrap I would call them up and insist they come in and grapple with some of the problems they had left us with.

As a freelance director, I had been thrown out of editing rooms all over town. Thanks to Elliot Silverstein and twenty-five years of

Directors Guild of America negotiations, directors have the right to their cut. I certainly wanted directors on my show to do their editing.

Since I was basically a director I was mindful of the problems created by scripts that were too long and on my shows always turned over lean scripts. It gives everyone a chance to do their best work in the time allotted. If, after tightening the show, we came up short, we could always write a brief scene of fifteen or twenty seconds to put us on time. Much wiser than shooting five or ten minutes over, with blood all over the stage, and throwing a day's work away.

After Room 222 *you moved on to* M*A*S*H. *How did this come about?*

Bill Self gave me the assignment to produce and direct the pilot of *M*A*S*H*. I asked my friend Larry Gelbart, who was living in England, if he would like to write the pilot. Larry was producing the *Marty Feldman Show* in London and suggested I come over there and together we could work out the story. Larry and I spent about ten meetings, working nights, deciding which characters to retain and hammering out an interesting story for the TV version of *M*A*S*H*. It was a great experience to work on rich material with one of the finest, most creative, and amenable comedy writers in the business. I came back to the States and started casting the show, working on the sets, assembling a crew. As the day approached I called Gelbart and said I really need the script. Larry said, I just mailed it. Then he sat down and wrote it in two days.

How did you feel working on this pilot when Robert Altman's movie version was so well known?

I was extremely excited by the script and by our cast with Alan Alda, Wayne Rogers, Loretta Swit, McLean Stevenson, and Gary Burghoff. We knew we couldn't be as graphic in the O.R. as the feature had been and we couldn't be as explicit with language but I didn't feel this limited us essentially. The important elements were available and those were the great characters, the setting, the humor dealing with the military and authoritarianism, and a powerful, serious theme which was the wastefulness of war.

The program was celebrated for its creative techniques but you still shot it in the classic three-day method?

Yes, we read and rehearsed (and did some rewrites) on Monday, shot Tuesday, Wednesday, Thursday and started a new show on Friday—a method that had been imposed on us by Fox. This four-day schedule was foolish because it pushed us for scripts but it made the season shorter for the company. Every third show I got a pick-up day where we did added scenes or pick-ups. I produced *M*A*S*H* for five years. After I left the three-day shoot stretched, but this isn't unusual for successful shows. The rehearsal day was strenuous but rewarding. They were a hard-working cast and used the day fully. Often, at six at night we had to be assertive about making them stop work. Alan Alda set the tone. He applied himself vigorously and the others did as well.

The one-camera show has great advantages. You're making a small movie. There is nothing more creative than the one-camera set-up where you light for that one shoot. Also, the acting can be far more intimate than in multiple-camera shoots.

We could shoot inside, outside. We shot as a rule, but not always, two days in the studio and one day on location. The one camera gives you great flexibility and variety. You could put the camera in a jeep, in a chopper, or underwater if you wished. We had ten to fifteen sets not counting swing sets (far more than multiple-camera studio shows), so we could really move the show. We had great areas in the studio and even greater outside so a director had countless visual opportunities.

The actors were outstanding. We had fine light comedians and they played well together, an excellent ensemble. The characters were rich and orchestrated. We often had two or more stories going in each episode and with the level of writing we enjoyed it was possible to have some fun.

What was the move like for you from M*A*S*H *to* Lou Grant?

When I came on board it had been decided to do an hour show with Lou Grant going back to print journalism. We were moving from the outstanding *Mary Tyler Moore Show* (a half-hour sitcom) to an hour format and this was a case where form determined content. It's usually the other way around. In an hour show you have four acts requiring much more story and you need more elements to sustain interest. And, as a drama, it was naturally more sober and realistic than a comedy form where you could be more outrageous. In a half-hour comedy Lou Grant could pull a bottle of booze from his desk; in an hour drama he'd get fired. The hour show became a seven-day shoot with (as a rule) five in studio and two in the street. Like *M*A*S*H*, it was one camera which allowed for creativity and flexibility in terms of staging and lighting. Journalism shows, prior to *Lou Grant*, had dealt with a crime story and a final act fight on a rooftop between the journalist and the villain. We chose to deal with life in the newsroom. We did heavy research, as we had done on *Room 222* and on *M*A*S*H*. We came up with stories, characters, and details of the life within the universe of journalism.

Here again, I handed directors lean scripts to give the actors, director, and crew every advantage. It gave them time to do their best work. If your script is long, it's prudent to cut on paper and not after the scenes have been shot. It takes guts sometimes to do it but it makes for better results.

After Lou Grant *you moved to made-for-TV movies. Did the work load double?*

Yes. An hour show is more than twice as tough as a half-hour and a two-hour movie more that doubles the trauma of an hour show. It's more like doing a pilot where you are starting from scratch. The characters are new, the sets must be found for the first time, and everything is being created. You look back on doing films for TV and say, "Boy, that was fun," but they're tough to do well in 18 days. I'm essentially happy with *In Defense of Kids, Doing Life,* and *The Whereabouts of Jenny* but they were mountains to climb.

Creatively, it's great to be working from square one. You are deciding what the show is all about, finding the theme, what must be emphasized to express the theme. Deciding how to find its reflection in everything at your disposal, in the casting, the sets, the wardrobe, the locations, the photography, the style of shooting, the behavior of the characters. It's very challenging and I've been lucky to have some good material to work with. You can dance lightly but you can't go far without a text that gives you and the actors and the creative team opportunity to deliver meaning, insight, personal statement, dramatic fire or humor.

We are always in search of "golden moments"; for me, directing is all about finding and expressing humanity.

Oz Scott

You'd had a lot of experience in theater, most famously as the director of the very successful For Colored Girls. *How did you make the transition to television?*

My first TV experience as a director was a PBS program for Ellis Hazlip featuring the World Saxophone Quartet. It was my first four-camera shoot, and I didn't have a clue about what I was doing. I always tell a story about a stage manager who had worked with me on a couple of plays. One day he said to me, "Oz, I've watched you and you always take these jobs where you don't know what you're doing. You don't have a clue, and yet somehow you survive and then you know what you're doing!" I've thought a lot about what he said and he's right. Sometimes you have to take that step into the unknown and you come out on the other side and you're there.

What made directing this show so difficult is that even though the four saxophones in the quartet all had different ranges, when one player would launch into an improvised solo he might hit a note that was in everyone's range and I wouldn't be able to tell as the director who was playing and who I should be shooting. I finally asked them if they could just give me some kind of nod right before they soloed so I could know who to shoot.

After this, I was called out to Los Angeles by Barbara Schultz to do two one-act plays for a PBS series called *Visions*. I'd been sitting in for a few months before watching Barnett Kellerman direct *Another World* so I was somewhat prepared.

What did you find about television drama that immediately separated it from your work on stage?

On the stage, you've got a proscenium, which gives things an inevitable flatness. On TV and film, you've always got to be aware of the angles and the depth. That's the greatness and versatility of the camera.

My first prime-time series was *Hill St. Blues*. I was introduced to the producers Greg Hoblit and Steven Bochco by my friend, Mike Warren, who acted on the show. I sat on the set, very studiously watching everything that was going on for about three months, and then was offered a show. It was a great experience, and I learned a tremendous amount about camerawork, which was something the show really emphasized.

Even though film and TV tend to emphasize beautiful shots and camera moves, I've always believed in going for the performance. When I was a graduate student at NYU, trying to choose between theater and film, I had a great teacher, Beyda Bodka. Beyda said to me, "There is a big problem with a lot of directors today. They don't know about acting. When you get out there to make a film, you can hire a great cinematographer and learn everything about camera work from him that you could learn here in school. Same thing with editing. But start right now learning your actors because it's going to take a lifetime to master that." That was the best advice I ever got.

From Hill St. *you moved on to comedies like* Archie Bunker's Place *and* Gimme a Break. *What was it like to now be working in sitcoms?*

It was a different experience. For example, I worked on the last two seasons of *The Jeffersons*, and I was surrounded by people who had basically spent the last ten years of their lives focused solely on this one show. I was offered the chance to do twenty-four episodes per season, but I only wanted to do about twenty so I could at least see what things were like elsewhere. I would go off and direct a few shows of *Alice* or *Gimme a Break* and then come back to *The Jeffersons* with a different sense of how to play things. Both of those shows had its own style of TV comedy, thanks to people like Bob Carroll Jr., Madelyn Davis, and Mort Lachman, and I was happy to be able to add those qualities when I returned to other shows I worked on.

I've always found humor to be very important, even when I'm directing drama. Identifying the comic scenes and working on comic timing with the actors in drama only enhances the serious moments that come afterwards.

Did you find you had a preference for one format over the other?

As a black director who had done a lot of "dramatic" theater, I was surprised that when I came out to Hollywood it was thought that all I could do was comedy. It's all I was offered in my first few years on the West Coast.

Before I began working in TV, I had done one feature film in 1979, called *Bustin' Loose*, starring Richard Pryor. After I shot the movie, I looked around and noticed that there was basically only one black film coming out every two years. I figured I could stay in film and, if I was lucky, between the other two black directors, my rotation might come up every six years. Or I could sit there and go to school and learn the camera, which is what TV was to me. That's why I liked doing twenty episodes of *The Jeffersons* because it allowed me to do ten full hours of production a season, and as a result, my knowledge really blossomed. I feel like I went to school on the industry's time.

Did you notice a change in production practices and style as you've continued your "education"?

There's been a gradual evolution in the television industry which I've had to adapt to as a director. When I first started doing dramatic shows, the basic approach was "line 'em up, shoot the scene, and get out of here." Then, slowly an emphasis on camerawork began to appear. An agent told me that every time I do an episode I should pick one shot that will be the beauty shot that I can add to my reel. *Hill St. Blues* may have been the first show to really emphasize good cinematography and directing, but by the late 1980s there was a definite transition in the "look" of TV drama.

Was this emphasis on style encouraging to you as a director?

Absolutely. Your shots now have to tell a story. Increasing the shooting time from seven days, which is what it used to be when I worked on *Hotel* and *The Scarecrow and Mrs. King* to eight days now has made a big difference. And producers now expect that with eight days you'll be able to give them more of a "look," even though it's more work.

Do you think it's easier to be a dramatic director on television now with the improved quality of writing and production values?

Not really. Basically, television is a closed shop, in the sense that every show has a group of directors that they favor, and you can't just walk in and say, "I'm here." Now we're beginning to find that film directors are even starting to do television, because it's quick, easy money and it can be very satisfying.

What do you think are the biggest challenges of directing episodic television?

As a guest director on a series, it can be tough. You come in on established characters, and sometimes you don't even get a script until two days before. I do spend a lot of time watching tapes of previous episodes so that I can get a feel for what it is that the actors and the show are trying to do. But it certainly can be difficult, especially because you don't get much time with the actors until you walk on the set. You're the guest. The one thing I always learned is that you're the last one hired on the creative team, and the first one to go. So that if there's a question about the show, who's the one to get blamed? Not the producer or the writers, because they're there all the time. No, they'll blame the director and say, "If we had a different kind of director, who'd taken us in a different direction, it might have worked." It's a producer/writer medium, because they have to maintain control week to week and keep the story and characters true to the way they see it.

Still, on good shows that I've worked on, like *The Practice* or *Picket Fences*, the actors are so good that they want to hear what I have in mind. When Norman Lear and Glen Padnick hired me to do *The Jeffersons*, I was really a novice—I'd only done about two or three half-hour episodes before. I was on a real learning curve, and I asked them early on why they didn't just promote the associate director to do the show, since he knew the cameras. And they told me, "Oz, we didn't pay you to know cameras. We paid you to see if you can inspire these actors, who have been doing this show for nine seasons. We thought it would be best to bring in a director who's an actor's director."

I've worked exclusively on one-hour shows during the last five years, with some of the best writers in the business. It's been wonderful to do these quality programs, but there is a small downside. One of my agents recently told me, "Well, Oz, now you're getting a reputation that you're a great director only because you work with great writers." I told him, "Do you know how many years I worked with bad material, making it better?" One of the things about working with David E. Kelley on *Picket Fences* and *The Practice* is that he listens. For me, part of being a director is being able to talk about a script. When I used to have bad scripts, and could see the producers did not want to hear what I had to say, I would sometimes get depressed and say, "OK, I'm going to be a good boy this time, and I'm not going to say anything about the script. I'm just going to shoot what they tell me to shoot." And that's when you usually get into trouble, because a lot of times they don't know, and they're looking for somebody to take control.

Still, despite some frustrations, I'd have to say that working in episodic TV has been a lot of fun for me. It's a wonderful place to experiment and it's very enjoyable to go from show to show and meet different people and work on different things.

The interview with Gene Reynolds was conducted by phone from his home in Los Angeles in October 1997. The interview with Oz Scott was conducted by phone from his home in Sherman Oaks, California, in November 1997.

Prime-Time Pilots

Bob Butler

In the fevered world of television production, a TV pilot is truly a special event, a chance to spend a bit more time, energy, and money to make a program look as good as it possibly can. After all, a pilot is a series' greeting card, and it is designed to attract the eyes of network programmers and preview audiences with a concentrated dose of all the show's best features.

Directing a pilot is of special importance, comparable in many ways to directing a feature film. Pilot directors are called upon to quite literally devise a series' style. Their work on this first episode establishes the visual blueprint and pace of the programs to follow. It's one of the rare times in episodic television where directors are given the freedom to think in broad stylistic and dramatic terms.

Bob Butler has been practicing his craft as a pilot director for more than three decades. In that time, he's helped create some of television's most memorable pilots, including *Batman*, *Star Trek*, *Moonlighting*, and *Hill St. Blues*. Butler approaches pilots with a sense of adventure and discovery, eager to see the material in fresh ways. Often his inspiration comes from classic films, such as the "canted" camera of Carol Reed for *Batman* or the rapid-fire dialogue delivery of Howard Hawks for *Moonlighting*. His directing is marked by its versatility and by its responsiveness to actors and atmosphere.

Though he's worked in feature films, Bob Butler believes that pilots can be just as challenging and, in some cases, even more rewarding. As he notes in the following interview, in a period in which Hollywood filmmaking is largely about special effects and star power, pilots offer a chance to mold an intimate dramatic environment that now seems to appear only on the small screen.

How did you get started in television?

I began at CBS and followed the usual progression. I started as an usher, then a receptionist, then a production person, then a stage manager, then an associate director, and finally a director. One of my first assignments was directing one of the last *Playhouse 90s*, which at that point was being done on videotape.

My first episodic directing assignment was *Hennesey*. The first day I worked for the show seemed like it lasted twenty minutes—I don't remember the camera reloading. Then I directed a couple of movies, some more episodic TV, then some movies of the week, and pilots. It's all been kind of random.

What was your first pilot?

It was *Hogan's Heroes*. The original pilot director fell out in late December, I think. A friend of mine, Eddie Feldman, was the producer, and asked me to jump in and I did. I had a great time with the cast.

What was the difference working in pilots vs. episodic television at this point?

It was twice as luxurious. Pilots shot at fifteen days per an hour, as compared to seven days for a regular hour episode. Plus, you get to set the tone and the pitch and the storytelling technique for evermore. You really are directing. The people involved are eager, they're hungry, they want the show to be a success, so they've very responsive. It's like a high-riding baseball team—everyone wants to pull together and they want the thing to be as good as it possibly can.

Did you now feel for the first time that you had creative responsibility in TV as a director?

You certainly have more creative room, because you're setting many standards. For example, on the pilot I did for *Batman*, it was my choice to "dutch" the camera, to make the horizontal level cockeyed. And that came right from the comic strip, where when the drama got high and the action gets high, very often the cartoonist will tilt the frame. The English director Carol Reed did that a lot as well in his films.

You also get to set the tone of the performances. I remember that in *Batman* Adam West kept bringing in jokes, and I had to keep telling him, "No, we've got to play this earnest and straight." That's the kind of managing and leadership you can apply to directing a pilot.

Describe your experiences in directing the pilot for Star Trek.

That was interesting, because there were two pilots made. The first one was with Jeff Hunter as Capt. Kirk, which was the one I did. I was told later that NBC had thought, "We like it, we believe it, but we just don't understand it. Do it again." It was great. I remember reading the script and not being that impressed with it. I felt everything had been hauled in but the kitchen sink, and I'm sure that's what Gene Roddenberry had done. He wanted to make a showcase of that pilot script, and as a result there were a lot of sci-fi chestnuts in it, probably to the point of confusion. Certainly to the point that it read like a smorgasbord. I kind of debated whether to do it or not, but my wife convinced me. So I did it, and had the appropriate slight disdain, which is always a good thing to have. I had a good time doing it.

I remember a couple of items to pick out. I tried to perform the thing very dry and very naturalistically, almost like Howard Hawks' *The Thing*, where the pitch of the performances is very low and very cautious. I tried that in the rehearsal period, but it just lay there. So after about two days I said, "Fellas, I'm wrong. You've got to put back the exclamation points." It was a melodrama, after all.

The other thing was that I wanted to dirty the show. It was too clean physically—the uniforms, the bridge, everything was totally pristine. I wanted to give it some age and some character. I also wanted some foreground pieces and structural pieces in the bridge.

In a way then you anticipated the type of look George Lucas achieved in Star Wars.

I guess that's right. But Gene Roddenberry didn't want to do it that way—he wanted it very pristine and sci-fi, which I thought was a drag. The show always retained that cleanliness, which I felt was kind of boring.

Gene offered me the second pilot, but I turned it down. I felt I had been there already.

Was The Blue Knight *your first TV experience with the police format?*

No, I had done other detective and police shows in my experience. But this was my first long-form. It ran for four hours. It wasn't called a pilot, in fact it wasn't really designed to be a series. It was called a special, and originally it was an experiment in long-form, running from Monday to Thursday at the same hour. It didn't do all that well, despite the fact that it starred William Holden. I think it probably proved the point that movie stars were not appropriate, or provably pertinent, for TV. And it also proved, because of its mediocre ratings, that long-form wasn't for television either. Given these liabilities, they decided to retool it, minus Holden and minus long-form, as a weekly series, but I had already left the project.

How did your involvement with Hill St. Blues *begin?*

I was in the process of selling *Remington Steele* to Grant Tinker, when Grant interrupted our conversation and said, "Let me send you this script to read." It was the pilot written by Steven Bochco and Michael Kozoll, and I thought it was some of the best melodrama I had ever read. Since their original choice for a director had turned them down, I was Grant's choice, and in a sense forced down their throats by Grant.

Did they know you at all?

Other than knowing I was one of the working guys, but beyond that I don't think so. I met them at a lunch with Grant shortly afterwards.

How detailed was the script you read in terms of visual elements?

It was a typical script in that the complexity of the storyline was there. You would see on the page a few beats of one story in a room, and then there would be a few beats of another story in the room. I don't think it was specified how to get from one to the other. So I kind of linked that all together and arranged that congestion and that staging pattern.

How did your directorial signature evolve in this show? How much freedom were you given by the producers? Was it a mutual decision on how the show would look?

No, I would say that decision was mine alone. They were very supportive. I felt that since the show was set in the east, we should use the congestion and the informality. For example, I talked to a New York policeman many years before who said about New York cops vs. Los Angeles, "In New York, we keep the peace. In L.A. you enforce the law." And that meant to me that the easy haircuts and the moustaches and the random uniformity was typical. So we used all of that colloquial character of the New York police force which does not exist out here. Out here it's rather rigid, rather G.I., clipped hair and all that.

The elements of congestion and colloquialness that I associated with the east I then applied to every area of the show. The look of the men and the women, the look of the crowd, the fact that there are beat-up cars on the sidewalk, the graffiti. I may have led this visual approach, but of course once everybody felt this was a good idea, the art director and costume people got behind it and contributed to it.

How did you capture this in terms of shooting?

I've always been very energy and pace conscious. I wanted as little shoe leather as possible; I don't want to wait and I don't think audiences want to wait. I want to keep the events coming closer on top of each other. To crowd and congest and keep the thing going was a very good idea in my mind for all reasons. So it thereby follows that as one scene is ending, let the other be beginning, so that the camera would be drawn to the incoming scene as it leaves the outgoing scene. I wanted a series of staged overlaps from one scene to the other. When you lay the congestion on top of that—namely a bunch of foreground and background busy people who aren't careful at all about the congestion on the precinct floor—plus in front of both of those is the layer of the rest of the living precinct, giving you four levels in all.

Didn't this add to your work as a director in terms of choreographing all of this congestion?

Only marginally because any good director will do his homework thoroughly and lay out all the staging and all the camerawork beforehand.

How did your decision to utilize so much handheld camerawork come about?

I originally planned to shoot the whole twelve-day pilot using handheld. But after shooting two days totally handheld, it became more and more of an affectation, especially after looking at the dailies and feeling like we were in the middle of a hurricane. So after that the guys asked me to use the handheld for the action scenes only, and use the dollies for the rest. I did a little pleading, but it was their nickel.

How influenced were you by the Susan and Alan Raymond documentary The Police Tapes*?*

Very much so. Greg Hoblit, the producer, had gotten it in and thought I might get a kick out of seeing it. When I saw it, I flipped and said this is the way we should do the show. What I meant by this was that the whole environment they captured was a mess. Every measure of scene making was sloppy and messy. And I felt that every element of our show should seem to be sloppy and messy. Of course, we would be creating that mess, which is a lot more difficult.

I worked closely with the cinematographer Bill Cronjager, who was a very savvy guy and knew all the tricks about how to make a show look any way you wanted it done. I told him at the outset that I wanted it to look ugly and messy, and every hour he kept coming up to me whispering "it's pretty bad," and I would say, "make it worse." And he ended up winning an Emmy for his work on the show.

After Hill St. Blues, *you went on to make the show you were originally pitching to Grant Tinker,* Remington Steele. *Did you have a distinct visual style in mind for that series?*

I had created the show and I felt it should be very "detective." In talking to Grant about developing it, Michael Gleason was brought in, and as writer and producer and co-creator subsequently he developed the script. I remember particularly liking the way the star, Stephanie Zimbalist, could wear a fedora, the signature element of film noir. It was fun to put her in a fedora in those first episodes, and we used a shot of her wearing it in the credit sequence.

You next moved to Moonlighting, *a show with a very unusual style. How did that evolve?*

That look was buried in the pages of the script as well. The script was huge—it was 150 pages long, compared to the typical hour-long script of 100 pages. I had known Glenn Caron on two other pilots that had not sold, and I knew the way he wrote, and appreciated it, and knew that it needed pace. That's just the way he writes—it demands drive and frivolity. The production geniuses were telling us to cut the script, but I knew that was about the right length, which indeed it was. So pace and energy and overlapping dialogue—the old Howard Hawks style—was very much the way Glenn Caron should be played, at least in comedy. Bruce Willis was new, and very adaptable—a good, sly guy. It was just fun to get him and Cybill together going 90 miles an hour.

How about the visual approach?

That too came from the pace. It was rather head-on. It was secretly a comedy, and my feeling is that comedy you can't get too elaborate, you've got to be a little head-on and let those people just bounce off of one another. I've always felt that in action sequences you go as boldly as you can, but in character sequences you go a little straight, so that those characters and comedy and that life energy and velocity can all play through. It's classically known that comedy works better in two-shots than close-ups so there was quite a bit of that.

The ending was originally going to be shot on top of the Capitol Records building, but they wouldn't let us up there. Our location manager suggested the Clock Building, which when we saw it we realized it would end up being a homage to Harold Lloyd, and it actually ended up being better. We rigged it so that we could use the hands of the clock.

Did you continue in episodic TV once you had done the pilots?

Insofar as I could contribute to the ongoing pattern of the show, I would stay with the show for a certain amount of time, maybe direct an episode or whatever.

In *Hill St. Blues*, for example, I was told that Barbara Bochco asked for me to stay on after the pilot and keep them on track, so I ended up doing the first four episodes as well.

Had the show moved away from the direction you had established?

It's always true to an extent, particularly in the performances. The actors take over to an extent because they've done so much work with the characters. They rightfully know what they're doing and what they should be doing. In that process, they're liable to stray a little.

Do you continue to watch the programs once you've shot the pilots?

Sometimes. I don't know if I'm fickle, or we all are, but once I've been there, I'm not that intrigued. I kind of know the score.

Do you find that you get critical watching what's happened to a show that you've set the course for?

Maybe of the performances. I certainly respect what the various directors will unknowingly and constantly bring in of themselves. I don't have much to say about the mechanics of directing, but I watch the performances closely to see if they're getting cute, which they often do. By cute I mean unctuous or precious or self-conscious or egocentric.

What was it like doing the pilot for Sisters, *which was designed to be an intimate family drama?*

I liked the writing, which was gentle, loving, and had a kind of glow to it. I respected that glow of love between those four women. When the show shifted gears to its gentle moments, I would make sure that the shift was clear and conclusive. There was one scene where the young women go back and sell their mother's house, where they'd grown up, and as they leave the empty house for the last time, there wasn't much written. It just said they walked through the living room, and take one last look around and walk out. But I adored the moment—nothing was said, they just take that final look and then leave. Still, it was the only time in my life that I've done eleven takes in a scene with no words. Nothing was spoken, but I just wanted to get the choreography of those four women and their last few footsteps absolutely right. I really tinkered around with it, and the women knowing the show from their perspective and knowing what I was doing were very cooperative. So we just kept fiddling with it, until it had that softness and sincerity and love that I felt was appropriate for the show.

How much input do you have in terms of the visual style of the shows since you are creating the signature of what will be the master for the remainder of the series?

A great deal. I mean we do discuss the look in very generic terms, but in terms of the camera work and staging that's very much my domain.

Clearly Hill St. Blues *was one of your most stylistically distinctive projects. Did you have the same type of freedom elsewhere?*

Not provably, because other pilots didn't lend themselves to as distinctively different a visual style as *Hill St.* It came from the material, which was random and congested and multiple. That suggested the visual style. Usually, shows are slightly more straight ahead than that one was. *Moonlighting* was different, but because it was essentially a duet, and because it was essentially a comedy, that prescribed simplicity.

How did you approach Lois and Clark*?*

I understood instantly that it was sweet feminism. I loved the idea that a young woman who is blindly smitten by our young man can thus be a little crusty about it. Terry Hatcher got it instantly too and played it crusty. She was delicious in playing that, because the crustier her exterior, the more vulnerable her interior. There was some discussion at the network about the degree of her crustiness, but I adored it, and we just ran with it. Her energy and smartness and vivacity helped propel the velocity of the show.

Working on pilots has certainly brought you a great deal of satisfaction.

Making pilots is the second best job in the business—feature films are the first. Pilots give you time and money, plus you really get to direct. I contend that you even get to do a little bit more real directing than in features. Assuming you want to shape performances and help the reality and the naturalism and the world that's being built, in my experience you do more of that sculpting in pilots than features. With features, the money is huge, the complexity is vast, and you hire actors who are known to be the characters they usually play, or people who are synonymous with their own characters. That's the way the casting is done. So what you do in a feature is shade and contribute and collaborate. You help the actor in the reality that he or she is making, and very often you tailor that reality to the actor. It's not that you're really doing less directing, but that your directing is slightly less of a personal or a behavioral nature in terms of the actors playing the lead parts. Whereas in television, you probably have more leading characters—five or six, instead of one or two. You get to sculpt more people, as opposed to tailoring an environment to a star, and then help that star meld with that environment. The nature of your directing in films is thus slightly less personal.

With a pilot, with the world you're creating on a television show, you're sculpting these four or five or six people together into this world. So I guess it follows that there's more sculpting with the individuals as well.

This interview was conducted by phone from Bob Butler's home in Los Angeles in September 1996.

Late-Night Talk Shows

Ellen Brown, Liz Plonka

Late-night television has traditionally been a place where the rules are eased—content is more relaxed, the style is edgier, the approach less mainstream. Over the last few years, late-night TV, at least on NBC, has also been a place that has opened the doors to women directors.

A distinct minority in the largely male-dominated world of television production, women directors in the past were often confined to daytime drama or news. Their rise to post-prime-time power at NBC came about not through political necessity but, like most decisions in television, because of sheer talent and opportunity. A skilled music and cable variety show director, Ellen Brown had worked with Jay Leno in the past when in 1992 he suggested she direct his Tuesday night appearances as guest host of *The Tonight Show Starring Johnny Carson*. Carson's surprise retirement announcement a few years later led to a permanent position, where, with Leno now at the helm, Brown played an important role in *The Tonight Show*'s current creative renewal and ratings dominance. Liz Plonka was an experienced comedy and cable episodic director who came to *Late Night with Conan O'Brien* in 1995. Since that time, she has helped turn the show into network TV's most endearingly quirky hour.

Both Brown and Plonka encountered the difficult task of joining programs already up and running, but a visit to their control rooms quickly reveals the easygoing camaraderie and strong sense of commitment they've established with their technical crew. The flexibility and openness to experimentation of late-night TV has clearly energized their work—a fact reflected in the sharper pacing and verve of their programs. While largely unsung, except when Leno or Conan asks them to roll tape, Ellen Brown and Liz Plonka have helped make NBC's late- night schedule one of the liveliest places on TV.

Ellen Brown

How did you get started as a director?

I started out as a production assistant, moved up to A.D., then made the transition to directing. Dick Ebersol gave me my first directing job doing talk and music segments on the *Midnight Special.* I went on to direct sketch comedy for Showtime's *Night of Almost a Dozen Stars.* My first big break was directing the Easter Seal Telethon in 1987, which was a great training ground—23 hours live. I directed that for three years with Liz Plonka as my A.D. (she now directs *Late Night with Conan O'Brien),* and then she took over when I left. That led to an HBO Special, *Women of the Night,* in 1988, followed by my first network prime-time special, *Get Out the Vote,* for ABC. After that I directed an assortment of comedy and variety programs.

How did your association with The Tonight Show *begin?*

I was directing the second of two late-night pilots for ABC, when I got a call asking if I would be interested in directing *The Tonight Show* when Jay Leno was a guest host. This was about a year before Johnny Carson retired. I'll never forget the moment when I was sitting at my desk at ABC and Peter Lassaly, Carson's producer, called and asked if I'd come in for a meeting and bring my music reel.

Why a music reel for a late-night talk show?

At that time, in addition to Jay performing the monologue and the interviews, the show usually featured a music act with one or two songs. My reputation as a comedy director was already established but Peter and

Fred DeCordova didn't know much about my music background. After sending them my music reel, I had the meeting with Peter and Fred, who offered me the job directing the shows when Jay was the guest host. I accepted immediately without any reservations. What was great about the situation was that I could continue to do my other outside projects.

Had you known Leno before?

I was the A.D. on a special he did from Philadelphia eight or nine years ago and we just hit it off. It was a tough shoot, but we got along very well and kept in touch after the special. When his original *Tonight Show* director was retiring, he recommended me to take over.

How did you prepare for this new position?

By watching the show on TV and observing the director I was replacing. It was a pretty simple show back then. Jay came out and did the monologue, and threw to commercial. There were no cutaways, no banter with the band, no comedy "drop-ins" during the monologue. After the commercial, Jay sat at his desk, did "Headlines" or a comedy piece, interviewed two guests, followed by a music set, and it was over. It was a very simple situation to slide into. Also I'd known many of the crew from working on various series and specials at NBC, and they were all very helpful.

Then in 1991, Johnny Carson makes his surprise announcement that he's retiring. What was this like for you?

I was asked if I'd like to direct the show on a permanent basis, since Bobby Quinn (Johnny's director) decided to leave when Johnny did. We went on the air live in May 1992, with Jay as the host, but almost everything else looked exactly like the old show. The opening changed and so did the band, but as far as how the show was produced and directed, it was still the same *Tonight Show*. It took a while to evolve into the current format. From a directorial standpoint one of the first changes we made was to bring in a handheld camera to supplement the three studio cameras, and after a while we dropped a ped and added a jib [ped—traditional studio camera on a pedestal; jib—a small crane-mounted camera, with a special mounting head that permits the camera to rotate 360 degrees]. But the biggest change occurred when we went to New York for the first time in November 1993, and used the *Saturday*

Night Live setup in Studio 8H. Jay performed the monologue on a "tongue" which stuck out into the audience. This called for a whole new way of shooting, in order to integrate the audience into the shots and translate the studio audience excitement onto the screen.

Did this make a difference to you as a director?

It did, because it gave me more freedom to include the audience and their reactions. Before the New York shoot we made a few changes to the Carson monologue format which never cut away from Johnny. But in New York there was a dramatic change, one that wasn't even planned. We had to build a simple set around the *Saturday Night Live* stage due to time constraints. *SNL* wrapped at 1:30 a.m. Sunday morning, and we had to be in and rehearse on Sunday to go on the air Monday night. One of the set pieces we retained was the "tongue" into the audience that *SNL* used for their host monologues. When Jay walked out onto that "tongue" Monday night, it was the most natural feeling in the world for him. It was as if he were in a comedy club again and you could see how much more comfortable he was in that setting rather than our L.A. studio where he was separated from the audience.

When we returned from New York, we sat down to figure out what we could do about the L.A. studio to open it up and make Jay as comfortable as he was in New York. The decision was made to move into the studio across the hall, build a new set, and make it truly Jay's show. We knew what had worked and what hadn't worked in New York and we looked closely at the tape to see what we could incorporate into the L.A. studio.

When we finally went on the air, Jay walked out, and it was just like he was home. The audience went crazy, because now he was right up there with them. It was exactly what he wanted to do, and he was comfortable with it.

How did this new style evolve for you as a director?

It began back with the shows in New York when I saw the excitement and realized we needed to pick up the pace of the show. The cutting became faster, in order to keep up with the energy of the audience. I brought in extra cameras as well, which made the cutting much easier.

One of the biggest challenges for me when we got back to L.A. was how to cover all the excitement and all the different performance areas with only four camera operators. We've come up with a system where the four cameramen operate six cameras, and so there's a lot of repositioning during commercials and sometimes within segments.

We are always looking for ways to keep things fresh. There's not much you can change in the talk segments, since you have to follow the conversation, so I've tried to make the bumpers [graphic billboards announcing the program's title, generally displayed before and after commercial breaks] in and out of commercials as visually interesting as possible. We go backstage to see guests getting ready before their appearances and we began taping their arrivals to use as bumpers. I've also tried to give the music a video feel by intercutting color and black and white, sometimes with a stutter effect [a computerized visual effect in which the image oscillates and appears to "stutter"]and letterbox [masking the top and bottom of the image to make the image appear wide-screen].

Take us through your preparation through the day.

Mornings are spent getting ready for the 5 p.m. taping. The writers will give me the scripts for that day at around 10:30 and if I have any notes we'll talk about it—how it should be done, etc. In terms of how far they can take a sketch technically, I have them talk to our technical director Mike Stramisky or Mac McAlpin who operates the Video Toaster [a graphics effect machine] to show them what we're capable of in this studio. We just added a video wall to our set, and we're still trying to figure out how we can best incorporate it into the look of the show.

At what point do you begin preparing the music segments?

I'll get a tape of the band, hopefully two or three days before they appear on the show and I'll listen to the song with typed-out lyrics and a band plot so that I can do some preliminary camera blocking. On show day I'll see the band at their 11:30 sound-check rehearsal. I can then make any changes from my preliminary blocking.

Would you say that most artists that appear tend to be pretty standardized in terms of how they're presented?

Yes. Once a musical act has recorded something and performed it, they tend to follow a fairly routine pattern. Plus we have limitations on time—about 3 ½ minutes, which is sometimes a bit shorter than their recorded versions.

After I watch the act at the sound check, we have our production meeting at noon, where we go through the rundown for the day, discuss the segments with the crew and segment producers. After lunch, we'll do a full-camera music rehearsal. That runs about a half hour, and then from 2 to 4 p.m. we'll do comedy rehearsals. Between 4 and 5 we have a second production meeting just to make sure there are no changes, and then we tape at 5.

Over the last few years, would you say there's been a transformation in terms of cutting and pacing?

Absolutely. For me it's a lot more fun now. We're on the edge of our seats the entire hour. There's a lot more excitement and spontaneity. Jay's so much more relaxed and we're always trying to capture the feeling of fun that he and the audience are having. I think the new *Tonight Show* has improved everybody's creativity and I hope it's up there on the screen every night.

Liz Plonka

In the past five years, you've worked on a variety of projects, from telethons, to comedy specials, as well as three seasons of episodic television for Nickelodeon's Clarissa Explains It All. *How did the chance to work on* Late Night with Conan O'Brien *come about?*

It was April of 1995 and I had finished the Easter Seal Telethon. Ironically, my friend Ellen Brown ran into the show's producer Jeff Ross, who mentioned they were looking for a director. Ellen suggested me to him. He checked in with NBC Burbank, they ran it by Don Ohlmeyer (now head of NBC Entertainment), who said "of course!"

Were you familiar with The Late Show with Conan O'Brien*? Had you watched it in the past?*

Yes, I'd seen it but, frankly, the show is on way past my bedtime. So I asked for about a dozen tapes—six of what they considered their best examples and six of their worst.

The program had been on the air nearly two years when you joined it in June. What were your feelings as you came on board?
I was excited, not only about doing something new but about doing something that was on every day, which I had never done before. My biggest trepidation was in leaving episodic, which is the area I've been focusing on. But I took the assignment not just for the challenge, but for the network credibility.

What proved to be the biggest challenge during those first few months?

Creating a quality program every day. For me that means a show that's technically flawless, artistically shot. It means doing the best you can do within the technical and spatial parameters available.

What I encountered immediately was the fact that the set was designed with no camera well [a carved-out area of the studio floor with three walls where studio cameras can placed without any obstructions]. It was taken up by the band, and that meant that everything was pushed forward, which proved very restricting. Another issue, which every director has to face, is "are the crew going to be on your team?"

Did you find the crew eager or apprehensive about you when you first came in?

They weren't eager at all. The first day I was there I was brought into a meeting with the whole crew, who were sitting there with their arms folded. I was prepared for their reaction, but I went in and said "I'm Liz Plonka, the new director, and I don't believe I can do this show by myself. So if anybody has suggestions, I'm open to hear it." Everybody has got to be working together to make it a functioning machine. I try to plant that spirit in the control room, and it's what helps make the job fun.

What aspects of the job did you find surprising?

The first thing you realize is what you're up against doing a show every day. You have to sacrifice certain things, while still maintaining the integrity of the show. You can't always be perfect. You can't always be an "Emmy-quality" show. Another thing that I realized is that there's a lot of room for experimentation in the style of comedy that we do on the show. I can try things and keep coming at it from a different angle directorially until it really works. Conan and the show's head writer,

Jonathan Groff, are really open to this approach, which has created a chain reaction, particularly with the show's other writers. Once they saw Conan could trust me, then they could trust me, and bring me a variety of ideas to try and pull off.

And this sense of trust that you developed has helped spur the show to much greater technical experimentation.

Well, the program is certainly more technically ambitious, and that's partly my fault for not saying no, but I don't want to. I want to let the writers go and do what they want to, because I want the show to be their vision. We'll try it together, and if doesn't work, then we'll back off. We'll sit in the control room and say, "This isn't working, we need to take it one step back." My technical director, Jim Marshall, is absolutely wonderful, and he loves a challenge almost as much as I do. I have a particularly close relationship with my A.D., Tracy King, who's my right arm and an integral part of the production of this show every day. She's technically astute and knows where all the "bodies are buried." I never have to concern myself with anything Tracy's handling. She really lightens my load.

The whole crew, if you approach an idea with enthusiasm, loves to experiment. My philosophy has always been it can be fun or it can be hell, so why not make it fun since we're all here together.

Given the program's edginess and willingness to experiment, is there ever such a thing as a routine show?

Well, maybe every two or three weeks we'll have a show where everything actually goes according to schedule, where the people that we've actually blocked we're actually shooting. But I equate this show with that scene in *Broadcast News* where Holly Hunter is madly chasing around the control room with the tapes to get the show on the air. That's the energy and pace I think we have on *Late Night*.

Discuss your relationship with Conan.

I first met Conan when I came to New York in April in my first go-round with the producer. Gradually, we've developed a real sense of mutual respect and trust. He rarely questions what I do or why I've done it a certain way, and if he does, I have to admit that 90 percent of the time he's right. He has an unerring sense of how things will play comedically. He takes his work seriously and I take my work seriously, and I think that's helped us build a good working relationship.

What happens during the course of a typical day?

By about 11 a.m. or so the script comes in, and I go over it to see what kind of technical or creative problems we might encounter. Writers will come into my office to discuss the comedy for that night's show. There will be planning for the Act I desk piece, which is always the heaviest comedy piece. Act IV is where we tend to put the riskier comedy. We may do something at the top of Act II if there's something topical or to sprinkle more comedy to the show.

I also have to plan the talk segments. The music can be really challenging in that limited space, and with the limited time, about 45 minutes, I have allocated to rehearse.

On non-music days, we start pretaping comedy bits for other shows at about noon, then break for lunch at 1, then from 2 to 3:30 we rehearse the show, followed by another hour of pretaping.

How many cameras do you have on the program?

Due to budget restrictions, I have five cameras, with four operators. This presents particular problems to us because we do so much comedy throughout the show. There are days when I need to add a fifth operator, or we just won't be able to do the show. I won't let the comedy suffer because of technical or other limitations.

One of the things that makes Late Night *so special is that the program is so willing to take risks, both in terms of its comedy and in terms of its production. In what ways have you contributed to this?*

I think that the writers feel confident in my ability and that allows them to try more. I'm in the habit of saying yes, let's try it, let's see if it can be done. Part of the fun of doing this show is the challenge of getting it done really well every day. That's true from Conan's standpoint and my standpoint.

If somebody says, "Do you think you can do this?," I'll go to the 11th hour before I say no. The writers appreciate this, and I think it encourages them to take things to the next level.

Liz Plonka was interviewed at the Late Show *studios in New York in*

February 1996. Ellen Brown was interviewed at the Tonight Show *studios in Burbank, California, in August 1996. This article originally appeared in the DGA Magazine, Vol. 22, No. 1, March-April 1997.*

Late-Night Talk and Comedy

Jerry Foley, Beth McCarthy

Long-running TV shows often resemble established monarchies, where all efforts are centered around the preservation of a ruling family (the principal stars and other significant above-the-line personnel). While maintaining power and control is always important, the continuing renewal of creative vision is perhaps the most daunting challenge. Long-term success usually depends on a delicate balance of talent and personality, both in front of and behind the throne/camera. Even small changes in personnel can greatly affect not just operations but also imagination.

Recently two of network television's most durable programs faced a similar problem in terms of their artistic ensemble. At virtually the same time, the original directors of *The Late Show with David Letterman* and *Saturday Night Live* decided to retire. Hal Gurnee had been associated with David Letterman since Letterman's first effort on NBC in 1980, and together they and the show's writers helped define an iconoclastic approach to the talk show that combined the wackiness of early Steve Allen with the slyly detached collegiate sensibilities of the 1980s. Dave Wilson had worked on *Saturday Night Live* since the first show back in 1975, skillfully directing the triumphant return of the live comedy-variety format, and sustaining its frantic demands and grueling pace for close to two decades.

Both Gurnee and Wilson retired in May 1995, leaving their respective programs at crucial junctures. Letterman had moved his late-night program from NBC to CBS about a year and a half before and, though riding high in the ratings and press attention, was facing a period when the program would steadily begin to lose ground to *The Tonight Show*. *Saturday Night Live* had just concluded a dismally received season, forcing creator and Executive Producer Lorne Michaels to embark on a thorough housecleaning to maintain the viability of his valuable late-night kingdom.

Though television is celebrated as a producer's and writer's medium, the contributions of Gurnee and Wilson were extraordinarily significant. They brought to their programs an alert sense of style and pacing, perfectly attuned to the friskier rhythms of "TV generation" television. Just as important was the continuity they provided night after night, week after week, year after year. They were true pioneers who knew the precise contours and "directions" of their shows because they had played a vital part in shaping them. Finding replacements would be no easy task.

Each program set about the search in characteristic ways. The community feeling that fueled the Letterman show (and revealed itself to viewers by the frequent appearances of most members of the production staff), made it difficult to conceive of a post-"Hal" era, especially given Gurnee's pivotal role as a founding father, Letterman-insider, and ever-so-unflappable control-room commander-in-chief. Nevertheless, when the time came to pass the baton, the solution came quite naturally from within the confines of the "family." Only a few weeks before he announced his retirement, Gurnee turned to his technical director of the past five years, Jerry Foley, and asked if he would like to direct the show. Foley, relatively inexperienced as a director, was surprised and gratified, and with just a brief period of on-air training, took over the reins of control. His atypical ascension (technical directors are rarely promoted internally to such a high-powered position) was in keeping with the camaraderie and esprit de corps the Letterman program fostered (at least until recently) among its creative personnel.

Saturday Night Live faced the issue of succession in a different manner. Dave Wilson's retirement coincided with one of the program's periodic efforts to recreate itself. Responding to a barrage of criticism, Executive Producer Lorne Michaels fired several of the previous season's cast members and writers and set out to replace them with fresh talent.

The choice for a new director would be an especially important decision, since it would be his or her job to recharge the show's "live" spirit and flair. In selecting the thirty-two-year-old Beth McCarthy, Michaels signalled his eagerness for change. McCarthy's years of experience at MTV (where she worked on virtually every type of format) and most recently at the cheerfully offbeat but little-seen *The Jon Stewart Show,* made her an intriguing choice to steer *Saturday Night Live* on its latest quest for creative renewal.

As they complete their first year, both Foley and McCarthy have managed to carve out individual identities within the confines of programs rich in institutional tradition. But establishing their new roles has not been entirely easy. They each faced intense pressure as they stepped into the shoes of beloved directors who were animating spirits of their respective shows. Foley's task was admittedly less difficult, since he had worked closely with Hal Gurnee, and as technical director had skillfully managed the program's large studio crew. His knowledge and their loyalty made the transition almost seamless (Foley simply took over on the Monday after the show's weeklong visit to London in May 1995, with Hal stepping in for a final night and salute on the Friday telecast). Still, in the months that followed, Foley discovered that navigating *The Late Show* requires a near-Herculean degree of stamina and imagination. The five-day-a week schedule is relentless, particularly given the multiple formats involved every night, from sketch comedy, remote pickups, pre-produced shorts, musical/variety acts, as well as a high-speed, restless style of talk/conversation. Mastering all of these elements and integrating them into a unified package would be a formidable task even for an accomplished director. That Foley, a directorial neophyte, has kept *The Late Show* sailing smoothly aloft, while imposing his own quicker visual pace, is a testament to his years of training at Hal Gurnee's side and his natural technical finesse.

By contrast, Beth McCarthy came to *Saturday Night Live* as a newcomer faced with a veteran production crew and a cast with little TV experience. She quickly needed to win their trust and confidence–a difficult position for any young woman entering the largely male confines of network television. The actors responded to her commitment and enthusiasm immediately; the technical staff proved a bit more challenging. Fortunately, Dave Wilson was a valuable mentor her first few weeks on the job, teaching her the rudiments of sketch comedy blocking and the contours of Lorne Michaels's sensibility. Where

McCarthy initially made her mark was in her dynamic approach to the music segments; and gradually after several months of working together, the production staff began to recognize the new creative possibilities she brought to their two-decade-old operation. By January 1996 she (and they) were becoming more comfortable with the demands of her multifaceted role.

In looking back on their first season, Foley and McCarthy recognize that their jobs are among the best and the toughest in television. The workload can be overwhelming (as their interviews reveal), but the pressures produce their own creative rewards. Both *Saturday Night Live* and *The Late Show* showcase a director's range and flexibility in unique ways. It's a high-wire challenge that Beth McCarthy and Jerry Foley clearly enjoy.

Jerry Foley

You'd been the technical director of Late Night with David Letterman *for five years when in 1993 it was announced that you all would be moving to another network. How did that transition work out for you and other members of the staff?*

I had been at NBC for thirteen years. When I started, just getting a network job was quite a feat. I settled into the standard path through the ranks and was lucky enough to become a technical director.

That's a pretty good run and I was grateful. I knew, though, that I didn't want the new experiences to end there and the fear of that happening kept me on the lookout for opportunities beyond what the system was offering. Then came this rather emotional evening when we gathered in the studio and found out that *Late Night* was moving to CBS.

Robert Morton, the executive producer at the time, made the announcement. Dave put his coat on, thanked everybody, and said, "To those of you who are able, we'd love to have you come along." With that he was off to the now-famous press conference. It was then that everybody had to figure out whether they really wanted to pursue the move, and how practical it was. The producers were left with the question of just how much of the show do you bring. It wasn't something that happened every day so there was no blueprint to follow.

How many of the technical crew came from NBC to CBS?

Just a few. Joe DeBonis, who does all our remotes and studio handheld camera, videotape operator and crash editor Kevin Drone, and lighting designer Ruth Roberts who's since moved on.

In essence, Dave's electronic nervous system made the move?

Some key elements made the transition with us and from that nucleus, the CBS personalities began to emerge.

How long did it take before the old NBC crew was able to meld with the new people at CBS?

It might have taken all of the first year and this is one of the areas where Hal Gurnee played a crucial role. Hal knew the importance of involving other people in the process. He had a great way of coming into the control room and setting a mood—dignified irreverence. He made people feel comfortable enough to contribute. So the personalities that you want on this show were drawn out by the setting Hal provided. He wouldn't issue a lot of memos and edicts, none of that. In fact most days we had no idea what the hell he was talking about. He'd arrive with nothing more than a pencil, and a cup of coffee. He was like a college professor and you were either going to buy into his teaching methods or you were going to be totally baffled. The people who bought in enjoyed the freedom, flourished, and those accustomed to a more traditional environment moved on.

Describe your relationship with Hal in the close confines of director and technical director.

The first year that I was his technical director at NBC—and remember he loved his previous T.D. —I just sat there with my mouth shut. There wasn't any great concept behind my approach other than I'm shy and Hal takes a little time to warm up to. I always kept in mind that he was older than me and he had this enormous reputation. He was doing Jack Paar when I was in kindergarten, and well, he was Hal. There was no way you could get mad at the guy. He was smarter and funnier and he had a great sense of what's important and what isn't.

When did you begin to feel more comfortable with him, and he with you, so that you began to feel like a team?

Well, he didn't let me off that easy. I don't think it was really until we came here to CBS. We had four years together at NBC and it was very much a working relationship—you're a technician, you're on a great show, you do a good job, and you're a nice guy.

Was Hal Gurnee involved in bringing you along?

I'll never know but I'm sure nobody would've bothered talking to me if Hal had shook his head and said don't bother.

And then, a little more than a year later, it's announced that Hal Gurnee is leaving. Was it clear once you made the move that this was on the drawing boards?

That was a very sudden turn of events. When we got here I was quite occupied with the responsibility and challenge I faced. I was at a new network with a clean slate and an unfamiliar crew. This is where Hal let me do my own thing. He said to me, on more than one occasion, "It's your crew, you're the technical director." I had to deliver the facilities to Hal but it remained an apprenticeship, in the classic definition of the term.

As part of my discussions about leaving NBC I made it known to Robert Morton and Peter Lassally that I would someday like to direct. But this was on a very informal basis, and certainly not obvious. I didn't want Hal getting the wrong impression. He needed a technical director, not a guy who was after his job. I never had the discussion with Hal out of simple respect. I wanted to make sure he knew I was loyal and was going to keep doing what I did.

As the workload at CBS increased, I came out front to Hal and asked to direct some of the outside remotes—St. Patrick's Day Parade, etc. Hal was a little uncomfortable but gracious in his response. We're talking about just a speck of directing work, but it put Hal in the awkward position of having to set some new precedents; technical directors don't typically get these kinds of chances.

I did some of this smaller stuff for a couple of months then, in May 1995, right as we're about to head off to London, Hal took me into his office and closed the door. This was not something that happened often. He just came out and asked me if I would be interested in directing the show. It was totally unexpected. I figured that certain people had some appreciation for my work but there's really no way to gauge the depth and reach of that respect. It was immediately gratifying, however, to realize that I had succeeded in being loyal to Hal without overreaching or being disrespectful. To have him come around and endorse me really meant a lot. For a while the excitement of him recommending me exceeded the excitement of the opportunity. Of course, he didn't want to hear any of that kind of stuff— not his style.

And then it became a very delicate social situation. You don't want to jinx it. You don't know the level of discussion that's gone on. You don't know how real it is. Hal advised me to lay low.

When was it made public?

The release announcing Hal's retirement went out the week before our London shows, about a month after Hal talked to me. There were some awkward moments but it was very well handled, very classy on everyone's part. One of the proud legacies of this production company is its great farm system. Interns, A.D.'s and technicians have been afforded great opportunities. Look at what they're doing. They're taking a guy and putting him in a key position on a multimillion dollar franchise, untested. I always wanted to direct and educated myself to that end. I had done some small-scale, no-name work. And here are these people who don't know me outside of being a technical director, and they're giving me one of the premier jobs in television. If it ended tomorrow, I would be forever in their debt. They gave me my first professional contract. There's no down side.

When the notice came out the production company wisely made no mention of a successor. I didn't have the pressure on me from outside people focusing on what I was trying to do.

What was this period like with Hal leading up to the final show?

Prior to going to London, I had directed a couple of segments and did one full show with Hal behind me. I flew to London, got preparations underway, and did the five London shows as technical director. I directed four more shows the following week in New York and then that Friday Hal and I teamed up one more time in our previous roles. After a nice on-air tribute from Dave, Hal was off into the sunset.

So by June of 1995, you were the director. How were you feeling during this initial period?

You don't look down because that's just going to scare you. There certainly was some pressure involved but most of it was from inside my own head. Like most people I work with I had been watching musical variety shows and talk shows since I was a little kid and this was something that I had a feel for and really wanted to be involved in. Now all of the sudden I'm there and like the guy who gets elected to high office you go in there starry eyed with all these wonderful things you want to do and you quickly find out that you're trying to move a battleship. You don't suddenly make a hard left and new graphics, camera angles and lighting schemes come up.

How long did it take before you felt (a) comfortable and (b) comfortable enough to start to inflict any of your own ideas?

I don't think I'm ever going to feel that comfortable, and I don't think I'm supposed to be comfortable. I have to be cognizant of what Dave wants, keeping his options open and leaving him with enough confidence to go out and perform and not be concerned with my end of the deal. You keep your eye on those goals and comfort doesn't factor in at all. It's also a producer's medium, so you can't let your ambition exceed your role. I have to be aware that as much as I am required and welcome to contribute, there's an understanding that only a small percentage of the suggestions are going to be implemented. I keep in mind that it's Dave and the writers who are driving this vehicle. You always pitch hard but ultimately it's their vision.

Do you feel the show has changed in terms of its direction since you've taken over the reins?

We've tried a couple of different angles and lighting conditions, tried to be more progressive in our music production but any changes I have effected are mostly not visible to the viewer. Specifically in the areas of information flow in preproduction and editing. We may have gotten a little bolder in our staging, for example, there's now a different opening, but the reality is and always has been that the guy behind the desk is what people are watching and it makes me a little uneasy when people pick up on the "direction" of the show. My job is to keep things moving; beyond that there's no room for a heavy hand in any area.

Take us through your typical day.

I'm usually in between 9:30 and 10 a.m. I'll start with a couple of phone calls, maybe deal with problems from the day before and they could be centered on personnel issues—the crew—ongoing technical issues that need to be resolved or improvements we're trying to implement. There's always a question about staging, band set up or something regarding the network.

The production meeting takes place at 10:45 and it is there that the days events are laid out along with the hopes and dreams of writers and segment producers. It's a great part of the day because nobody's been injured yet.

At 2 p.m. all issues concerning lighting, microphones, set construction, wardrobe, camera angles, staging, etc., should have been thought through so that Dave and the writers can take the stage and be free to concentrate on performance and embellishing whatever material we have up to that point.

In a sense, you work in a liaison capacity, relaying technical issues to producers and to the network.

Yes, that's part of it. There is a pool of very talented CBS people who will do absolutely anything you ask. They're phenomenal. After seeing and hearing the various descriptions about what a piece is supposed to be, I have to relay to the crew and CBS exactly how that may or may not affect a given show and what the requirements will be. In many ways it's like having the Pentagon at your disposal. If you can articulate what you need, the sky's the limit. If we've planned a bit where a guest, Alec Baldwin in this case, is going to ride a snowmobile on the roof of the parking lot down the street, that may be as far as the writers and segment producers have developed the idea. They know that when Alec shows up he'll add to it himself and after we've run it a few times other ideas will present themselves while earlier concepts will be discarded. What I need to do is facilitate the skit; we know there will be communication issues, microphones, speakers, etc. There will be concerns about cueing with the stage managers, and timings with the associate directors. There will be prop issues—we've got to get a snowmobile down there. These are all details that the writers and Dave shouldn't be encumbered with.

So you're kind of the nexus, where all sorts of technical and production information flows back and forth.

Well, maybe that sounds a little too important but the description is accurate. Throughout the day people will pass along a variety of related details. Information is flowing all over the place and you have to be flexible enough to accept it from wherever and whomever it may come. You can't worry about why somebody found out something before you or after you. You just have to be kind of gently corralling people and resources and try to get everyone focused on getting it into a state where Dave can go off in any direction he wants.

What happens next after you've marshaled your production resources and you're feeling comfortable about the technical strategy of the upcoming show?

That's Dave's time. That's the writers' time. That's the segment producer's time. With any luck we're prepared to give life to any one idea that's been kicked around in the morning meeting or further develop an idea that's been through several previous rehearsals.

What's your relationship like with him during the rehearsal period? Are you sometimes just the man in the booth who he relies on to get the shots right?

Most of the time that is the best role for me to play. Hopefully he knows there's a loyal, energetic guy downstairs who's done the degree of homework I've described and is going to represent his inclinations and his aspirations creatively and cleanly. Then he doesn't have to worry—he can just relay his feelings to the stage manager, who's in communication with me about where he might want the camera or which way an actor should be facing.

Letterman will take this much control over directing stage business then?

Sure. Once we've given him something to work with it goes through a wonderful, and sometimes exasperating, process of fine tuning.

So one way of looking at it is that during this rehearsal period there are two directors—you and Dave. Your collaboration is in being able to instantly execute his impulses.

There are many directors but as any successful collaborator knows, you have to be very careful when you weigh in with an opinion and just how important your contribution will be to the entire piece. If I want to obsess on something that may be bothering me as a director, that's not necessarily going to give Dave confidence that the piece will go well. On the other hand nobody wants you to wimp out because you're afraid people will be uncomfortable by the challenge.

In a way, you're the Paul Shaffer of the control booth. You're mirroring his moods and impulses and executing them instantly, but with camera shots rather than music.

You have to get away from these lofty descriptions—I may start to believe them. Again though there's some truth in the analogy. This is very much a part of my responsibilities and I in turn have to delegate the detail work to the very able people around me. I have to be freed up to do what you just described. I can't worry about technical issues when I call for a camera or satellite feed or sound effect or tape roll. By the time we start taping, my concentration has got to be strictly on Dave's performance. And what makes him unique and still very exciting is that he doesn't know where that performance is going. My best moments are when he's up there after all the preparation and rehearsal and he feels secure enough to go anywhere he wants. Of course there are those less exciting moments when I totally derail him because I'm a boob.

You've given him the scaffolding and he has the opportunity to fly.

This is what we hope to do. Giving him that confidence is as important as making sure there's a signal from the garage roof or the remote camera on Broadway. Convincing him that it's going to be O.K. is an important part of the job. A lot of times rehearsal is this weird hybrid of blocking—letting the lighting and sound know where people will enter and exit—but you're equally committed to the conceptualization happening at that time.

That's what makes the show unique, at least for a daily program. You're putting on a play, a comedy, every day, with writing, creating, directing.

And this is where you always get into some exciting, high-energy conflict, and I mean that in the best sense of the word. There's the craft end of it—getting a good presentation, which everybody realizes is important. But that can't overshadow or overburden the creative process. And that's a fun struggle. A writer will come up with a great idea—let's dangle an elephant from the catwalk. But then you have to go out and explain that the follow spot [the principal spotlight, generally at the rear of the auditorium, which follows the main performer on stage] doesn't reach the catwalk and the cat walk can't support the weight of the elephant. So, you're sometimes dismantling at the very moments they're trying to build.

So you're in the control room, while the creative forces are out on the stage, and during the period there's this constant electronic give and take going on between the floors.

Well, I suppose. There is after all a process at work that puts an idea in one end of the machine and on a good day some fun comes out on the other side. I feel very protective of the writers' ideas as they evolve and if a writer spends some time in the control room he can see what I see and I can offer up options for camera angles and actors' positions. We can work out how a character is brought onstage and find out early that we may be tipping the joke or not staying with it long enough. What we're trying to do is hammer this thing into something that feels right and is close to what the concept was or easily absorbing what the changes might be to the original idea.

It's a plus when writers are coming and going between the stage and the control room. One of the few disadvantages that the physical plant of the theater dumps on us is the distance between the two areas. We're in the basement, at the back of the house. Even though I can be on the stage in twenty seconds, it's not like most TV studios or like it was in our days at NBC, where we were literally right outside the door of the stage.

And that makes a difference?

Oh, yeah. I feel bad sometimes for Dave and the people on the stage during rehearsal because their entire connection to the facility is one monitor. It's frustrating for them. They're so removed from the engine room activity it's tough to understand why things take as long as they do. Everyone appreciates the effort but that separation lends itself to more anxiety than we need.

After the cobbling together of the rehearsal period from 2 to 4, you then begin the music rehearsal period. What's that like?

Dave will go upstairs and now have gone from broad concept to something a little more focused, but we still haven't nailed down the show. Ideally we've given him more than he needs and he'll sort it out with the writers sometime around 5.

In the meantime, the work downstairs doesn't stop. Paul Shaffer gets the stage at 4, and he typically will spend about 15 minutes with his band working out play-on for the guests. Simultaneously, we're setting up a guest band, for the second time that day. The crew has previously set up the drum kits and stage monitors at about 11 a.m. One of the key points, which evolves during the week is working out stage plots, which we try to vary from band to band. Unlike other shows we don't have the luxury of a huge space to work with nor is there a lot of storage for props. In tandem with that is a production decision that we really don't want to make it look like something other than *Late Show*. It's a very delicate balance between trying to give the thing some pizzazz and some production value, but not making it look like something you've never seen before if you were flipping through the channels.

You're very aware as a director, then, of making it look fresh night to night?

One of the worst things you can do on a show like this is to fall into repetition, and we fight that every day. You can do an awful lot with lighting, camera angles, and camera moves. Our musical producer, Sheila Rodders, does a great job of finding out who's hot and what's out there, and I try to keep an ongoing dialogue with her about how she sees a particular act presented. She also has very valuable insight into what managers may or may not want to do in this particular venue. For example, when we had Bruce Springsteen on a few months back, I prepared by listening to the CD, while Sheila was working with managers and Dave on song selection. After that's done, I research through reviews any information that may help me out on production. I read that during his performance of "Youngstown," which was the song he selected to perform, they'd done some very dramatic lighting onstage. I mentioned that to Sheila, who then went back to his management, who said they didn't want to make such a statement on the Letterman show. They wanted something more sparse and stripped down. So, by the time he finally gets here, we've all reached a decision that since he's going to be onstage alone, it's going to be minimal lighting, with a lot of close-ups to emphasize the face. But the question arose: since there's no musical accompaniment, no chorus, no musical breaks, how do you make that interesting? What we discovered was you want some relationship with the audience, and how they're totally wrapped up in what he's doing. His management just wants close-ups, but we wanted to make it clear that this wasn't a tape—it was Springsteen performing on the Letterman show to the Letterman audience. Ultimately, there were some compromises, but I think we came up with something nice.

At 4:15, the feature musical act will come on, and I'm trying to get the cameras to show me what we can do that may be a little different than last night. In tandem with that, the lyrics of the song have been transcribed by my assistant Amy Cherin. She's had musical training and has broken the song into bar counts.

It reminds me of Live from Lincoln Center *music-style direction, where you're conducting musically through the camera and switcher.*

Another lofty comparison, but I'll take it. One of my associate directors, Jessica Santini, is in the audience taking edits and doing research on who is singing at what moment during the choruses—is it two singers or three singers? Where are they positioned? She can then come down and tell me the configurations by line. But let's not forget that musicians are devils, and things change from rehearsal to rehearsal and even during the actual show.

How often would you say you have to wing it?

Maybe about 75 percent of the time you can script it, but 25 percent of the time you better be flexible enough to grab it as you go. I can only approach it by trying to be as perfect as possible, and then when it's time to go off the page, well then, you go off the page.

We shoot it twice in rehearsals, the group may then go down to the sound booth, listen to a playback, and come up and perform again. Hopefully by that time I have a rough idea, but I'm still shopping. By 5:15, if I'm not encumbered by a particularly intricate production problem I can go through the lyrics, factor in the edits and do a shot sheet. Jessica will number and transfer the shots to a form for the camera people, and more often than not, we'll be able to stick to it. Typically, we're using five cameras, three studio, a handheld, and a Jimmy Jib [a small crane-mounted camera, with a special mounting head that permits the camera to rotate 360 degrees]. A three-minute rock number may have thirty-five shots. But what makes the job great is the variety of music you have to be familiar with, from klezmer to rock to pop.

In the course of about 2 ½ hours, you shift from sketch comedy direction to musical direction, then, with a fifteen-minute break, it's show time.

It's the best of all worlds, but if you spend too much time thinking about what you're doing you'll never get through the day. By the time the show starts taping live at 5:30 p.m., I've availed myself of the expertise of all the people around me, especially lead A.D. Randi Gross and T.D. Tim Kennedy. This is one of the hardest things a guy in my position has to learn and remember. The biggest mistake you can make is to try to do it all yourself. There are wonderful people working here, and as long as you've been clear and fair about what we're trying to accomplish in the next hour, it can be the greatest ride on earth. The lights go on, the band kicks in, Dave hits the stage—where else would you want to be! It's just wonderful, and I'm grateful for it every day.

At that moment, at 5:30, I have a little speaker next to me, and it's just Dave's voice, and that's what I'm glued to. One of the things I've discovered over the last few months is to concentrate on Dave's mutterings, which could take the show in an entirely different direction. He'll be starting a little riff on something. You've got to be ready. If you're not there's no place to hide.

I noticed that it's a very oral control room, in the sense that everything's focused on what Dave's saying, almost to the exclusion of anything else. You've got to follow that direction, since things could quite literally change on a dime.

And often do. So at 5:30, I've done all my shot sheets, spoken with the segment producers and writers, and we've dealt with the stage managers and whoever else might be helping us out as an actor that night. We try to be as organized as we can be so we can concentrate on one guy.

And that guy is like a rocket because in one way he can suddenly veer right, and everything—the dozens and dozens of technical people—have got to follow.

Based on my experience, I can safely say, with the greatest affection, it is like no other show anywhere.

On Letterman, *you function not only as a sketch director, and a musical director, and a talk show director, but also as a remote director. What is that situation like?*

Again, it's a very fortunate situation I find myself in. You go from multi-camera studio work to essentially making a movie. It's a single-camera shoot most of the time. It is done on the fly and on the streets. My main contribution is to make sure there's coverage there, so when the writer gets into editing he has options. Occasionally there's a script to break-down and some choreography and stunt coordination. Sometime actors are involved. The variety of situations is quite broad but like the rest of the show it's all about Dave and the writers. You try to help without confusing things further.

How many nights a week does this go on?

Two or three. But again it's all this role playing. You're not a film director in the sense that you have complete command of the set. There is no set. The best thing I can do is to make sure that we got it done in a reasonable amount of time and nobody got hurt.

Your job then is to make their vision work?

Exactly. And if I at some point can impart my own sensibility, well there's a bonus.

Beth McCarthy

You got started at MTV, which proved to be an absolutely invaluable experience for you as a director.

Yes, the beauty of being at a place like MTV is that you learn how to do a lot of different TV directing. You get paid no money, you work the most insane hours in the world, but it's an incredible atmosphere to learn in. It's like going to school and getting paid for it.

I was at MTV at a great time, right at the point when they began seriously launching their own original programming. When I started out directing here in 1987 (after working as an associate director and producer), I quickly found myself directing virtually every type of programming. I did news shows, entertainment shows, quiz shows, all one day after the other. We might shoot 15 episodes of *Club MTV* on Sunday and Monday, and then I'd be back in the studio directing VJ segments on Tuesday. I also got a lot of experience directing live programming, such as our *Spring Break* which we would shoot live from Florida for five days, or pregame shows to our big events. Plus, there were lots of new shows getting started—we'd do pilot after pilot, new show after new show. I was very fortunate to do the pilot episode of *Unplugged*, which at the time was three cameras and a walk-down camera hung in the ceiling. Nobody knew what that show would turn out to be, and I ended up doing a lot of the programs, including the ones with Tony Bennett and Nirvana.

In many ways, you were the having the kind of experiences in television directors haven't had since "The Golden Age," literally doing a lot of everything, acquiring valuable skills in every format.

Well, that's why it was so extraordinary to be at MTV when I was there. I was able to do so many different styles of directing.

My next big project at MTV was the *Jon Stewart Show*, which proved to be an incredible experience. Jon is a fantastic talent, and is one of the few creative people I've encountered who can handle the nuts and bolts of production. His creativity is matched with a real understanding of the mechanical process, which helped us work together beautifully. Ultimately, the show was picked up for syndication by Paramount in the spring of 1994, which meant I had to face the most difficult decision of my life—leaving MTV. By this time I was senior director, and it was very hard, and it probably shouldn't have been that hard, but I was such a sheltered child there. Shows came up, and I did them. What I loved was the variety—I was never bored.

You did decide to leave, but unfortunately, syndication didn't prove to be a pot of gold.

We lasted ten months, going on September 12th, 1994, and ending in June 1995. It was very sad, because it was such a great show, primarily because Jon was the kind of person that made you want to put your heart and soul into it. The problem was that syndication demands good ratings numbers in the first three months. We didn't have the luxury that Letterman had when he started out to get a chance to grow. We had bad affiliates and bad time slots. We found out we were canceled when we were on a break in May 1995 and we still had two weeks of shows to do. It was devastating, but right after that I got a call from Lorne Michaels's production office. *Saturday Night Live*'s longtime director Dave Wilson was retiring, and I was recommended by Keith Raywood, who was the show's production designer, but had worked with me on a number of MTV projects. They were talking to one director, who had no interest in doing the musical segments—was afraid of doing it, didn't want to do it. So Keith told Lorne that I was going to be out of work in two weeks and you should meet with her. Originally they talked to me about just directing the music pieces and "Weekend Update."

How did you feel about that?

I was fine with that—it was the easiest gig in the world for me. But then that director wasn't a contender anymore and they asked my agent to include more comedy on my audition reel, and I asked why, if all I'm doing is the musical segments. It turned out they wanted one director for the whole show, and I was so scared. At the same time I wanted to stay in New York, and here was the quintessential New York show. So this process of negotiation continued throughout July and August of 1995, and didn't conclude till right before Labor Day weekend.

And the first show was scheduled when?

September 30th.

What was the month of September like for you?

I was cramming for finals. I watched every show I could, guided by one of the producers of the show, Kenny Among.

Did they tell you they wanted continuity or were you given a mandate for change?

I don't think they would have hired me if they didn't want it to change a little bit. Lorne definitely wanted a different look. When he hired me he told me he really liked my reel, but the one part he didn't like was my use of tight close-ups on musicians hands. I was surprised he liked my work, because the reel had a *lot* of close-ups. He certainly didn't sound like he wanted to curb and guide me in any way, and I had a sense that he felt I could pick up everything I needed to know as I went along.

I studied those tapes closely because I didn't have a large amount of sketch-blocking experience. I shot everything on the *Jon Stewart Show*—all the single-camera pieces, all the remote pieces—and that was the most intense comedy work I had done. I learned a lot that year, but there's a big difference blocking something for single camera where you're getting pickup and blocking something for multi-camera live.

What else did you feel you needed to do during that month before the first show?

I started meeting with people. I met with Lorne Michaels a few times. I began working with Jim Signorelli, who's the show's film director, and Keith Raywood, the set designer, designing the new opening and logos. I was also meeting with the writers and all of the different crew people as well as the show's very talented set designers. It was intimidating as hell. These were people who had done the show for twenty years.

What was it like to come into a show that had been on the air for two decades and quite literally be the new kid on the block, facing this seasoned production crew?

I think it would have been difficult for anyone to come onto the show and fill Dave Wilson's shoes. But by and large they tended to be supportive, once they got used to a thirty-two-year-old woman coming into a program that they had been working on for so long.

One problem, and this was inevitable, is that this crew, or any crew, were used to a routine way of doing things. If we were going to do a store setup, they knew from two decades of working on the show how a store setup should go.

Did you consider it your role to fit in with this culture, or do you feel your mission was to change it?

I definitely had to fit in. It's important to remember that I was on a huge learning curve, and these were people who had done the show for twenty years so they weren't quite as accommodating to your mistakes as if you had been with them right from the start.

Do you think Lorne Michaels was eyeing you warily at this initial stage?

Not really, but he definitely had a lot more comments about shooting in the fall than he does now. Which to me is great because I needed to figure out what he likes and what he doesn't like.

This was all very hard for me because I haven't been in this kind of position for a long time, where people weren't saying "that's amazing" or "don't change a thing." I got a lot of criticism, and it was all very constructive and right on the money, and it's really helped me be better, week after week after week.

Ken Among, the supervising producer, was so supportive of me, and always is. And I had tremendous support from the set and lighting designers, who were really helpful. But it just takes a while. These are people who have been in the same place for twenty years, and all of a sudden somebody else is coming in. They are understandably a bit wary.

How did you get up to speed then on what was a very different approach to directing?

They brought Dave Wilson in for the first four shows, and he sat with me and helped me out when I had any questions. He was the nicest man I've ever met, so sweet and wonderful to me, and it made for a much smoother transition. Basically, we don't have much time for blocking. The sketches are completed Wednesday night and Thursday we go out to the studio and begin blocking them for the next two days. It doesn't make for a lot of time to be creative. Davey would show me how he would set up the scene—where the people would go, where the furniture would go.

Did you have any theater background to draw on?

No, but I work very well with talent, and that's what's been helpful this season. It's a new cast, and we get along great. We all learned along the way together. During that first month of working with Dave, he would watch me block, and I would ask him after the sketch if there was anything he noted that could make it better. This was very helpful to me in addition because he knew Lorne Michaels's sensibility inside and out, and at this point I didn't know Lorne very well. He would let me know the things Lorne would like and wouldn't like.

I also drew a lot from my experience with Jon Stewart in terms of camera positioning and cutting, such as the cardinal rule that if you're going to go to a close-up you better have a *reason* to do it. The thing that was so different for me about *Saturday Night Live* was that I was used to capturing the action, not creating it. And now, I had to create it.

How did you make that transition to literally becoming a theater/sketch director?

It was hard. I wasn't very good at it, I don't think, and I'm still not great at it. But the beauty of it is that I hope I'll have more than just this season to get good at it. And I'm an insane perfectionist—I'm very self-critical. I come in on every Monday and watch the show and the dress rehearsal from top to bottom, and take note of everything that was bad, and try not to do it again.

I welcomed the comments I got during those first few months. I'd been learning where you need to cut to reactions in sketches or where you need to see more close-ups, and which writers and producers wanted things done a certain way. This was a lot more helpful than just hearing "oh, that sketch is OK."

What was your relationship like with the talent, particularly since many of them started on the show at the same time you did?

I have been so lucky to work with a cast that has proven to be so talented. It's been wonderful. It's been a complete team effort; they want to help, and they want to do anything they can to make the show a success. It's a great atmosphere to work in.

What needs to be mentioned is that the new cast members had no TV experience; they all came from comedy troupes and the stage. I think they're a really strong group of performers and very funny. I'm very pleased with the way they've come along and how talented they are. And it's because of them that I think the show is phenomenally better.

Where do you feel you were given the most creative freedom? The music segments?

Absolutely, and that's where I felt most comfortable. I didn't feel comfortable having creative freedom on the sketches because I didn't feel I had a grasp fully on the situation. I'm the kind of person that loves to be right, but I have to be 1,000-percent right before I feel I can barge in with my expertise. For me to go in and make drastic changes on the sketch shooting when I didn't feel comfortable with the blocking and shooting was ridiculous. I had fun blocking the music, but when I was blocking the sketches I stressed out from the first part of the day to the end of the day. I didn't like not being amazing at it. I didn't like not being perfect.

It took almost all fall until I felt I really could add to the sketches from a directorial standpoint. Or even blocking and giving the writers suggestions. I was basically treading water the first four to six shows. Starting in January with the shows hosted by Christopher Walken and Alec Baldwin I began to feel much more comfortable about being out on the floor, blocking talent, grasping the sketches.

The music I had no problem with, since I did so much of it at MTV, and Jon Stewart had a band on every night. I'm happy that when I shoot a musical program most of the people I use have some kind of musical background; in fact one of the cameramen on *Saturday Night Live* is a percussionist, and so he's always in the back shooting drums and percussion because he knows what to go for.

I was particularly impressed with your sensitivity to lighting during the musical segments.

I think the lighting staff has enjoyed my being there this year because we've been trying to do different things. We work very closely together—sometimes they'll show me their ideas for an upcoming sequence, and other times I'll make suggestions. It all depends on the nature of the song and the performer. For example, we did a segment with Tori Amos and her second song was just her and piano on that huge stage. I suggested that in order to emphasize the intimacy of the performance, I'd rather not light the walls, and instead have the overhead Vari-Lights all pointing at her, closing off the set a little bit. It looked beautiful, and it was something vastly different than what had been done before.

I try to use lighting cues to emphasize key points of a song, when you're going to the chorus now, or to the musical bridge. Or when something drastic changes in the song.

I think anything that I try to do musically is basically just a way to enhance what the music is doing, and if I can do that, great. If I'm not going to take that approach, I'd rather not do a lighting cue or a camera move.

Do you try to change your style each week depending on the artist?

Not every week. Sometimes the bands might be very similar and I can guarantee the segment is going to look almost the same, but not exactly. Obviously, it all depends on who the artist is and how the song sounds.

How would you compare how you directed the musical acts on Jon Stewart *with the way you direct on* Saturday Night Live*?*

I think it's a little more toned down now. But it's a nice happy medium; we have some very interesting lighting cues, and I'm able to get a lot of movement out of the cameras and out of the crane. I also particularly like using the handheld with music. I love having the camera right on top of the artist, it just makes you feel like they're right in your living room. It's a different style than Dave Wilson's, people seem to like it, and it's fun for me.

Davey blocked all of his music according to a script, and I don't block music. What I do is tell the camera people what they're going to focus on—the horns and backup singers, let's say. Then I cut the song but it's not exactly the same way each time. The way I block a song during Thursday's music rehearsal is not exactly the same way I do it at Saturday's dress rehearsal or on air.

I have a production assistant who counts the bars of music, which is very helpful in terms of telling me when the guitar solo is coming up or when the chorus is about to start. I'm partial to wide sweeping shots, particularly on choruses if there's a build [an increase in intensity and volume].

Will your planning in terms of lighting cues have been done prior to the music rehearsal on Thursday?

I listen to the music on Tuesday or Wednesday, and if I have something specific to suggest I'll mention it to the lighting people on Wednesday. We'll try to then set it up before the rehearsal the next day.

Take us through your week.

I come in on Monday, watch the shows, and have a pitch meeting with the host. On Tuesday, I work with the writers about anything they might like to try for a sketch or have questions about. They've been writing all day Monday and Tuesday. This is very beneficial for me so I can get a head start on what the sketches call for and tell set design what they need to do if it's something difficult. By Wednesday night, after we pick the sketches for that week's show, I go into set design and we place it in the studio. Then we start talking about specific sets. If writers have specific ideas they'll come in as well, and all three of us will talk. The writers are basically the producers of the piece.

As a director, how do you like working that closely with writers in terms of their having this much input in set design and shape?

I've never had a problem with input. Jon Stewart had an incredible amount of input in his show, so I'm very used to that. Plus two of the writers on *Saturday Night Live* are from *Jon Stewart*, and the other writers are just great. I'll block a sketch, ask if they have any problems with anything. I'm interested in hearing their ideas or comments. I always feel the best idea wins, I don't care whether I had it or not.

Thursdays and Fridays are devoted to blocking the sketching, with constant rewriting going on as the sketches begin to unfold. I'll have blocked all of the cameras shots during those two days, and on Friday night I go to a hotel with a master blank script and I block the whole script out, which everybody then works off for the show.

On Saturdays, after a few hours of sleep, I get to the office about 11:30 in the morning and see if there have been any major changes. Some weeks we haven't even done the cold open or the monologue by this point, and so I'll try to get one of those scripts so I can take a look at them. Then at around ten after 1:00 I head off to the studio so we can begin the run-through of as many sketches as we can, with a fully dressed set, and as much costuming and makeup as we can put together. We break for a meal, during which time the band rehearses, and I'll often go out to the studio and take a look at that. Then I block my "Weekend Update" script, rehearse that and the monologue, and then it's time for the dress.

One of the things that surprised me in watching you block the show is that you utilize the entire setup of Studio 8H, with sets in virtually every corner and wall area. How do you coordinate all of this traffic, and getting cameras from set to set in time?

It's very difficult, especially considering how small the studio is, and how much activity is going on in there. Plus, we'll usually cut four pieces between dress rehearsal and air.

Saturday night's dress rehearsal starts at about 8, and this is a crucial time to see what works and what doesn't. This is a place where Lorne is especially vital. He'll give notes to the writers as the sketch is going on, and the writers will have to make changes as their work is being performed. At a little after ten, we're done with dress, the production assistants grab my script to add the revisions. If there's something that didn't work in dress that I want to go over with the technical director, I'll ask that they get me a script back so we can have a chance to clear up the problems. Then they'll be a meeting in Lorne's office with Lorne, the head writers, and the host. I'll be called in and we decide what's going to be in what part of the show. Lots of time your air show at 11:30 is completely different than the dress. Then we call in the whole cast and the crew, and Lorne gives all of us dress notes. If I have any dress notes, I give them as well. I then get my book in order, run downstairs, talk to the camera guys and the stage manager about any changes.

What do you think the main differences are between a show you shot in March vs. one you shot during your first month?

My comedic timing is much better. My cuts are better. At first I think I overcut, and Lorne might point that out to me, and the following week I would then undercut. I'm now getting a grasp of what sketches need to work best on the screen—what sketches need reaction shots, etc.

Can this be done by looking at the script or does it depend on seeing it in rehearsal?

Sometimes you need to see it before you figure out the editing, but often the nature of the sketch determines your cutting. For example, on our "cheerleaders" sketch, we tend to go with a very basic approach—wide shots for the choreographed cheers, a tighter two-shot for their dialogue on the bench. That's great for me, because that skit makes me laugh so hard I can just sit back and enjoy it, instead of worrying about complicated cutting patterns. Sometimes there are sketches that go by and I don't know what's going on because I'm so involved in getting the shots and cutting right.

One of the things I noticed about your shooting style for the sketches is that it's very minimalist and unfussy. It works well for the show because you trust the comedy and let the sketch live, without trampling it to death through overt style.

A lot of that I learned from working with Jon Stewart. Jon liked the frame to be there and to let the comedy happen in the frame. Lorne also follows a similar approach. He always says that if you're going to cut to a close-up that puts a lot of emphasis on that moment and gives it a lot of responsibility—it better be there for a reason, it better be smart, and it better be funny.

It's certainly been the most unique experience of my life, but I have to thank MTV for helping me acclimate to the incredible pace of production on *Saturday Night Live* so quickly, or at least quicker than somebody else who had never done this style of programming.

Jerry Foley was interviewed in his office at the Late Show *in April 1996 in New York. Beth McCarthy was interviewed at the Brooklyn Diner in New York in March 1996. This article originally appeared in Television Quarterly, Vol. XXVIII, No. 3, 1996.*

News Magazines

Arthur Bloom

As it reaches its thirtieth anniversary in 1998, *60 Minutes* is still the most successful news program in television history, continuing to earn high ratings, journalistic awards, and an enormous fortune for CBS. The show defined the concept of the TV news magazine, thanks to the pioneering vision of Executive Producer Don Hewitt and Director Arthur Bloom, who have been together since the very first "issue" in 1968.

Maintaining the program's classical look and method of storytelling may look easy, but it's extraordinarily demanding work. Each week's installment presents special challenges, which Bloom tackles with an engaging sense of energy and concentration. A master of detail, he's involved in every aspect of the production, whether it's the visual placement of a story in the opening preview box, the lighting of an interview, the pace of an introduction, or the overall structure of a report.

While *60 Minutes*' spare and elegant appearance might seem constraining to the man responsible for the dazzling sets and graphics of CBS's campaign and election night coverage from 1976 through 1990, Arthur Bloom clearly relishes his work with one of television's most distinctive programs.

60 Minutes *is a unique program in many ways. It was the first, and still*

is, the most successful news magazine on network television. It was also a program whose creator, Don Hewitt, was also a director. You were there from the very beginning—what was it like for you as the program's founding director to collaborate with such a well-known producer/director?

It's interesting how I got the job. I was mainly an assistant director at the time, who occasionally directed the Sunday night newscast with Harry Reasoner. It was 1968, and I was doing the Oregon primary, with Vern Diamond directing and Don Hewitt was the producer. During the broadcast we had one location with Roger Mudd and Bobby Kennedy and another location with Eugene McCarthy, and while we had McCarthy on the air, I could see Kennedy on the monitor with Mudd, listening and getting upset. So I said to Hewitt, "Let's split the screen; we could create a debate." And Don said, "No, no, we can't do that. We promised them." But I said, "You're wrong, this is great television,"and we started to fight—a great situation, as the A.D. and the producer began screaming at one another. Finally, Hewitt said, "You're right, goddamn it, let's split the screen." And we split the screen, and it worked—it was great TV—and the next day we got written up. And Don wrote a memo saying it was Artie Bloom's idea—I've still got that memo.

Don then came up to me and said, "I'm starting this new show, I'm supposed to be the director, but I don't have time. Would you do it? You may have to start as the A.D., because I don't have the budget, but I promise to make you the director." That was the nature of Don and my relationship—he feels very passionate and strongly about things, and so do I, and we always fight about what we believe in, and we continue to have a strong and passionate relationship.

What did you do as a director in helping to shape what would turn out to be one of the most influential programs in television history?

The director was really in charge of the look of the show, and of developing that look. If you go back and watch the first show, you'll see how much things have changed. For example, there was no ticking stopwatch—that idea came quite literally out of my pocket and we began to use it on the third program.

It was a very small unit back then, and it was very interactive and very involving. I was basically a producer/director, and often would cut the stories as well. Sometimes I'd go out on the road, like for our story with Richard Nixon opening up the family quarters of the White House for Mike Wallace and Harry Reasoner.

As a director, I was essentially a problem solver. If something didn't work, you made it work, whether it was a producer who couldn't figure out how to get the right effect for a story or our original film editors who were unused to working with our medium of 16 mm film.

One of the qualities of 60 Minutes *is that it has an almost classical look. You defined what a news magazine was—it was not going to tamper with reality, there would be no gimmicks and no special visual effects.*

When we started back in 1968 we couldn't do any effects because we didn't have the technology—if we had started the show ten years later it might have looked very different. We were very limited in what we could do.

But out of those limits evolved a very clean and direct approach.

Don Hewitt, remember, was a pioneering director, and he helped invent graphics for television. He got the idea for lower third of the screen supers [superimposing graphic information at the bottom part of the screen, usually to identify the name of the person speaking] by looking at a sandwich board and figuring the idea out for television. He was an inventor of TV graphics, and I also had a strong interest in the area and later brought real-time computerized graphics to television. So we both had a strong visual background. But it's also essential to note the tradition we came out of at CBS News, which was storytelling.

So for *60 Minutes* Don had the very logical idea that since it was a magazine concept, make it look like a magazine. To that we added the clock, which added a punctuation to end the stories. And it worked, and we loved the way it worked. Six months into the program, we realized, "hey, this is good," so we kept the basic approach and spent the next years refining it.

For example, take the letters segment. People today think our letters graphics are electronic, but they're not. We're still using the method I came up with twenty years ago, which was actually our third attempt. One time I had the camera show a letter actually being typed at a typewriter, but I didn't like that. What happened is that I typed out a letter and told the artist that I wanted to figure out a way to reduce the size of the magazine page as I flicked it on top of it. We still use the same approach today where we have to reduce the size of the book, put it on a slight angle, and then have a stage manager flick the letters (which are now typed on a computer) on cue as the camera zooms in. I believe it looks better than any other letter graphics I've seen on TV and does it in a way that's true to the show—clear and precise.

One of the things I noticed as I was watching the show being put together is that even though so many of the program's signature elements grew out of expediency, and you now utilize the most sophisticated computerized technologies, the show still looks essentially the same, in the sense that it remains uncluttered and clean and stately.

Don Hewitt and I once had a conversation that I think is the key to the show. We both feel that while everything in this world is changing at a radical pace, *60 Minutes* is comfort food. No matter how much is changing in people's lives, they can turn on CBS on Sunday night at 7 and hear a clock ticking and know they're going to get solid stories on the air. That's what we want to give them. We don't want to change; people have enough change in their lives. We think we can tell the stories better and our quality is better.

Now we do make little cosmetic changes, but they're very little. For example, thanks to computer technology, we were able to create the ticking clock totally in the paintbox, which gave the clock a more three-dimensional look. I asked Don if he noticed it, and he said, "Yeah, I was in a cab and driver said to me, 'Mr. Hewitt, did you see that new clock,'" laughing at the question. That was the last cosmetic change, but Robert Corujo and I are working on some changes for next season, like maybe making the *60 Minutes* type a little slimmer and mildly rework the clock.

Your involvement in the show is comprehensive; everything that appears in terms of audio or video is your bailiwick.

Right. I do the final edit of the show, the studio portions, the teasers. I sometimes go out in the field, though not as much as I used to. This would happen when there was a late-breaking story, especially during the Nixon era, when we did interviews with Ehrlichman and other Watergate figures. We had to use remote trucks, because this was before the mini-cam, and we'd set up big, bulky cameras. There was a lot more field work in those days that I was involved with. Now, if we do multiple camera shoots, say at the White House, I might be involved with that, but other times we might handle that with satellite lines for the camera feeds.

What are your responsibilities as a director with the producer pieces? Do you direct stories once they've been handed in?

On some pieces there is no directorial involvement whatsoever. On other pieces I'm involved in before it even gets across the street to the studio. They may have a problem and they may come to me for help or expertise, or we might change some shots for them, or they might need some graphics. It's one big family—they're left alone and if they need help, they get help. If once the piece comes in and we feel there's a problem, we'll call them up, we won't try to change anything without giving them the courtesy of saying "we think we can do this better." Most of the time, nothing is done, because we've seen the piece before it gets across the street, but occasionally we may tighten things up.

What's involved in directing the segments between the produced pieces?

It's important to remember we have a new set every week, because we're a magazine and new art has to be prepared. The art department reports to me, but Robert Corujo is a great artist and we leave him alone. If he does something we don't like, we tell him, but that's rare. He gets carte blanche.

What struck me in being in the control room is how much attention you and your team devote to the most minute detail, such as the way the opening teases are positioned within the graphic frame. I don't think viewers are aware of how carefully everything is polished and presented.

I think a good director is not noticed. If your work isn't noticed, you've done a very good job. It just blends in as part of the show; it's not over-directed, things aren't done that get your attention and takes away from the story.

We take great pride in our product. People don't realize it and even here at the network they feel we've got it easy and don't work very hard. It's not true whatsoever, it just looks simple.

Where did that aesthetic notion that you weren't going to let directing stand in the way the story is told come from?

That's the way CBS News was in 1960 when I came to work here. We were in the news business; directors put the producer's show on the air. That's what CBS News was—we were journalists. The director's training, when I got started, was first as a journalist. Then it was how to get the show on the air without interrupting that flow. This was the house that Ed Murrow built, and *60 Minutes* is the Murrow ideal. That's why the show works just as well on radio; it's now simulcast on the CBS radio network and it works perfectly. Audio is very important; sometimes we'll look away and just listen.

It's been thirty years of excellence, which comes from the CBS News tradition, and I don't want to be here when it's not excellent anymore. In our editing suite we can do many things—when the picture's too dark, we lighten it. When the audio's not right, we work on the audio.

But not for the chance to demonstrate technical wizardry?

No, the goal is for excellence, which to my mind is just fine quality. One of the reasons we stayed away from special effects is that we could not do them well when we got started, but we also realized it wasn't needed and it takes away from the stories. We separated ourselves from other shows by not going in that direction.

So you never had a crisis of the soul where you said, "Maybe we should just reinvent the whole thing?"

There was a pressure at times from management to try to change things. But we owe a lot to Bill Paley, who kept us on the air in the early years when we didn't have good ratings. He supported us and it paid off.

We have a great luxury. There are lots of magazine shows, but we're the only one that looks like a magazine. We have a cover, we have our magazine stories. We look the way a magazine looks, and since we were first, we really couldn't be copied. The bigger question is, why would you want to change that? We have to make a new set every week, we have to change our book, but that helps us. When you lead into a story, it helps you to see a title and what you're talking about. The entire set is part of the story.

Producers may come to us from other shows, and they come in and want graphics, but we always call that lazy producing. We say, go out and shoot it and don't use graphics to make up for what you don't have tape to cover. After they're on the show awhile, they know they have to shoot enough to cover it. We're not going to put in graphics just for the sake of graphics—graphics are used only when they will enhance the story and help you understand the story.

60 Minutes, *like a magazine, has a publication date, which tends to mean everything is ready a few days in advance of Sunday night. But there have been times when you've scrapped things and gone live. When and why?*

In the early days it was almost like a live show, where we did a minimal amount of editing. Thirty years ago, the correspondents used to come in live for their intros and we used to roll tape live. Then this began to change because of the unique nature of the show, where our correspondents do the studio work plus the field work. This means they have to travel, and we said we can't keep having them come back to the studio on Friday. So we taped them to accommodate their busy schedule, and put the show together in pieces. We're now trying to figure out a way for them to do their introductions from remote locations to limit the need for additional travel.

There's also the factor that in television you have to be prepared to do anything, because anything can happen. A princess can die, there can be a presidential emergency, and you have to change the show and the way you do the show. You have to be prepared to go in any direction. One Sunday I wound up at the White House producing and directing a segment and feeding it back to New York for air. While you might get used to doing a show one way on a week-to-week basis, you have to really be prepared to do anything.

This interview took place in the control room of 60 Minutes *in New York in October 1997. It originally appeared in the DGA Magazine, Vol. 22, No. 6, February 1998.*

Special Events

Arthur Bloom, Max Schindler

Covering special events—whether it's a political convention, presidential summit, or the funerals of presidents or princesses—is among the most demanding and specialized of directorial tasks. On the one hand, it's the equivalent of marshaling an army, as several dozen cameras are put into position and strategies are devised to anticipate every contingency. But on the other hand, since it involves live news, it calls for skillful improvisation as directors try to keep up with the twists and turns of unplanned reality.

There's certainly no area of directing that can be as tense and as exciting. With enormous amounts of information pouring into the control room, the director must act as the central processor, weaving together remote locations which may span the globe. When it's breaking news, such as an assassination attempt or a disaster in space, rules are often being made up as the story unfolds, and coverage can last for long, uninterrupted hours, or even days.

Though the situations may vary, from the months of planning involved in televising a political convention to the seat-of-the-pants nature of a special bulletin, special events directors must exercise a sense of authority and imagination. In times of crisis or commemoration, their efforts are just as important as those of the anchors, the reporters, and the executive producers. The decisions they make in the control room will quite literally make history—the images they select will become etched into the nation's TV consciousness.

The directors interviewed in this chapter played crucial roles in a number of television's most remembered events. Starting in 1976, Arthur Bloom directed all of the political conventions for CBS, as well as the network's primary and election night coverage through 1990. Max Schindler of NBC has covered the assassinations of John F. Kennedy and Robert F. Kennedy, the signing of the Camp David peace accords, the Apollo and Gemini space launchings, the welcome home parades for Alan Shepard and John Glenn, as well as the inaugurations of every president since Lyndon Johnson.

Arthur Bloom

You covered all of CBS News's big events from 1974 to 1990. What do you recall as the most challenging and ambitious?

Political conventions were very big shows in those days. I used to have as many as 30 cameras. And we used to do them out of one control room, while the other networks might use two.

Election nights were also difficult; the planning for them would take two years. The computer animation alone back then might require months of execution. Let me give you an example. My first election for CBS was in 1974, and for that I built this new set. At the very end I came up with this idea to make our giant map somehow light up with a color indicating which party had won. So I went to the shop to see how it could be done, and found out it would cost $50,000. I told management it would run $30,000. They said "No, you're already over budget." Gordon Manning was in on that meeting, and a year later he went over to NBC, and asked me to join him. I said no, but he did take my map idea with him, and for the next election, they used it and it worked wonderfully for them. Bill Leonard, who was then the president of CBS News, called me in and said NBC beat us and how did this happen, and I told him that was our map and pointed to the vice president and said "he vetoed it." Leonard asked him if that was true, the guy said yes, and Leonard then ordered us to beat the idea next time.

So I realized the only way I could beat it was to get into motion graphics, which we did by using these devices ABC had tried out called Dubners. Writing the software for that took six months in those days, and that's why planning for these events took two full years.

For these events you had the enviable role of both producer and director, being able to direct the vision that you had conceptualized?

Yes. It was important to be able, at least for me, to take it all the way through. The hardest thing for me as a director was to execute someone else's work. You're better at executing something you have passion about and believe in strongly.

How did this work in terms of covering conventions, which can't really be planned as tightly as election night coverage?

Conventions are really a director's show; it's great cutting [selecting which camera shots to broadcast] cameras (and I had 30 at one point) and they're great fun to do. The first convention I did was in 1974 in New York, and the way that everyone did it back then was that they shot the podium. We used to be on the air from 6 p.m. until 2 a.m., four or five nights of this. I'd do these shows and say, "God, is this boring." And I realized that I had a couple of cameras on the floor for the roll call, and then all the rest of the cameras shooting the podium. So what I decided was that there was a better show on the floor than there is on the podium, and by the time we moved to Kansas City, which was the second convention that year, I moved all my cameras. I left two shooting the podium, and had the other twenty roving over the floor. I began cutting away from the speeches and showed the conventioneers wearing crazy hats or what not.

I looked at the convention as a kaleidoscope, and I think one of my talents was that I was able to become part of the event—if they got bored, I got bored, and I showed bored people, sleeping or dozing.

Your cutaways and reaction shots were done during the floor speeches. What about while Walter Cronkite or the reporters were talking?

I took my cue from what they were saying. It's all audio based. You have to listen to do a good job as a director.

After the success of your coverage in 1974, were you given carte blanche to do what you wanted in covering these political events?

In 1976, I was approached to take over political coverage after CBS had had three disasters in covering the early primaries. But I said no, I can't do any better job, and I told them that I resented the fact that they had blamed the current director. They asked me again and I refused. Finally on the third time they asked me under what conditions would I do it, and I said I would only do it if I could change the look, change the way it was done, and that I wanted to be left alone. They said OK, you'll become the producer/director of the shows. I always found it interesting that I got a lot of power from refusing to do the shows.

From then on they really let me do what I thought needed to be done. You need freeedom to do really good work, and trust. For a director to succeed, you need to take risks, and you need to know that the management that hires you is supporting you. When that support is taken away, you can't do your work.

Still, I sometimes would hide a lot of the work I was doing. I was always looking for new ways to go and other types of changes, and I found it very hard to show management types work in progress. They didn't seem to be able to picture the final product. And I learned that if I showed them things they would try to stop me. What I used to ultimately do was to show them things when it was too late to change them.

I worked with a wonderful vice president, Joan Richman, and we did great work together. I look at 1984 as the peak, because it was really the end of the growth of television. After that, the satellite dish and the paintbox helped make every local station equal to a network, since they had exactly the same tools. At any rate, starting in 1984 we had the budgets to really start to do wonderful computer graphic displays, which led a few years later to extraordinary interactive graphics (after one program, I got a call from Microsoft to head up their interactive graphic divisions). They were flashy, maybe flashier than news should have been, but it was still an era when we were experimenting and taking off in new directions.

It's interesting that unlike the excitement of being on location for conventions, for elections you were locked in a fixed studio, and yet this spurred you on to tackle really new approaches.

But they're also two different types of shows. You have to ask yourself what can you do to make this show special. In conventions you can do it in terms of cutting cameras, and using that as an art form. On election night, you can use graphics as an art form, because it's a graphic show. There's no show which needs graphics more, except perhaps a halftime sports show.

Clearly the graphic look of these programs was one of the most vital aspects of your work as producer/director.

Absolutely. But as a director it's important to remember that though you can build beautiful sets, it's really hard to show them, because so much of the program is done in tight shots. I would have this beautiful set but I couldn't show it except in the opening wide shot. So the very first set I designed in 1974 for election night, I made sure that we would take wide two-shots, as the anchor would go back and forth with the on-set reporters. The set was made from plexiglass—a concept I got when I was out shopping with my wife at a towel store which had lots of plexiglass holders, etc. I then decided to design a set which would have people behind Cronkite working on raised tiers in working areas made of plexiglass. The entire thing was designed based on what shots I wanted. This was also the first time we used bumpers which displayed the whole set from various angles before the commercials—prior to that, it would simply be Cronkite saying, "We'll be right back," with a dissolve to black.

In terms of graphics, I'm a great believer in talent. I will go to an artist and say "here's what I want, but don't you dare give me back what I want, because you're the artist." I rely on artists and on their talents—I try to push them in a certain direction, but I think a lot of directors make mistakes when they try to tell an artist exactly what to do.

What about covering events that can't be planned as carefully as election night or conventions? What challenges does that present for a director?

I learned from the best, Don Hewitt. I was as an A.D. and Don Hewitt was a producer, and it was a summit meeting at Glassboro State College in Glassboro, New Jersey. We got there, and Don was a master of these kinds of situations. Instantly, he started figuring what we could do, since after all, we were CBS News, which everyone always looked up to. The other networks used to follow us to see what we were doing. This was in the era before mini-cams, so we had these ten big cabled cameras and a remote truck. We rented a house, and gathered information, and then started to hide our cables and our big studio cameras, in bushes. And that's how I learned to do special events. You couldn't always hide in bushes, but you tried to get the best positions, up on rooftops, so that even if you didn't know what was going to happen, you could get coverage. Coverage was the key, and the ability to be flexible.

One of the first things I did that made me into a director was when I was sent to Chicago to direct a remote for a 1972 primary. I had three cameras, and four correspondents, and what I did was cable six different areas of the hotel. When we went on the air at first, we were in one room. But when they came back to us an hour later, we'd be somewhere entirely different. All I did, of course, was move the cameras to another room. Management called me and asked how many cameras I had with me, and when I told them three, they said, "But you sent us back 12 pictures." That's what you can do when you have some time and a lot of cable.

It was a great growth industry when I started here, and you learned an incredible amount on the job. Plus this was CBS News and the talent here was extraordinary. You learned very quickly to go for it and to beat the competiton. It was instinctive.

How did this high level of training prepare you to cover the unexpected?

You have to ask youself, what are the possibilities? What can happen? For example, during the 1968 Democratic convention, I was sent to Washington to cover the final illness of Eisenhower, who was dying in a hospital. Everyone else was in Chicago covering the convention and I was just a 26-year-old kid planning for all the networks Eisenhower's funeral. You learned quite quickly how to figure out what can happen, because no one in the family wants to tell you what can happen. So what you do is look at the hospital and determine all the exits and entrances—you just look for anything that can happen and where you can get coverage. You have to figure out how you can do things and how many cameras would you need to do it. It's always looking for information; you're a newsperson and you're looking for information any way you can.

So how do you cover events? You have to give yourself flexibility. It's frightening because sometimes you have limited resources and you're worried whether the other guy is getting this before you or whether you made a wrong call. But that's the adrenaline that makes you work hard and love it—it was very exciting.

Max Schindler

How did you get started directing TV?

I began in TV in 1954 and at a time when no one knew what they were doing. I had gone to a school in New York called Television Workshop, and it was something like the Actors Studio for TV—five hours a night, four days a week, and every weekend we did programs. We had singers, dancers, actors who all wanted to work in TV. At the end of a year, I went to a small station in Wisconsin as a cameraman, but I did that job for less than two months before they made me a director, since I was the only one there with TV experience—the others had all worked in radio.

There weren't any rule books to follow. We'd just try something and if it worked out well, we'd say "gee, that worked out fine, I'll remember that and use it again," or if didn't work out, we'd try to remember what we did wrong. In those days, a director was very much like a general practitioner—you did a little bit of news, a little bit of sports, a little bit of everything. But as the years went by, like doctors, we began to specialize.

When did your specialization in news begin?

I was working at a station in West Virginia in 1960 when a young senator came there to try to win the presidency of the United States. His name was John Kennedy. I spent a lot of time with Bobby Kennedy doing statewide hookups for his brother's campaign. And because of my time with Bobby, and the fact that I was working for a CBS affiliate, I was able to arrange that on the night of JFK's primary triumph in the state, the Senator was interviewed exclusively by CBS News's anchor, Douglas Edwards. NBC had sent a whole flock of people there from the *Huntley-Brinkley Report* and they had all gotten beaten pretty badly. So the next thing I knew, I got a call from NBC News in Washington asking if I'd like to come to work for them. I said yes, and the first thing I worked on for them was *David Brinkley's Journal.* And that's how I began to specialize in news.

Were your duties just on this once-a-week program?

No. As a staff director you may have regular show assignments, but if a press conference comes up, or a crisis situation, you're part of their organization and you can be assigned to other things. For example, I directed *Meet the Press* from 1965-85, but I also covered conventions, parades, etc.

What were your first large-scale live news events?

I guess my first events must have been the parades for returning astronauts Alan Shepard and then later John Glenn. I was in charge of covering their landings at Andrews Air Force Base prior to their parades to the Capitol. I remember that for Glenn we were all set to go live at 10 a.m. when he landed, but at about 9:40 the plane was in sight at Andrews. I started screaming at the P.R. officer that they couldn't land yet because the networks weren't going on until 10. So here we had the hero of outer space circling Andrews for twenty minutes before he could land.

A landing and a parade can in some ways be preplanned. You can set up your cameras and anticipate, in some ways, your shots. But what about an event that no one can foresee. For you, the first, and certainly the most dramatic, was the assassination of President Kennedy.

If the networks had tried to plan their coverage of that event, we would have had meetings for one year at least. I first heard the news of the shooting as I was driving into work and a woman at Ward Circle in Washington yelled at me to turn on my radio. I heard the bulletin that the president had been shot. I got into the newsroom about three or four minutes after that and it was a scene of complete pandemonium.

At first, I was told to pack a bag and go down to Dallas. When the news came that the president was dead, they said "never mind, you're going to Andrews Air Force Base. Air Force One is going to land. We don't know if the president's body is on the plane, whether Lyndon Johnson is on the plane, or if Mrs. Kennedy is on the plane. All we know is that you need to get out there."

So I jumped in my car and got on the road and luckily a highway patrolman on a motorcycle happened to be driving by. I yelled at him and told him who I was and what I wanted to do. The cooperation on that day was extraordinary. He said, "You follow me," and he turned on his red light and drove over the grassy median in the middle and got me to Andrews in record time. But once I got to the gate, I had trouble getting in, even with my White House pass, because the Secret Service was so understandably jumpy that day. Luckily Nancy Dickerson of NBC was there, and she knew all the agents and told them that unless I got in, we wouldn't get on the air.

All the networks had cameras there, and as luck would have it the lines that went in were to NBC first and they couldn't get lines to the other networks. So at the last minute we became a pool [when news organizations decide to "pool" their resources and allow one reporter to cover the event for everyone] at a time when they didn't do pool coverage all that often.

As the plane was approaching, I had two cameras set up and they had lights on on the field, which they made us turn off. The noise of the plane was so great that the cameramen couldn't hear me, and if you look back on the tapes, you'll see swish panning [a sudden camera movement back and forth, often when the camera operator is in a difficult remote situation] because they didn't even know if we were on the air. As soon as the plane landed, they let us turn the lights back on, and the cameramen could hear me. I had one camera on the plane, and as the back door opened, I cut to the other camera which showed a close-up of the casket being lowered. I remember being struck as we saw that casket that now it was really true, that for me and most of America here was the first solid evidence that the President was really dead.

As the casket was being lowered from the rear, the front door opened and Jackie came out, and Bobby and Teddy came up the steps to greet her. I followed them all the way up and then all the way down, as Jackie moved towards the hearse.

Were you watching this through a window as well or were you focused solely on the monitors?

I guess I saw what the American public saw. I may have occasionally looked up and out the window where I could see what was going on, but I was too intent on what we were doing.

Jackie got into the hearse and it drove away. We had set up a microphone but nobody had gone to it, and I didn't know what else to do with the camera. So I said to the on-air camera, very slowly pan back to the plane, and then, much to our surprise, at that moment Lyndon Johnson came out and went over to the microphone and he made his first address as president of the United States. Later, one of the news magazines said that television had graphically portrayed the passing of the old to the new with that pan, but in actuality, it was because I didn't know what else to do. A month after that, I was the pool director for *A Conversa-*

tion with Lyndon Johnson and I related this story to him during a break while we were setting up. I said to him, "Mr. President, I know you're an avid TV watcher, you have a console with three TV sets tuned to the networks. Were you sitting in the plane watching me?" And he said, "Yes. When you panned back to the plane, I thought that was my cue."

During the next three days, you were being sent on remotes all over the city, from the Capitol rotunda to Dulles Airport, working at a feverish pace, with little sleep. What do you think you learned as a director in this kind of extraordinary and completely unprecedented situation?

You learned to cope as you went along, and how to pick up things on the spur of the moment, always looking for something that would be telling and symbolic. Sometimes I don't know how we did it since I was fairly numb with the pace and the emotion. I think we did it largely by instinct since we had all done so many events, but of course none like this.

For example, I looked at a monitor once as the funeral cortège was going by, and I had a camera at the back of the crowd and I saw two hands raised held up together—one was black and one was white. They were united in their grief, and I was instantly struck by it, particularly since this was in the pre-civil rights era.

Did you mostly rely on your camera people for the types of shots you wanted or were you constantly giving instructions to your crew?

A lot of both. You're asking for things and telling them what to do, but a lot of times with an event like this you've got cameramen, they sell you shots, they find shots for you and they're on top of things—they know what you like and don't like.

When those three days of funeral coverage were over, did you all get together and discuss what you had learned?

Not really. We were so numb when it was over and we were launching right into coverage of the new president in the White House.

Unfortunately, there would be more funerals to come in terms of network coverage during the 1960s. What do you recall of these experiences?

Bobby Kennedy's funeral was very memorable. I was at Arlington Cemetery all day waiting for the funeral procession to come down from New York. As you may remember, it was coming down by train and someone was killed on the tracks, delaying the event for hours. We were scurrying around, and what should have been a daytime event was turning into a nighttime one, and I had people frantically getting lights so we could cover the ceremony.

How did you approach this second Kennedy funeral?

The night before the funeral, Charles Octavius Jones, who was the pool director, and I were waiting for a call, which finally came at about 3 a.m. We were told to come to Arlington Cemetery, where the Kennedy family had at last picked a gravesite. When we got out there, we were informed about what our restrictions would be. I walked around with Charlie, who was putting stakes in the ground where each one of his pool cameras was going to be. After he finished, I then went around putting my stakes in the ground where the NBC cameras were going to go, because I now knew what his cameras were going to show and I wanted to supplement. CBS and ABC weren't there—they didn't come until the next morning—so I guess their positions weren't as good as ours.

We started putting up our platforms that night, and I remember Charlie and I climbing a ladder and with a carpenter's saw sawing off the branches of a tree, which was unheard of at Arlington Cemetery. When the officials yelled at him, Charlie, from his lofty perch up on top of the ladder, said, "Millions of Americans are going to want to see this martyred hero laid to rest, and this branch shall not stand in their way," and he continued sawing. A little while later, another man came over and asked him what he was doing, and Charlie went into his whole spiel again. The man said, "Mac, I don't care who you are. I'm a carpenter, that's my saw, you took it out of my box, and you're making the blade dull." I was laughing so hard I almost fell out of the ladder.

Still, I knew Bobby Kennedy from a long time back, and I found his funeral a very trying experience for me to cover.

You've covered many inaugurations beginning with Lyndon Johnson. Given the rather formal, predetermined nature of the event, did they get to be routine?

Yes, which was frustrating, since each time you cover the inauguration you would have more ideas of what could be done but for various reasons you weren't allowed to exercise them. It wasn't until Bill Clinton, and the influence of his friend and TV producer/director Harry Thomason, that things began to change.

For Clinton's first inauguration, I was, as usual, the pool director for the Capitol. It's always been broken down through the years that ABC provided the pool coverage for the White House, CBS had Pennsylvania Avenue, and NBC had the Capitol. This was my fourth inaugural there, and I knew the Capitol very well. I knew the routine, and how to get up to the roof and where the cameras should go. I was determined at this particular inauguration to get new positions which we never had before. You've got to realize that as director for this kind of event, you're working two or three months before. You go to meetings with the Metropolitan Police, the Capitol Police, the Secret Service, the Congressional Inaugural Committee, the Senate Inaugural Committee, the pool representatives from all the networks, and it's here that you try to work out all the problems that you have. But my biggest problem was working out these new camera positions. One of them I wanted was on the dome of the Capitol at the upper balustrade level. We'd never had a camera up there. From that level, you can see all the way down Pennsylvania Avenue to the White House, but you can also see the whole inaugural—the mall and everything else. When I went up to survey the site, I had picked out a position where, if the wind were right, you would see the flag fluttering on the right-hand side of the screen but you would still be able to see in the foreground the whole inaugural scene, including the President taking the oath of Office.

We went round and round about having a cameraman on that scene, but the Secret Service was adamant, saying that was where they put their sharpshooters. I argued that we might be able to squeeze a platform back against the dome—even though there was only about five feet of room overall in width. When I climbed up there to scout it out I realized it was too precarious, but when I looked out over the balustrade I noticed there was a ledge that we could put a robotic camera on. After more arguing, they finally agreed. Then I had to find riggers who would go over the side of the Capitol to lash down the camera, and that's how we got our first new position.

I also wanted to use a jib for the first time over the crowd in front of the president, rather than our usual routine of handheld cameras. The officials argued that it would be intrusive and block people's views, but finally I pleaded long enough with the Architect of the Capitol to let me show them what it would look like. After a demonstration, where we brought a twenty-one foot jib instead of a fourteen foot one as I had originally promised, they reluctantly agreed. As it turned out, during the actual Inaugural, all of the Senate and House families were sitting in that section, and rather than being upset about being obstructed, they were all looking at our camera and waving, hoping to get their picture taken for their constituents back home.

We also were able to get a lipstick camera [a miniature camera the size of a lipstick tube] inside the bulletproof glass next to the presidential podium that could look up at the president as he was being sworn in.

Given these successes, was there more openness to innovation for President Clinton's second inauguration?

Yes. Harry Thomason was very understanding of our needs. For example, during the planning of the first inaugural I had tried to convince him to change the carpeting on the inaugural platform. When he wanted to know why, I told him that when the president is making his big speech, the background we see from our camera positions is the burgundy carpet on the center steps coming down to the podium, and that looks terrible for flesh tones. He told me it was too late since the carpet had already been bought.

So when we started meetings for the second inauguration, I raised the issue again and after a great deal of back and forth, they bought the blue carpeting (after sending me a selection of six different swatches). When the inauguration was over, everybody agreed that, yes, it looked better than it did four years ago.

Political conventions also try to follow a script, but there's a lot more room for improvisation and variations. Tell us about what it was like for you as a director.

One of my most vivid memories was covering the Democratic convention in Chicago in 1968 when the riots broke out. I was having dinner at the time, and I rushed to the nearest NBC mobile unit—it wasn't even mine. We had three or four cameras spaced out at various locations, but obviously they weren't planned to cover a riot. Basically, we covered what we could see of the riot. At my location we didn't even have a correspondent, we were just feeding pictures with natural sound. Practically every picture we took was of mass mayhem, so it wasn't very hard to put pictures up.

Space launches are another type of event you've covered that also seems to have a fairly standard format. Were you able to add your own elements as a director?

I covered a lot of them, Apollo and Gemini, and we tried different things to make the coverage better. I would go down to Cape Kennedy, and we would basically have access to certain of NASA's cameras (there were three feeds) and we had our own cameras. And every time you saw a space shot you would see the vehicle lifting up off the ground, and we would follow it, then you would cut to NASA's cameras which would take it out into space.

I was frustrated because I always wanted a shot that would look down on the rocket and see it lifting off, giving a new perspective. So I got this bright idea—there was another launch pad about ten miles away and I went up to the top of it. And sure enough we could see the other launch pad, but the problem was how we could get a camera up there. I was able to talk the Air Force into loaning us a helicopter, and we lifted an old-fashioned, very heavy color camera and put it on top. And it worked beautifully—for the first time, as they were counting down in the last five seconds, I was able to cut to this shot and you could see smoke coming up and you could look down and see all the ground in a real wide shot at the moment of liftoff.

What about the relationship between directors and producers?

There are all kinds of different relationships, but I look at it basically that the producer's job is content and the director's part is how it looks. Take the case of a producer that you've worked with for a long time, as I did with Bob Asman, who I started with right when I got to NBC in 1961. A lot of times he overlapped my job and I overlapped his job. Some producers that you don't know as well will draw a line, but Bob and I were always backstopping and overlapping one another. If it were a producer job and I saw that it wasn't done, I would do it. If he saw there was something hadn't been ordered that I needed, he would do it. We just knew each other that well that we could speak for one another, and so we had a very good relationship and worked together for many,

many years and many, many specials. We very rarely argued about anything and always saw eye to eye.

NBC seems to utilize you as a director whenever there are great logistical issues.

Yes. One I remember in particular happened in 1966, soon after I began directing *Meet the Press*. They told me they were going to do a show where the Secretary of State would be questioned by foreign journalists in five European cities, and we're going to do it live, and they told me I would be controlling the whole thing from Brussels, where the European Broadcast Union had a big technical setup.

So I had to go to London, Bonn, Paris, Rome and survey the facilities, talk to the people there and tell them the set that we wanted. Each country had their own methodology of how they approached TV, and it was difficult, to say the least, to find a way to negotiate it all. The rehearsal was a disaster—the French weren't on time, the British didn't have what I wanted, and the Germans were giving me grief, only the Italians were right there when I needed them. Finally, the show was ready to go, and I remember when I said into the microphone, "Standby London, standby Rome, standby Paris, standby Bonn, standby Washington" thinking, "damn, I'm genlocked [a technical term for locking various remote TV signals together in the early days of televison] to the world." It was the first time NBC had ever tried such a complicated international hookup, and ultimately it worked very well. At the end, Lawrence Spivak, the program's very serious host, even smiled—I don't know if it was because the show was good or just relief that it really worked.

What special talents do you think make a great special events director?

A director of special events is a different breed than other types of directors. A director of a drama program will place cameras in certain positions and will have his or her actors walk to a mark, say their lines, turn a certain way, give a certain expression, and then walk to another mark where another camera picks it up. A director of special events tries to figure out what is going to take place at the event, and what they might be able to get that no one else might be able to get. Then the director places cameras in these various locations and hopes the talent will come to the mark, so to speak. You can't stage the news event, but you try to put cameras in places where you can catch the most dramatic shot. Every once in a while, you get lucky and capture history in the making—whether it was President Kennedy's casket coming out of Air Force One or the hug between Menachem Begin and Anwar Sadat at the White House peace treaty signing.

Do you get a thrill in the control room when moments like that occur?

Yes, for me it's like a director of a drama program who feels that they've gotten the kind of performance out of the actors that will win everybody awards. It's the "money shot," capturing the right shot and the right time. It makes the whole process worthwhile.

The interview with Arthur Bloom took place in the control room of 60 Minutes *in New York in October 1997. The interview with Max Schindler took place in the New York offices of the Directors Guild of America in September 1997.*

Sports and News

Roger Goodman

During his thirty years at ABC, Roger Goodman has directed just about every type of event in live television, and earned 18 Emmy Awards for his efforts. From Super Bowls to the Inauguration, from superstar interviews to award-winning town meetings in South Africa, from the Indy 500 to the Kentucky Derby, from the Olympics to the conventions—he's covered them all, and in the process, helped to revolutionize what it means to be a TV director.

Right from the start of his career at ABC, Roger Goodman demonstrated the rare talent of seeing the world with television eyes. At ABC Sports, he quickly recognized how TV could bring viewers directly into an event through strategic camera placement, a heightened awareness of cutting, and a gripping sense of presentation. The intensity and the excitement of live competition thrilled him, and he consistently found new ways to make that come alive on the small screen, whether it was horse racing, championship bowling, the New York City Marathon, or the Olympics.

When he was asked by his boss and mentor Roone Arledge to join him at ABC News in 1978 (while continuing his work at ABC Sports), Goodman brought the same energy and drive to the political and world arena. He directed conventions, debates, and inaugurations with a dramatic flair, making full use of multiple cameras, satellites, and innovative new technologies like Quantels [a video effects machine] and paintboxes. ABC's numerous news magazines and specials also permitted him to expand his expertise in areas such as set design, lighting, and graphics. The look of ABC News is largely his creation, starting with the revamped sets of *20/20* in 1978 to the bold style of *World News Tonight, Nightline, This Week with David Brinkley, Prime Time Live,* and dozens of others. Lately, he's been extensively involved in the areas of virtual reality set design, launched with ABC's coverage of the 1996 election and continuing with the Discovery Channel's *Discovery News* and a series of specials entitled *The Twentieth Century* in 1999.

Goodman's directorial style is at its best when it confronts one-of-a-kind challenges. His coverage of events such as the Olympics, the Gulf War, the funeral of Princess Diana, or *Nightline* specials from Jerusalem or South Africa helped set new standards for the medium, but what viewers didn't get to see was the incredible marshaling of resources, the creative flexibility, and the nerves of steel required to get these telecasts on the air. Television directors are like commanding generals during special events, and nothing seems to make Roger Goodman happier than the ability to connect the world through the electronic tentacles of his control room.

Not content with his triumphs in sports and news, Goodman recently expanded his work to entertainment as well, directing the ABC special "Michael Jackson Talks to Oprah," the 1993 and 1994 Daytime Emmy Awards, and then went on to design the new look of *The Oprah Winfrey Show.* He's currently Executive Director of Special Projects for the ABC Television Network, where he supervises the direction, design and overall look of all of the network's special programming. When I talked with him, he was busy designing new sets for *20/20* and *World News Tonight,* as well as planning ABC's new studios in Times Square.

You arrived at ABC Sports in 1964 at a very exciting period. What was it like back then?

Sports was brand new, and we were given incredible freedom to create. I loved creating and dreaming up things. Take graphics, for instance. In 1964, graphics largely consisted of restaurant menu boards—you go down to some place on 42nd St. and buy the blackboard with the white letters. On my first graphics assignment I went down to cover a golf game in Ligonier, Pennsylvania. The camera would be on the 18th tower, it would shoot the ball coming up on 18 and then swing around and shoot a menu board and it would say "Arnie Palmer +5, Jack

Nicklaus +3," and then go back to shoot the game. Then we invented something called the drum, which was a magnetic drum which would have names on it and every time you clicked it, it would turn.

We constantly kept thinking up new solutions to problems. For example, with bowling we did some bizarre things. We didn't have any videotape machines, but we did have a magnetic disk that could store thirty seconds worth of replay footage. We figured out where to stop the disk in recording and playing back so we could put other things on it—like faces or animations. For instance, we took a bowling ball, painted half of it chroma-key blue, put it on a turntable, and then when it was time to go live, we would carefully time it so that you would see the name of the tournament, then the ball would be turned and you would see a guy's face in it, then turned again and you'd see the next player and so on until all five players were shown on the face of the ball. This was all before the invention of computerized animation.

Sports was an environment where we were told to be as creative as we possibly could be. If the technology wasn't available for what you wanted to do, you created and developed it yourself. You literally created your own world.

What lessons do you think you learned as a director from Roone Arledge, your boss at ABC Sports and later at ABC News?

His attention to detail was truly amazing. He was concerned with every aspect, from the smallest shifts in lighting to camera angles. He was always giving you directorial suggestions and he still does—you're shooting too fast, you're shooting too slow. Roone not only gave you the problem, he gave you the solution, which I found to be very interesting. I remember once I was shooting an individual in the early days and Roone whispered in my ear "pedestal the camera up." I asked him why, and he said "to minimize his double chin." Roone would bug you if there was lint on someone's shoulder, or if their tie wasn't straight.

He's been a very big influence on my career as a director.

You covered virtually every type of athletic activity during your years at Wide World of Sports. *Did you try to approach each sport differently or was there some kind of common denominator?*

It depended. When I first began covering pro bowling, for example, I came up with some new ideas. The budget for the shows said I could only have four cameras, but a television truck had eight. I asked if I could use them, and they agreed, but they wouldn't give me the extra four camera people. So I placed the cameras strategically around the bowling alley—I put an unmanned camera on one of the alternate lanes so you could see the ball coming. I called it "Bruce"—a name which is now used all over the industry for unmanned cameras. I took another camera and put it on a ladder so you could see the full arm swing of a bowler. We turned bowling into an eight-camera extravaganza.

Was this your basic approach, to add as many cameras as feasible in the belief that the more eyes you had, the more you could see?

That's exactly right. But sometimes you can also shoot something with four cameras and make it look like ten, depending on how much you can move the cameras around and how many different angles you can get. I love cranes, I love blimps, I love helicopters. But I also love the challenges of getting cameras where they haven't been before. When I was doing the Indianapolis 500 I put a camera on the end of a broom so that when a guy came into the pits, you take the camera and extend it out and you could see the driver's face and you could see the cockpit. Sometimes things would be upside down, but that was an experiment.

Clearly, it was the challenges of trying something new that thrilled you at ABC Sports.

I did three Super Bowl halftimes, with the most challenging being the one in 1995 featuring Indiana Jones, which was all special effects. It was hundreds and hundreds of cues, with guys jumping out of airplanes and hitting the ground at a precise time and beat. I told them at first they were crazy—there was no way they were going to hit the ground on time, so I decided to record it. I'm glad I did because during the event the guy missed his mark; we quickly went to the tape from the rehearsal the night before and nobody noticed.

In addition to the Super Bowl halftimes, I also did the pre- and postgame shows. I never directed the actual football game.

You've worked on four Olympics, directing your first one in 1980 at Lake Placid. Did you feel the need to right from the start to define your signature and approach to the broadcast?

Yes, and I think I did. For the first time ever I helped design a brand new device with a company called Quantel that gave us five picture boxes on the air live. Now the announcer could say we're showing you a live picture of hockey, from downhill, from figure skating, from speed skating, and from the luge. We also premiered a brand new version of a device which I'd helped to work on for two years called the Dubner Graphics Factory. It gave sixty-four colors, which we then thought of as a big deal; now it's in the millions. So that was my mark—the graphic look. We had graphics that moved, plus we also had miniature cameras in ski helmets.

For the 1984 Olympics we tried something different by building and constructing the show's set starting back in September 1983. The set was originally designed in Los Angeles, put together and tested thoroughly in New York, then later shipped to Sarajevo for the winter games, then shipped back to Los Angeles for the summer games.

In 1978 Roone Arledge asked you to join him as he expanded his duties to include the presidency of ABC News as well as ABC Sports. What did you find that you learned in sports directing that you could instantly apply to the news?

Just about everything. When I came to news, you really had to direct, you really had to ask for stuff. At first, it was hard to go from thirty cameras to the two or three cameras then being used at ABC News. It's important to remember that back then the camera people (who in those days shot on film) were always looking through the eyepiece of a handheld camera and they were kind of producing and directing within the camera themselves. When we finally started using twenty cameras for a news event, I had to tell them that I would be doing the thinking for them. Their orientation had always been shooting an individual sitting down, but now that we need elaborate shots and pans for conventions, it just wasn't happening the way I wanted it to. I started to bring sports camera people with me to news, and it worked beautifully, since they were used to the pace and action of a live event.

I was also frustrated by the fact that the producer in news used to sit behind me. I couldn't take it, and told them "I'm in the front, I'm not turning around to talk to you. We have to sit here together. You've got to guide me, I've got to guide you—we've got to do this as a family." And with the exception of a scripted show like *World News Tonight* most of the producers at ABC News will now sit next to the director and talk.

What other changes did you make once you moved to news directing?

Originally when they were covering a big event in the field, there might be ten cameras and each would have a director. I said, bring it all back to New York, and let me direct the events from here. Now when we do an event like the funeral of Princess Diana, we used thirty cameras with thirty videotape machines, did it all from here, and it was no big deal. This approach was all something I brought from ABC Sports.

While you were at ABC News you also continued to work at ABC Sports. Did you find it a bit confusing to work on the Olympics and then move on to directing the conventions and the elections?

Actually, they were rather similar. One of the other things I brought to convention coverage from sports was the idea of a centralized control room. Previously in covering conventions they had a pre-set control room and a main control room. I got together with Jeff Guralnick and said "you're out of your mind. Let's do it out of one television truck. What are you building a separate tape room for? I come from the world of sports where we do everything with a television truck equipped with tape machines." Now, everything comes from one television truck. You can drive in, do a television show, and leave.

I found it tremendously exciting to work in news because of the variety. For example, I was working on the Olympics in 1984, and right afterwards, we decided to do an international town meeting called *Capital to Capital.* It was certainly one of the most difficult things I've ever done. It involved directing five cameras in the Soviet Union, coming back on eight separate satellite paths, plus eight cameras in a Congressional hearing room. We had Senators and Congressmen and some public; the Soviet Union has their officials and an audience of 500, and the Americans are asking the Russians questions and the Russians are asking Americans questions. Plus there was the issue of translations, and the fact that many of the Russian cameramen didn't speak English.

How did you direct them then?

What we did was to memorize four or five basic phrases, such as pan left, pan right, tilt up, tilt down, zoom in, zoom out. We had about thirty minutes to practice with each cameraman.

What are your techniques in directing multi, multi-camera events, such as the thirty cameras or so you use for the elections or the funeral of Princess Diana.

Let's use the Princess Diana coverage. I was in New York, directing about thirty cameras from all over the world. The first thing I do is I must talk to the camera people, since it's impossible to hold a meeting. I try to find out if they've ever done sports, since that tends to make them exceptionally good camera operators. Then I tell them what I think I want, and make sure they can speak English.

Then I come up with a plan of what I want to do with the cameras, which was a bit different than covering elections or inaugurations. First there was the difficulty of coordinating the various satellite feeds, plus I had a sixteen-plex monitor, showing the sixteen cameras out of London being fed to me on a high-speed ISDN modem. [Integrated Digital Services Network, which transmits data at a maximum speed of 128 kilobytes per second]. I then categorize the cameras. I do graphics in certain colors, I take speaking people and color code their monitors. Everything is then put into different sections on the monitor wall, so I know where everything is—and it's usually the same arrangement from event to event. So my talking heads are on the left, my beauty shots on the upper left, the middle are my meats-and-guts shots that I know I'm going to need, and bottom right is where I keep my graphics.

How did your interest in graphics evolve?

I didn't have a graphics background, but my dad and sister were artists. I've always loved graphics, and after my early experiences with the field at *Wide World of Sports*, someone asked me if I wanted to do some animated openings. I liked the work, and from 1968-80 I created all the animated openings for ABC Sports, and for ABC News as well. Then my duties expanded to set design—I did all the sets for ABC News, ABC Sports, and for the Olympics.

You designed the sets for every ABC news show, including World News Tonight, 20/20, *and* Prime Time Live. *What look were you striving to achieve?*

Roone Arledge gave me a directive and it's still true today—newsrooms. So if you look at the original tape of *World News Tonight* from 1978, you'll see it there—all three anchors were situated in newsroom environments. I've put together newsroom sets all over the world, from Johannesburg to Israel to every ABC bureau.

Tell us about your involvement with virtual sets, which are sets created entirely with a computer.

I started working with an Israeli company called Orad about four years ago, who had come up with a system that permitted you to pan, tilt, and zoom on a chroma-key screen. We first used it three years ago. Now we use it for our program *Discovery News* for the Discovery Channel—we tape it every Friday morning at an independent production house. It cost us about $45,000 to create the set, and we use a room 10 feet by 17 feet which looks like it's 110 feet wide.

The advantages are absolutely enormous, in terms of costs and versatility, but it's very difficult to direct virtual sets, primarily because you lose a sense of time and space. You don't know where you are. You can mix in three-dimensional objects and real props and walk around them, but it's still difficult to get oriented. Plus there's a seven-frame delay, which takes some getting used to. I haven't had the chance to work with actors and actresses with it yet, but anchors and reporters seem to get along fine.

We'll be using virtual sets for a new magazine show coming out in February 1998 and for a series of specials called *The Twentieth Century* in early 1999. I see the day that soap operas, for example, will build all their sets in virtual, especially since it's a third of the cost. I also can't believe every local station in the country won't be using this, since you can get a completely different look for every newscast, with an infinite amount of chroma-key screens and every type of moving object. There are some inherent problems with it—it still gives a somewhat cartoony feel, but the Europeans are way ahead of us.

In addition to sports and news, you've also been involved in directing entertainment programming at ABC, such as the specials with Oprah Winfrey and the Daytime Emmy Awards. What changes did this mean for you as a director?

Again, one of the biggest changes was adapting to new types of camera people. There was a different type of formality; they would request our shot sheets, for example. I also found the lighting people to be more formal, approaching their work more like a director of photography. Frankly, I found the pace too slow.

How would you characterize your approach to directing?

I'm very specific—I'm specific about the music, I'm specific about the lenses. I want to know as much as I can about the television switcher, as much as I can about the lighting. I usually memorize all the lighting cues so I can call them, and if something doesn't look good I can ask for something else. You talk to people now and they will say "he is so anal, he drives you crazy." And it's true, I go over things, it's got to be my way.

This interview took place at Roger Goodman's office at ABC News in New York in October 1997. It originally appeared in the DGA Magazine, Vol. 22, No. 5, January 1998.

Sports

Bob Fishman, Doug Wilson

Versatile, flexible, creative, nomadic. These are the defining qualities of TV sports directors. No other area of television directing calls for the range of skills or the grueling, on-the-road existence required of those who cover sports. Unlike their studio-bound counterparts in news or entertainment, sports directors are constantly shifting gears and locales as they are called upon to tackle everything from baseball to wrestling to skating to the Olympics.

Traveling from city to city, and sometimes from continent to continent, they must quickly establish control over a bewildering variety of circumstances, including setting up the best camera positions, mastering the available technical resources, learning everything they can about players, coaches, and strategies, while also coordinating plans with producers and on-air analysts.

Directing the event itself can be equally as daunting. Working with anywhere from six to several dozen cameras, sports directors must be constantly on the alert to follow the action and make sure that it's clear for viewers. This means continuously scanning the monitors searching for the liveliest shots, while anticipating what might be about to happen next. It's not an easy task, particularly in sports which are fast paced, like auto racing, or downright unpredictable, like baseball.

In addition to their command of logistics, sports directors must also have a flair for the dramatic. They need to be able to capture the emotional impact of each event, making viewers feel a direct connection to the athletes in the heat of competition. Like directors who work on episodic series, they must know when to go for a close-up, how long to hold the shot, and when to cut away. Their theatrical instincts, however, must be especially sharp since, with the exception of figure skating, there's no script or rehearsals in the drama of live sports to fall back on.

Bob Fishman has directed virtually every major competitive event in nearly twenty-five years at CBS Sports, including NCAA basketball (for which he won Emmys in 1982, 1988, 1990, 1991 and 1992), the Daytona 500, the U.S. Open Tennis Championships, the World Series (winning an Emmy in 1993), thoroughbred racing, and figure skating at the 1992, 1994, and 1998 Olympic Winter Games. He's also won the 1986 Emmy Award for Outstanding Live Sports Special, and the DGA Award for his coverage of college basketball (1988), the U.S. Open (1989), and Major League Baseball's ALCS Game Four (1990). He joined CBS in 1972, working as a production assistant and associate director at CBS News.

Though Doug Wilson is most closely associated for his innovative direction of figure skating, he's also covered every sport from bowling to wrist wrestling to gymnastics to Ping-Pong. Wilson has been a producer/director for ABC's *Wide World of Sports* for thirty-five years, winning sixteen Emmy Awards and the DGA Lifetime Achievement Award in Sports Directing. He's also participated in the coverage of ten Olympic Games, including directing the coverage of the closing ceremony of the 1988 Games in Calgary.

Bob Fishman

Were you always interested in being a sports director?

Well, I knew I wanted to do something in sports, and like most kids, my dream was to be a sports announcer. I got interested in television at the ripe old age of 16 when I went to work for a station down in the Virgin Islands, where I grew up. I anchored the evening news on the weekends, and by the time I went to college I was very focused on what I wanted to do.

When I graduated from Boston University, I realized I wasn't going to be an announcer, but I became increasingly interested in what was going on behind the scenes, thanks to some college production courses. I started out as a stage hand and floor manager at the CBS O & O in

Philadelphia [WCAU-TV, owned and operated by the CBS Network], and then I went on to the network in New York as a commercial coordinator. My first break came in 1972 when I met CBS News producer Robert Wussler, who was a legend in the business. He hired me as a production assistant, and from then everything kind of fell into place. I worked as a P.A./A.D. and was directing inserts for the news division by the time I was 26.

Then as luck would have it, Wussler became president of CBS Sports and soon after offered me a job there.

Did you immediately start directing once you got there?

Pretty quickly. Coming from news gave me an advantage over the A.D.s who were already in sports because of the experience in working with film-to-tape transfers and with mixed tracks that had little application in sports. Having worked on elections and space shots and *60 Minutes*, etc., I had learned to work under pressure and racing the clock, which was invaluable experience.

My first directing assignment after the transfer was the studio portion of the *CBS Sports Spectacular*. From there I ended up directing the *NFL Today* for six years.

Did you find studio directing in sports similar to studio directing in news?

It was pretty similar, though it was a little more creative because we had more equipment and more talent on the set. Still, I knew all along that working the studio was only going to be a temporary stop and that what I really wanted to do was to go out and direct live events in the field. I was able to do some inserts, like ten-minute segments on horse racing and auto racing, and by 1981 I made my complete break with studio directing and became exclusively a remote director.

What did you find to be the biggest difference being out in the field as a director, compared to your previous work in the studio?

The biggest difference is that in the studio everything is formatted—you've got a teleprompter, you've got a confined area, and if something's not working right you just get out of your chair and fix it. On remote, you rely on the talents of lots of different people and you confront the unexpected at every turn. There are thousands of new variables and it's a bit of a scary experience the first time.

The other thing I found is that I was now suddenly directing legends in the business, people like Jack Whittaker and Pat Summerall. Here I was a twenty-seven-year-old kid and I'm supposed to be in charge. It was a little bit unnerving at first.

My first fully remote broadcast was a horse race from Saratoga. I had some ideas that had never been tried before. For example, I was the first director to use a handheld camera in the starting gate. I always felt the most thrilling part before a race was the loading of the gate and seeing the tension of the jockeys and their getting ready to start, but nobody had ever captured those moments. I made inquiries with the track supervisor and he reluctantly let us try it. It worked wonderfully that day and is now part of everybody's horse racing coverage.

Your work at CBS Sports called for you to cover a variety of sports from week to week. Did you have your own ideas about how to approach each one of them?

There have always been proven ways to cover each particular sport, and I think all networks cover the basics the same way. But everybody likes to put their own stamp on their coverage, and it's become so competitive that each director would like to come up with something that's new. In my case, I'm most proud of the new ideas that I began in horse racing, but I also have received credit for things that were not my ideas. For example, the use of cameras in race cars. This was an innovation credited to me, when in fact, Ken Squier, who is our lead auto racing announcer at CBS, had gotten wind of the fact that the Australians were using this technology. It wasn't long before we were working in concert with them and now, of course, the cameras in the cars are standard.

You try to approach every sport creatively. And in many cases, we attempt to put cameras in places they have never been seen before. Sometimes it's successful, but sometimes we're met with reluctance on the part of the leagues or organizers. In some cases it's like pulling teeth, and in other cases we're allowed to place equipment wherever we want. But you're always trying to improve your coverage.

No other directors are called upon to do as many different activities as sports directors. How do you know what to do when you may not be completely familiar with the sport you're assigned to cover?

You talk to people who've done it before. You watch tapes. You go to events. You spend a few days before you do it watching the preliminaries. The key ability you need is to be able to see things in a broader, fuller way than a studio director sees things. It's a talent you have to cultivate, and it basically comes down to sitting in the chair and doing it over and over again.

I had limited experience with auto racing when I was thrown into the task of directing the first live, flag-to-flag coverage of the Daytona 500 in 1979. This was going to be three hours, and it was a huge assignment for somebody who was as young as I was and as inexperienced. My preparation was to spend a week down there beforehand, and to spend a great deal of time with Ken Squier, who had covered a lot of auto racing and had a vast amount of knowledge. I also watched a lot of tapes and quickly saw that there were two ways to cover auto racing: you could focus on the lead car, ignoring the other racing and quickly drive viewers away from the TV set. Or you could try to cover the race within the race, meaning getting your cameras further back into the pack where the best action is generally taking place. Furthermore, unless you also wove in stories that were taking place in the pits or in the garage area, you just weren't delivering the full picture.

So it's important to have a sense of drama?

Sports is a great form of drama, and sports directors should know how to bring that drama alive. Sports is the story of winners and losers and I think what separates a good sports broadcast from an ordinary broadcast is the way you make viewers have a rooting interest. It's important to do your research and so that when the events are unfolding through your lenses you have a plan of how to capture the drama. Close-ups of the athletes reacting during tense situations are, I believe, the essence of drama in sports.

Sometimes drama presents itself in the most unexpected ways. The 1979 Daytona 500 was a perfect example of that. Here I was directing this very important event and on the last lap of the race a crash between the two leaders allowed Richard Petty to sneak through and win. Suddenly on the backstretch the two drivers who had crashed—Cale Yarborough and Donnie Allison—have left their cars and are embroiled in a fist fight. That specific incident propelled stock car racing right to the front page of the *New York Times*. Here I was, lucky enough to have the Goodyear Blimp hovering above the race track, isolating these two grown men, punching each other. It was a great piece of luck and a great piece of drama.

I guess after the complexity of auto racing you were now prepared for anything?

I was feeling fairly confident after this assignment, and I now started to get the chance to cover the sports I was more comfortable with, like football and basketball. These are sports that are easier to cover than auto racing because they're predictable. There's a predictability in sports that are played left to right and right to left, anything that goes from point A to point B. You can anticipate with sports like football and basketball, because (a) they're playing in a confined area and (b) they're only moving in one of two directions—left to right or right to left—and therefore you don't have to worry much about the camera that is following the play.

It wasn't until 1990 when CBS acquired baseball for the first time that I had a chance to direct a sport that is totally unpredictable, and that, like auto racing, became the biggest challenge. There's a total unpredictability about baseball which makes it, in my opinion, the most difficult sport to direct. There are only two cameras in covering a baseball game that have automatic assignments. These cameras are your center field camera, which covers the pitch, and the camera above home plate, which follows the ball. Aside from those two cameras, there are many combinations that are used to cover the game.

Directing baseball may start out very simply. A batter walks to the plate, there's nobody on base, and your only responsibility is to concentrate on the batter vs. the pitcher. Suddenly, two men get on base and the whole complexion of your coverage changes. Now you have to worry about your runners, you have to cover the pitcher, you have to cover the next batter, you have no idea where the ball is going to be hit, and there is very important timing that you must use to document the ball and the runners at the same time. This unpredictability makes baseball very challenging.

When you're watching a baseball game the impression is that things are happening very slowly. For a director, this is not the case. There's so much going on within the game, so many subtle things, like the signals being given between the manager, the coaches, the catcher, the batter, the pitcher, and the fielders and these can provide some wonderful close-ups before the ball is even thrown. This to me is the ultimate challenge of directing baseball—to capture all of those shots and then be ready for the actual play as it unfolds.

I've always enjoyed directing basketball, especially college basketball during the NCAA tournament. It's always been very refreshing in this day and age to see kids trying their best and getting as emotional as they do, which provides wonderful television moments. Directing football is also interesting because of the various isolation patterns that are the essence to directing a game. But I'm passionate about baseball. I grew up playing baseball and I find it more challenging to direct than other sports.

What's the minimum number of cameras you need to cover baseball?

There are local baseball directors that use as few as five cameras, and I admire those directors a great deal. In some cases at CBS we employed only five cameras, and any director will tell you that the fewer cameras that you have, the harder you have to work. For network baseball playoffs or the World Series, you're into a whole new kettle of fish. Even with the extra equipment, perhaps anywhere from fourteen to twenty cameras, many of the shots that you need are easier to get, while at the same time as a director you have many more monitors to look at. With that much equipment, you can plan a series of all the shots you need more easily than if you only have five cameras to work with.

You started covering college football in 1981 and then moved to covering the NFL. Were there any major differences in the way you approached them?

NFL football is a little bit more predictable than college football. In college you have more varied offenses that the teams run—some teams run the "option" which makes it difficult in some cases for the camera people to pick up the ball because there's fakery going on between the quarterback and the running backs. Plus there are so many more players that play and dress that you have to know who's on the field and what their skills are and are they more likely to catch the ball or run with the ball, etc. In the NFL there is more familiarity with the teams and often you see the same teams on repeat weeks. In college, you might see one team and not see them again until next year and by then everyone's graduated and you've got new players to learn about.

What kind of preparation do you need to do for football?

You watch tapes. You have meetings with the coaches and players to get a sense of what their team is about—are they a running team, are they a passing team, are they an offensive team, are they a defensive team, are they going to throw the ball sixty times, are they going to run the ball sixty times. This gives you a good guideline for going in and for helping your camera people when you meet with them about who they should focus on for various types of plays.

In a sense, a sports director is the visual play-by-play analyst. You have to be every bit as informed as any of your commentators.

Absolutely. There are situations where you see a formation and have a pretty good idea about what play is about to unfold. Generally, though, we take our lead from the analysts, because in network television the analyst is someone who has either coached or played the game and understands better than any director what's happening on the field.

How does the director function not only in terms of working with the announcers, but also in terms of working with the producers and the camera people? Are you the computer that keeps the elaborate operation up and running?

I think of myself as the air traffic controller. The producer is in charge of the overall look of the broadcast, and the announcers are responsible for the information flow of the broadcast. But the director has the ultimate responsibility to show you what's going on and simply to get the best picture on the air at any time. This can be frustrating at times, particularly when the announcers or the producer is leading the broadcast to a particular story line. There have been instances when the announcers are telling a story about a particular player while there are other things happening on the field and you, as the director, must choose what is the most important thing to show. My main focus, however, is never to miss live action just for the sake of somebody telling a story. In any sport, you can't fall in love with close-ups on the sidelines if the players are ready to play ball.

The announcers and director also work closely in choosing the isolations in a football game. Your analysts, especially, might give you a list of players that need to be followed during the course of the game. Sometimes these isolated shots, which become replays, work out and sometimes they don't, so there is a dialogue during the entire course of the game to change these isolations.

It's the same thing in every sport. You have to pay attention to what's happening on the field. If you understand what is going on in the game, you have a good chance of being successful. But directors often make the mistake of trying to use all of their cameras and force in a lot of shots without grasping what's happening on the field. The director really has to have a sense of what's important right now and cover it in a manner that doesn't disorient the viewer. Over-cutting is the most frustrating thing I see in sports coverage today. Less is often more. One day I would love to teach a course on over-cutting and switching angles. I'm not foolish enough to think you can cover a game properly with one camera but there is something wonderful in the simplicity of single-camera coverage. I suppose MTV has created a lot of this over-cutting, but for me the best sports telecasts are the ones where you know a director has twenty cameras to work with, but has the patience to use them correctly.

How did you come to terms with directing figure skating?

As we approached our first Winter Olympics Games in 1992 in Albertville, France, CBS had to come up with a crew to cover skating. The network had not done much of it before, and I was elected. Right away it became apparent to me that this was something very different than anything I had done before. I believe that figure skating takes more creativity than other sports.

Skating is very personal, it's very dramatic, it's one person alone on the stage, and for that reason you cover it differently. Figure skating is about beauty, it's about music, and it's about passion, and you have to cover it in a more sensitive way.

Did you approach skating as a departure from your previous sports directing?

My directing has always centered on getting emotional shots. These shots generally present themselves only at the climax of a close game. Skating is different. In an Olympic competition, for example, that emotion is there throughout the performance. Because of the lifelong preparation needed to reach the Olympic level, skaters, alone on their frozen stage for three or four minutes, exude that emotion throughout.

ABC director Doug Wilson was probably everyone's teacher. Even though I had some idea of how to cover the sport, I did need help so I asked Doug's associate director, Meg Streeter, to come aboard for the 1992 Olympics and help me understand what the sport was about. She taught me about the different kinds of jumps, the terminology. We sat and talked about how to cover the sport and what types of approaches to use in cutting and when to cut.

Different directors will approach skating in different ways, but I think there are some rules you need to follow. Number one: I think it's essential to cover all jumps head-to-toe, and to try to be on a camera that's low to the ice to see the height of the jump. Number two: I think it's important to cover any spins head-to-toe, because the whole body is the essence of the spin, and not just a close-up of the skates. Number three: I think it's important to never interrupt the flow of a particular move. For example, there's a move called the spiral, where a skater will go from point A to point B in a circular movement, and to chop that up with lots of different camera shots is not the way the choreography is intended to be shown.

I think directing figure skating is a lot more challenging creatively. You spend a lot more time studying what the skaters are doing. We have very long blocking sessions, where I'll have an assistant videotape practices, and then bring the tape into a viewing room. We'll watch the tape, and labor over which camera we'll use for each portion of the routine. You never do that in other sports. Each skater is unique and each routine is unique, and you're drawn into the sport more than any other because of the degree of preparation that it demands.

There's probably no area of television as directly affected by new technologies as sports coverage. How have the changes over the last few decades changed your work?

The advancements, particularly in lenses, have been extraordinary. So have the advances in graphics, digital tape, and high-speed cameras for replays. What this has meant for sports is the ability to see things more clearly, to get into the eyes of the athletes, and to bring the viewers a sense of what the athlete is feeling. In the old days, everything had to be shot in a fairly wide perspective. You would basically see the same view at home as you would if you were sitting in the stands. Today there is nobody, including the people who have the best seats in the house, who can see with the naked eye what the camera lenses we now have can see.

On a negative note, I can't stand what has happened to sports coverage because of the abundance of new special effects. I admire the hard work that goes into the creation of these devices but they are being overused to the detriment of every director who cares most about a good picture. Also, the cost of doing business has necessitated a glut of commercial information during action. We now shrink the screen for lineups, other scores, statistics, etc., because everything is sponsored. This goes against everything I enjoy about directing. I think I learned the basics of good television from working on *60 Minutes* as a production assistant. The trademark of *60 Minutes* has always been a good story, an uncluttered presentation, and a focus on people in close-up. Have you ever seen a graphic or a special effect on any *60 Minutes* piece?

Let me give you one example. I recently watched a feature piece on a college basketball coach who was recovering from a heart attack. No sooner had this feature begun than the frame was squeezed to allow for scores of games currently being played. This basically told the viewer that this piece is not important enough to give it your full attention. For me, directing sports has always been about conveying drama, and so in this day and age of information saturation my job has become more and more difficult.

Doug Wilson

What led you into directing?

I originally wanted to be a performer, and hoped to be a singer or actor. Still, I was always fascinated by the production aspects of entertainment, especially after watching Perry Como do the rehearsals for his TV show when I was just a teenager. After graduating from Colgate University I ended up as a page at NBC, where I discovered how much I truly loved broadcasting. I then got a job as a production assistant at ABC in 1958, and after two years moved up to being an associate director.

I worked on a number of programs and then was assigned to ABC's Sunday religious program *Directions*. I couldn't have had a more wonderful start in terms of hands-on creativity, since the show tackled a different topic each week, with every type of approach from documentary to photo essay to drama. The producer Wiley Hanse became my mentor, and in a storybook fashion, I got the chance to direct when Jack Sameth, the director of that week's show, had to leave the day before and they let me take over. I had never directed before, but I kind of wanted to, and there I was in 1962, twenty-three years old, with a full crew, a Houston crane, a big studio, and I was scared to death. I remember I told *International Skating* magazine a few months ago when they asked me what it was like to direct this first show that it was a little like the first time I had sex—I was a little confused and a little frightened but I sure was looking forward to the next time. I ended up directing a few more episodes the next season, which I greatly enjoyed.

How did you move from public affairs to sports—it's not really a typical route?

I worked on *Directions* as an A.D. for three years, and then I was informed that there had been a request—to this day I don't know by whom—to go to work for sports. Back then, sports was called Sports Programs Inc., and it was essentially an outside production company that would make shows for ABC, using ABC's production support for their programs. Later it was sold directly to the network where it became ABC Sports Inc. I had worked once before for the unit in February 1963, doing the New York AC Indoor Games, where I sat next to Curt Gowdy handling the cue cards.

I hated to leave *Directions* because of its enormous variety, but I felt like I was reaching a dead end there. So I went to sports as an associate director, which was still a step up, and the first thing I was assigned was the AAU Synchronized Swimming Championships on *Wide World of Sports*. Roone Arledge was in charge and I realized immediately that he gave everyone—producers, directors, associate directors—the freedom and the encouragement to do your best. He wanted to nurture our creative juices. If you had ideas, you went with them. There was no one there to say no. For example, I thought of an interesting way to start that first show by using our underwater camera and have a girl swim towards it holding up a plexiglass sign saying *Wide World of Sports.*

Time passed. I did football games and all sorts of *Wide World* activities. I began to have a lot of creative input, and working with Jim McKay was especially nurturing for me, because he and I thought a lot alike about our approach to sports. I approached sports as theater and music, because that was my background. McKay gives me credit for being the first to put sports to music on TV.

And you were doing this still as an associate director?

Yes, they let me do it. The directors would do the event and leave, and we'd be left in the tape room to create the show with the producers. A lot of that still takes place today.

I helped pioneer the idea of a tease for *Wide World of Sports.* One of my first was for a show commemorating the 100th anniversary of the climbing of the Matterhorn. I booked a studio, set up easels, shot a series of old photographs, edited it to music, and made it a tease. I had to convince them that when you came out of a station break you should grab people—a concept which had never been done before. Previously they just played the standard opening, "Spanning the globe to bring you the constant variety of sports." But every time I did the show as an A.D. we had a tease preceding it, then others picked up the idea as well.

I was also quite proud of a piece I did for the Muhammad Ali/Brian London fight which took place in London, England. Chet Forte was the producer and he knew I was the music guy, and he said to me, why don't we use "A Foggy Day in London Town." I said fine, but couldn't figure out how to use a love song in connection with Muhammad Ali. Now, I knew Frank Sinatra's version like the back of my hand—I bet I had played it in my life 400 times. And a week later as I was driving home, I kept thinking of the lyrics and it came to me how each line of lyrics could be fit perfectly into a visual counterpoint. I scripted what I wanted line by line so by the time we got to London, it was ready to be shot. Ali was incredibly cooperative and we got some beautiful shots, which coordinated precisely with the lyrics and the rhythms of the Sinatra version. *Variety* later reviewed the telecast and said the fight was lousy but "whoever did the opening film of 'Foggy Day' really had a sense of style."

How long did you remain as an A.D. before they recognized, and you recognized, that you wanted to be a director?

In the swashbuckling days of ABC Sports in the 1960s and '70s, we could do everything. If we saw a need, we filled it or if we had a creative idea we went and did it. We were not as shackled by financial yokes, because Roone gave his producers, his directors, and his associate directors creative freedom. He wanted them to be thinking about the creative side of their jobs, and not be inordinately burdened by the financial side. So, this meant that I was an A.D. who often took the bull by the horns and just directed stuff, like the Muhammad Ali montage I just mentioned.

Gradually I began to be upgraded to do a directorial job or a producing job. What's important to note is that ABC Sports was much more a producer's medium than a director's medium, and the first hint that I knew I had potential was at a National Football Foundation dinner, which I went to with my dad as guests of a family friend. Roone was there and said to my father, "Doug is going to make a great producer some day."

In 1967 he had me direct a U.S. National Figure Skating Championships from Omaha, and I didn't do a good job. But Roone was kind and instructional, analytical, not critical. He mentioned to me in a car ride later that a director has to have something beyond a method, he has to have a sixth sense.

This was followed by a meeting I had with Chuck Howard, who was vice-president in charge of production for ABC Sports, and he said they'd like me to produce their bowling series. At first I was a bit perturbed, moving from my international beat at *Wide World of Sports* to bowling for 13 weeks. But it was an opportunity I couldn't say no to.

What's the difference between being a producer and director in sports?

It's a question I get asked a great deal, and the answer is, at least at ABC, that it overlaps a great deal. The producer decides what we're going to do, the director decides how we're going to do it. But the producer can also decide what the best kinds of technical requirements are, what kinds of cranes to use, etc., because he's where the buck stops.

During the next decade I ended up producing much more than directing, but I still did some directing. The flattering thing was that, at least in those days, while Roone had tremendous respect for directors, his people really were the producers. They were the boss, they were responsible for what went on the air. If the producer didn't like what a director was doing, the producer could tell the director, "Don't do it this way." There might be fights, but that usually didn't happen, because everybody was on the same team.

What were the main differences you noted as you moved from directing to producing?

As a director, you could concentrate on one project at a time. As a producer, I was in charge of four or five shows at once. It was total life immersion, at least at ABC Sports. You never could get away from thinking about your shows—twenty-four hours a day, seven days a week.

You mentioned that your first experience directing ice skating was a failure. When did you realize that skating was something that you actually were born to direct?

I always felt it, from the time I first saw it, because I wanted to be Gene Kelly. I was aware of Sonja Henie and Dick Button when I grew up, plus the fact that I'd taken all sorts of dance lessons growing up. Skating to me was an amalgam of all the athleticism of sports and artistry of theater that I'd been drawn to my whole life.

I believe I always had what Roone referred to as "a sixth sense" about skating, but I didn't at first have the methodology. I was so concerned in that first show with the cameras and getting them right that I didn't see the skater.

When did this begin to change for you?

There were a couple of influential events. One was the opportunity I had after the 1976 Olympics to work as a creative consultant on Dorothy Hamill's first TV special with two director/producers who had been my idols: Dwight Hemion and Gary Smith. I learned a tremendous amount from just watching them, seeing their control, the way they handled people, and their use of lighting. It was also a wonderful experience to be able to work with Gene Kelly, who was a guest star on the special.

Then a few years later in the fall of 1979, I was called to do an assignment with Peggy Fleming and Dorothy Hamill, which would take place in the brand new Lake Placid Arena. I was producer and director for this event, which ended up showcasing Peggy doing three spectacular numbers. The show proved to be a breakthrough for me in how to shoot skating in a way that captured what was actually going on in the rink. I had been trying for twelve years to figure out a way to get directly on the ice—I had tried hand Zambonis and all kinds of stuff. Finally, I took the advice of someone from the movie industry and just put one of my camera men on a wheelchair, with someone very skilled pushing them. Now you could be on the ice, with the skaters, and it was quite powerful and effective.

There was another important event. During the 1980 Olympics, I saw Peggy diagraming her performance. I had never seen anything like it before, and it was like a comic-strip lightbulb going off in my head. One of the frustrations of directing ice skating up to that point was that if you saw, let's say, Dorothy Hamill going into a spiral position, leaning forward with her arms back and her back leg up in the air, and I wanted to take a quick shot of her face because it's just exuding emotion, you couldn't do it. By the time I got the camera ready and took the shot, it would be too late, and I would be looking at the north end of the horse going south. I didn't know what was coming and I had no method or technique in finding out and making notes about it.

Now, with the possibilities of the diagram laid out before me, I would go to practices and ask the coach and the skater to come afterwards. We'd sit at a table, play the music for their routine, I'd give them a pencil and a diagram of the ice surface, and I told them, "Mark where your start position is." Then we would begin the music and I would start a clock, and they would draw a squiggly line for their double lutz and I would take notes and write down "twenty-three seconds from the start," and so on through the whole four-minute routine.

This proved to be a wonderful approach, and I got to know the skaters very well. But ultimately, it was inefficient. I would end up with lots of pages of spaghetti lines, and I'd go back to the hotel room that night and could only use about 40 percent of it. Still, I used this method for about three years, and it helped me prepare, and it helped me do a better job.

What finally caused you to abandon it, given that it was still the best way to know what the skaters were going to do in advance?

Fate took a step in my direction. We were doing a show in Madison Square Garden called "Pro Skate," which featured professional skaters. It was a very rushed and pressured affair, with rehearsals out in Staten Island, and I never had the time to sit down with the Janet Lynns and the John Currys and go over their routines. And now it's the afternoon of the night of the performances and I've got no preparation. The skaters had practice time in the Garden between 2 and 4 o'clock in the afternoon. I said to my associate Ann Uzdavinis, who had been an amateur skater herself, "Grab a stop watch and when the music starts you start the watch and write down what I tell you and note the time."

In my mind's eye I camera-cut the skater's performance. For example, from the moment the skater would be out in the center and getting ready to start, I'd be saying "OK, camera four gets a tight face, camera two head-to-toe right frame, dissolve to two. The music would start and I'd say stay on two, stay on two, OK, we're going to dissolve to four, and so on." After Annie had written this all down, I told her that when we went back into the truck tonight, I wanted her to start her stopwatch when the music starts, and tell me how many seconds I've got until such-and-such camera move or cut. I would then be able to warn the camera people what's coming and they'd have some warning.

It was only a guideline, it had nothing to do with exactness, like in a drama. This was my best guess at the time, and, even though it may not be how I'm going to do it, and I may change it as I watch the monitors, it was still a very useful guideline.

Still, the method was very archaic at that time, especially compared with how intricate this process has since become. Now, I've got a camera guy who works with me, shooting with a Hi-8 camera, and we tape it. The advantage is that if there's some real complication, or I didn't get the thoughts fast enough, I can check it. Or if because of production needs and I can't be there, I can watch the tape later on in the hotel.

So in many ways your approach to skating has become more simplified?

Yes, now all I need is time. I need to see the skaters perform, which can be frustrating because they may go to practices and not do their routines. It's important to also emphasize that the process of refining this technique continues to evolve. I continue to discover things, I continue to change nuances.

What's your relationship like with the camera people, who haven't seen the rehearsal and don't know exactly what to expect?

As all of us directors know, we're only as good as the camera people who are working with us. Before every show, I sit down and have a camera meeting. Each year, I give the same speech and apologize for it, because they've heard it again and again. But what I do is explain my basic philosophy of how to make things look seamless. There are a lot of techniques—there are left-right dissolves, there are "let-em-go-aways," etc. I try to emphasize the nuances, the subtleties. Hopefully, they'll be unnoticeable, but they need to be explained.

This is a very important thing. If in any way my camera work becomes inordinately noticeable, I have failed. If the guy at home comes to me and says, "Boy, that shot of so-and-so was great," I consider that the equivalent of getting an "F." However, if he says to me, "Did you see Michele Kwan? When she did that lay back spin, that was so beautiful," then I've done my job.

It strikes me that the approach you have to ice skating mirrors the approach Fred Astaire wanted when his dancers were being filmed—he wanted the audience to be able to see him, full figure, without anything fancy getting in the way.

A director once asked me how to do skating and I said to him, "Just let the skaters skate." If you're going to the ballet and you're sitting twelfth row center, and the dancer comes downstage left, you don't want to suddenly be thrust from your seat and be sitting orchestra right. You want to sit in your seat and watch the dancer flow—have him move upstage, get closer, far away, etc. We can do that with skating competition. And once in a while we can go one better and momentarily be on the stage with the skater.

It's very easy to cover figure skating in a mediocre way. You've got at least four to six cameras, maybe up to fourteen or fifteen, you've got one or two human figures on the ice surface, and you can certainly keep them in frame. What I learned starting in the early 1980s is that when you do figure skating, you're not there to have cameras come to an arena and look in on the skater. What we have to do is to make each camera an extension of the skater's choreography. Our job is to enhance the dance, not look at it.

When you think about the incredible discipline and skill and training that go into each skater's performance, we, as the conduits of their performance and their moment should do the damnedest, deepest, most analytical job we can to make them look as good as they really are.

The interview with Bob Fishman was conducted by phone from his home in Boca Raton, Florida, in December 1997. The interview with Doug Wilson was conducted at the offices of the Directors Guild of America in New York in October 1997.

Specials: Dance

Merrill Brockway

For the first three decades of American TV, dance and television weren't the happiest of partners. Though there had been many full-length programs devoted to ballet, and numerous appearances by noted dancers on variety shows during the 1950s and 1960s, basic problems remained. The largest concerned the issues of design and scale. How could choreography created for the stages of grand theaters be reshaped, and re-edited, for a two-dimensional medium? Added to this was the question of visibility—how could dancers, let alone a company of dancers, clearly be seen on a screen no bigger than a breadbasket?

The medium took a giant leap forward in the mid-1970s with the launching of PBS's *Dance in America*. Here at last was a series dedicated to "serving" ballet and modern dance by attentively collaborating with the country's leading choreographers. Rather than watching from the sidelines as their pieces were squeezed onto the small screen, masters like Martha Graham and Merce Cunningham could now work side by side and step by step with skilled TV craftsmen in rethinking and redesigning their ballets expressly for the limits and the possibilities of television.

George Balanchine and his company, the New York City Ballet, were initially reluctant to participate in the series. Through the years, Balanchine had had many unhappy TV experiences, from scaled-down telecasts of *The Nutcracker* in the 1950s, to a critically disastrous CBS commission of *Noah and the Flood* in 1962, culminating in a brutally directed and edited series of dance programs from Germany in the early

1970s. Fortunately, the task of persuading Balanchine to work with PBS fell to *Dance in America*'s series producer and director Merrill Brockway, who was eminently suited for the job. A former classical piano accompanist and a skilled director of many award-winning arts programs, Brockway was able to convince Balanchine that he would "trust the dancing." Together, the two men would create some of the most memorable hours of dance on television.

The key to their partnership depended on a shared sense of musical logic and structure. In devising his shots and editing patterns, Brockway instinctively responded to the internal architecture of Balanchine's choreography. His carefully conceived camera movements mirrored the lyrical pulse of the dancing.

To capture the intricacy and formal coherence of Balanchine's work, Brockway employed an elaborate production "system," initially developed during his previous work on CBS's *Camera Three*. What the "system" entailed was a detailed inquiry into every aspect of the ballet and how best to capture its spirit in the transition to the small screen. The result was an approach to tele-dance "translation" that was unusually responsive to choreographic intentions and to the care and nurturing of the dancers themselves. This attentive approach became one of *Dance in America*'s signatures.

For Brockway, working with "Mr. B." proved to be an exhilarating experience. Balanchine grasped the medium's potential almost at once and eagerly embraced its challenges. He was not only excited by the production process but eminently practical about its consequences. Rather than adhere to his stage designs, he was more than willing to alter his choreography to suit the circumstances, going so far as to add a new, more "TV legible" ending to *The Four Temperaments* and a new promenade for *Jewels* (additions he liked so much they became the official City Ballet version).

George Balanchine and Merrill Brockway's artistic collaboration led to four programs on *Dance in America* as well as a later program for CBS Cable of *Davidsbündlertanze*. Little seen in recent years, the shows are fortunately now being released on home video by Nonesuch, along with several other tapes of Balanchine-related material. Though nearly two decades old, the programs still seem newly minted and remain unsurpassed examples of how to make TV dance.

When Dance in America *was in the preparation stage, Jac Venza, the executive producer, approached Lincoln Kirstein to request the participation of the New York City Ballet. It is reported that Mr. Kirstein responded: "I hate television; it's a vulgar invention." Against this opposition, how did you finally go about convincing George Balanchine to work with you?*

I was appointed series producer of *Dance in America* in 1975 and learned that Balanchine appeared to be cool to the project. I assumed the reason was an unpleasant film experience he had in Germany in 1973. Nevertheless, I wrote him a letter telling that I was the new boy on the block and "for us to call a series *Dance in America* would be unconscionable without his participation." My boldness amused Barbara Horgan, his personal assistant, who arranged a luncheon at Balanchine's favorite restaurant.

We didn't immediately talk about dance or television. First he wanted to know about my training, especially my musical background as a pianist; then he wanted to tell me stories of his film experiences in Hollywood. Near the end of the meal he insinuated the subject of television, and I invited him to collaborate with us on this new dance series. His response was a curious question—"but will you trust the dancing?" I, of course, assured him I would.

On our walk back to the New York State Theater, Balanchine invited me to see any performance of my choice during the season just beginning. He told me to come to him when I had an idea about "what would be good for television." He was a television watcher (his favorite program was *Wonder Woman*!) and he knew that all of his ballets would not be comfortable on television.

I walked back to our offices overjoyed that I had gotten through the big gate, but I wondered what he meant by "will you trust the dancing?" I continued to wonder several years before I understood what he meant: "Will you serve the art of dance?"

Did you have any expectations of which works would be most suitable for television?

No. So I saw many performances during the season. The first piece I thought might work for television was the "Melancholic" variation from *The Four Temperaments*. It had a sense of space, a sense of character, and the dancing was vivid. Even now I think it was perhaps the most successful piece we did for the series. When I told Balanchine, he was agreeable, but he gradually convinced me that the whole ballet could work. I was especially wary of the number of people in the last movement. His response was, "Don't worry; I fix."

To complete the first program, he suggested the duet movement from *Divertimento No. 15* and *Tzigane*.

How did the actual production process itself work? Did you meet before you went into the recording studio to figure out how this would be shot?

After I had done a considerable amount of viewing record tapes and pacing, we rehearsed for a week in New York a week before going down to Nashville to record. In the rehearsal we used a single handheld camera to show what each ballet would look like. I wanted to get all the shots set before we went to the television studio.

What was it like once you left the rehearsal studio and moved down to Nashville for final production? Did you map it all out in terms of camera movement and cutting and then present the master plan to Balanchine?

Well, yes, in a way. I started doing this with *Divertimento No. 15*. I had the sequence of shots mapped out, and I took Balanchine from camera to camera and showed him my plan as the dancers performed their steps. He could then make suggestions: "higher, lower, tighter, wider." He didn't change any element of the basic shot plan. Often his comment would simply be "millimeter, millimeter." It was all a matter of exquisite adjustment, which is what my plan was all about.

What we were doing was working out a "system" and Balanchine was integral to it, both in shooting and editing.

And what did this system entail? Was it something new for you as a director?

I had always been a systems person, one who likes to search through the loose strands and weave "the organizing principle." I started with that, drew upon my encounters as an analyzing musician, and added my experiences as a worker in television. The system was designed as a series of guidelines that would help channel a director's individuality.

The system actually developed during my work as a director at *Camera Three* at CBS; it expanded and became more formalized at *Dance in America*, especially through the input of Emile Ardolino, who was the coordinating producer and oft-times director.

The system was divided into a number of parts and questions. The first involved determining how well a given piece would translate from the stage to television, and if television could reveal new aspects of the work. After a piece had been selected, we closely analyzed it: What was it about? What was its generating principle, its subtext? What shots would best serve it?

We asked ourselves questions about presentation: What would be the best way, the most supportive circumstance, to present this work? What works should surround it? Then we began to separate it into sections and explore the shot possibilities of each camera. We wanted to work closely with the choreographers to understand their intentions and how their participation could help us translate their work from one medium to another. We very early understood that there could be no one-to-one translation. Soon the credit read: "Choreographed and Reconceived for Television by...."

The system also carried over into postproduction where the tapes were watched with the choreographer. We were always looking for the accident that would enhance the original plan. In addition to Emile I was blessed with Girish Bhargava, editor extraordinaire. Together we developed an approach to editing dance that responded in a musical way to the choreography.

How did the limitations of TV affect your approach to choreography?

You have to remember that in 1976 directors were tremendously aware of the small screen, a fact largely forgotten now that we have 51-inch screens. Back then a 9-inch and perhaps a 12-inch television screen was standard and directors were very concerned about not putting too much detail on the screen. You never used a foreground and background with detail—you just told your story simply.

What impact did this have on your "choreography" of shots in terms of angle, position, movement, etc.?

A visual sequence for television is usually an arrangement of wide, medium, and tight shots. Each type of shot is needed to avoid monotony. The close-up is clearly the most utilized. But Balanchine was a neo-classical choreographer, which meant that dancing wasn't about the face. The drama is in the full body which called for a different visual orientation for me as a director. The tight shot was no longer only the face; it might be the entire body or from the knees up to and including the face. We developed a rule: if a body part is not doing anything (the legs and feet, for example), it's not necessary to include it in the picture. That gave me the release I needed as a director.

One would think that Balanchine would want his dancers to be seen whole, without any fracturing of the body.

But you see he knew his intention. You'll see a lot of "from the knees up" in these programs. Most often the close-up was port de bras, arms and face. And this came about because I would ask him, "When can I get a tighter shot?"

There was one other continuing, gnawing question that we both faced. If a body is moving at Balanchine speed, as his bodies did, I would track them in a full-figure shot. And he would say, "No; if you do that, only the scenery moves!" This is true; so I developed a fixed frame shot in which the dancer would move from one side of the frame to the other. No pan. You frame the shot wide enough that the space the body operates in is fully visible.

Now we had two ways of seeing the body move through space: one was tracking, the other was through a fixed space. When we met one of those situations, I would say to Balanchine, "It's your call." My preference was the fixed wide shot, but he would often say, "It's too wide!" Each time he would evaluate how he wanted to see that body move through space. This was the kind of discussion that we had; there was no rigid rule, each situation was evaluated. The joy for me was to be able to have continual conversation with the man who created the choreography.

Was there an evolution in the way Balanchine approached TV during the course of your years working together?

He certainly became more comfortable with the medium. *Dance in America* was the first time that he'd worked intimately with television. He'd had ideas, but he never had the chance to try them out.

What kinds of ideas?

Programming ideas—what kinds of pieces he'd like to see televised and what he'd like to see in the pieces. It had all been theoretical before.

When we first began working together, we worked with a half-inch camera in the rehearsal studio so we could see what we might expect. As he became more experienced, he became bored with this procedure. He knew what he could expect. He was eager to get to the recording studio. I, of course, needed as much preparation time in the rehearsal studio as I could get.

Your final project together was Davidsbündlertanze, *which was done for CBS Cable. How would you characterize that experience?*

By that time we had done enough together so that we could read each other's signals. I only misread him once, and that was during the double duet section of the piece. I treated it like two separate duets, and he said, "No." He wanted the four dancers to be seen together; so we corrected it.

Soon after his death, you put together a two-part documentary for Dance in America *on his career. Did working with him influence the shape and texture of the program?*

Of course. I don't think there's any question of it. Each one who worked with me on the biography—Holly Brubach, the writer; Judy Kinberg, the producer; Girish Bhargava, the editor—had worked with him and was familiar with the way he thought and what he wanted to see. We all felt his presence.

Looking back, what experiences as a director do you think best prepared you for your work with Balanchine?

Clearly my musical background as a musician, and my interest in musical analysis. Balanchine made his ballets on the music. They had a logic and a sequence that followed the musical architecture. I then built my piece on his piece built on the music. Putting together the sequence of shots was where I constructed my sense of "form."

So Balanchine responded to your ability to recognize his construction and to translate it in appropriate television terms?

Yes, to discover his architecture and his intention. We used to have long conversations where I would ask him "what was your intention here? What were you trying to do?" And gradually over time he would release more information about what he intended and why he liked working with us. We wanted to know what he was about, what was important to him and why?

And of course, he being who he was, he would change things if he could see they didn't work for the screen. That was the joy of it, since we didn't feel beholden to do it as it existed, but rather how it could be reconceived.

Did you have differences of opinion?

Oh, yes. I wasn't always fond of his sense of building a sequence of shots. He saw shots as individuals; I saw shots as part of a phrase. During a camera rehearsal, he would be looking at the monitors of the three cameras, see a shot and say, "That's pretty; let's use that one." It might be a shot that I planned to use later; so often I would tell a cameraman to "cap up. I don't want him to see that shot yet."

Balanchine had no trouble changing his choreography. Sometimes the ballet mistress did not feel the change was an improvement. I finally found a way to confront that situation. I'd say, "It's fine, but not very pretty." His immediate reply was, "I change." For him "pretty" was the highest compliment.

Did you have to rethink your directorial style as a result of working with him?

I had previously televised dance on *Camera Three*, working with choreographers like Twyla Tharp, Maurice Bejart, and Merce Cunningham. By *Dance in America* I was beginning to speak the rudiments of a language. I recently looked at a tape I made with Dance Theater of Harlem, and I said, "Good! the basic structure is there. I wouldn't change anything, but it needed more shots." I had the tree, and Balanchine's gift was to show me how to put more apples on it. He validated what I was thinking, and stimulated more thinking and added to the thinking. It was the same thing he used to do with Stravinsky—they turned each other on.

So he did approach dance differently than other choreographers you worked with?

It's not quite fair to say that because both Twyla and Merce were interested in video and film. But Balanchine was a problem solver. He loved to have problems presented; he would try this, try that—and he would solve it! He had an inquisitive spirit and unflagging energy.

With Balanchine I began to learn to direct in a new way, a different way. At the beginning he said to me, "How much do you know about ballet?" I replied, "Nothing." He smiled; "Good; I teach you." When you're being taught by Mr. B. it's a highly conscious process. Before, with dance, I was simply being intuitive.

Describe the process of working as a director with Balanchine.

As a director, I am an accompanist—that's how I started out as a musician, and that's my nature. Our collaboration was my working closely with someone with a strong vision, someone I felt totally in touch with, and someone I respected and supported. But then it goes both ways because he encouraged me to be more than I could be without him.

Did Balanchine's visual sense influence your directorial "eye," both during production of the programs and in your later work?

Absolutely, he changed my "eye." He taught me what to look for and what to look at, and to trust what I saw. Balanchine once quoted the poet Vladimir Mayakovsky that "I am not a man, but a cloud in pants." What Balanchine taught was not one single thing or several. He was a cloud that settled over you and forever changed your way of thinking, your way of doing.

This interview was conducted by phone from Merrill Brockway's home in Santa Fe, New Mexico, in August 1995. It originally appeared in Television Quarterly, Vol. XXVIII, No. 1, 1996.

Specials: Music

Steve Binder

Once upon a time, there was a golden age for music and variety on television. The airwaves were filled with great performers, whose talent transcended demographics. The commercial networks showcased the artistry of these entertainers not just on talk programs, but on single-star variety series and, most importantly, on lavish specials, complete with carefully designed original concepts and high production values.

Steve Binder was lucky enough to have played an important part in this now largely vanished era. At the age of twenty-one he was named director of Steve Allen's innovative syndicated talk show for Westinghouse. Two years later, he continued his long interest in pop music by helping to launch *Hullabaloo* on NBC (while also actively working in the recording industry). After a brief stint at CBS with the *Danny Kaye Show*, he decided to move on to the more creative potential of music specials.

Acting as both producer and director, Binder's first special featured Leslie Uggams, fresh from her triumph on Broadway. His second special in 1967 followed along similar tracks as a showcase for Petula Clark and guest Harry Belafonte, but, thanks to Ms. Clark's unplanned touch of Mr. Belafonte's forearm during an emotional duet, managed to ignite a nationwide racial controversy. His third special would prove just as momentous, as it singlehandedly revived Elvis Presley's career through its intense focus on the singer's roots and his explosive performing style.

During the 1970s, Steve Binder continued to work on musical specials and extravaganzas, featuring artists as diverse as Liza Minnelli, Mac Davis, Patti Labelle, and Barry Manilow (which won the Emmy Award for Best Special of 1977). In 1982, he did his first program for Showtime—Diana Ross's famous Central Park concert in the rain—which was televised live around the world. The program earned him a Cable Ace Award, but also helped symbolize the move of the traditional music special away from the commercial networks to pay cable. In the following decades, there would be little call for this once potent format on either ABC, CBS, or ABC. Instead, Binder turned his talents to various awards programs (including the Emmy Awards telecasts from 1984-88), a movie-of-the-week, *Pee-Wee's Playhouse* (as executive producer), and a Super Bowl halftime show with Diana Ross.

Lately, he's worked on several Disney TV ice specials and is planning Luciano Pavarotti's first network TV special for ABC. In this interview, he looks back on the glory days of network music specials.

What led you into directing?

I was born and raised in Los Angeles and never knew anybody in show business. I was in pre-med at USC, and applied for a summer job at both CBS and ABC. I interviewed at both networks the same day. ABC was like a little barn out in North Hollywood and seemed to me like it might be a more fun place to work environmentally. I got a job in the mail room, and one day started talking to Selig Seligman, who was then president of the local ABC affiliate KABC-TV. He asked me what I'd like to be doing, and right out of my mouth I answered "I'd think I'd like to be in your chair asking *you* these questions." He thought it was quite amusing, and he asked me if I'd ever like to be a director. I didn't even know what directing entailed, but he still said he'd like to introduce me to a few people. One of the first I met was Steve Allen, who'd been canceled off an ABC show and he seemed very depressed and was thinking about producing a show that he would not appear on. He had a young guy with him named Jimmie Baker, who was a jazz aficionado. Jimmie and Steve were planning to launch a series of twenty-six, half-hour jazz shows called *Jazz Scene U.S.A.*, which Steve was financing. Somehow I got offered the director job, and went from the mail room to directing the show, which we taped at CBS using the old *Playhouse 90* technical crew. It was a great experience. We taped three shows a day and I met everyone in jazz.

How did you know what to do in the control booth if you'd never directed before?

I didn't. But I was real smart in being able to say I didn't know, and I had a lot of people to help me. I must say when I first walked in the control room, it sounded like a language from Mars or Jupiter, but it very quickly began to make sense. I guess I was like a duck thrown into water the first time and found you either sink or swim.

What about the process of directing music? Did you develop any techniques to guide you in this first venture?

Somehow in my mind I saw video with music. Traditionally, everyone would tend to "play it safe," and they would shoot music shows from a distance. I felt jazz music was so intimate that it needed to be shot extremely close, and I started to montage close-up to close-up to close-up. I wasn't going for the usual master shot, medium shot, close-up, but rather for something that reflected the intimacy of the artist and the instrument. I used close-ups of their fingers, the sweat on their brow. Even though there wasn't a big audience for it, the show did do incredibly well in terms of critical reviews.

In the middle of all this shooting, Steve Allen called me up. He'd just gotten a contract to do a syndicated late-night show for Westinghouse and asked if I'd like to come with him. I ended up staying for two-and-a-half years—that's where I went to grammar school, high school, college, and then got a master's degree, so to speak, in directing. I was directing five ninety-minute shows a week, and got a chance to meet everybody in the business.

You were directing one of the most varied of all talk shows. What challenges did this pose for you as a director?

I credit Steve Allen with teaching me that you never ever stop until there's nothing left to shoot. We shot a ninety-minute program live-on-tape, with no editing, no isolated cameras. It always appeared to me that if you left the mistakes in, everybody loved it. I always called the show organized chaos—we knew where we were going with the road map, but we never knew what was going to happen when we got there. That's what really brought out the excitement and the energy. I had total freedom and creativity. Steve Allen once said in an article in the *New Yorker* that he had a young director who shoots from the hip and somehow knows what I'm going to do before I do it. Steve and I just had an instinctive sense of mindreading. When I put the camera out on the street I could somehow mentally anticipate what he was going to do, so I could make sure the shots were there. And it worked vice versa. He had great instincts in terms of where the cameras were going. We just had a tremendous amount of fun and when I look back on my career now, I realize that working on that show is why I chose this business as a profession. I never look at my watch to see what time I get off work but when I can go to work.

You took a different direction after Steve Allen *and returned to music, in this case rock and roll.*

I got an offer to go to New York to launch a show on NBC called *Hullabaloo.* I came with a very talented choreographer named David Winters, who had worked with me on our movie project *The T.A.M.I. Show* (which featured the Rolling Stones, James Brown and the Flames, and the Supremes). One of the first ideas I introduced was the notion of girls dancing in go-go cages, which I stole from the Whisky À Go-Go in Los Angeles. I also pushed the idea of using all of New York's top models in some of the songs, because I felt that would make an adult statement about contemporary rock and roll. But David and I also had to convince the producers that the show's appeal was to young people, moving it away from stand-up comics and marching bands (who were among the performers on the first program). The dancers were sensational, and both Michael Bennett and Donna MacKechnie were in the show's dance chorus.

After Hullabaloo *you went back west to help CBS resurrect the* Danny Kaye Show. *What was it like to work on a traditional prime-time variety show?*

Though you learn something new and positive from *every* experience, it was a horrible time. Basically, the problem was that Danny Kaye didn't respect me. Even though we started out with a wonderful relationship, the more creative I got, the more the antagonism grew. For example, we were once doing a musical parody of the poem "What is a Boy, What is a Girl," and I decided to shoot it as a remote out in Griffith Park. I went to great lengths to prepare it and organize it, and this was something that wasn't ordinarily done in studio-bound series. Shirley Jones was the guest, and she loved doing her sequence, which was shot separately from 9 in the morning until noon. Danny was going to do his part after lunch from 2 to 5. The choreography was all blocked out, and so were the camera moves from Shirley's part earlier in the day. All we had to do was rehearse Danny, but he was mad because he'd had to drive so far from the studio. I walked him through the blocking, and then he does one take, in which he makes three mistakes. I said let's do it again, but the stage manager said, "I don't think we're going to get him again," and the camera operator said "look at my camera" which showed him getting in his car and driving away. We had to air the segment as it was, mistakes and all. I told Danny's manager I would never do a remote with him again.

This would be your last series, after which you began working on specials. Was this a planned evolution?

I realized early in my career that movies are a director's medium, theater is a writer's medium, and television is a producer's medium. So I knew I had to become a hyphenate, though I knew little about producing, in order to have the power to direct the way I wanted to. That's why I began to say I won't direct unless you let me produce. I got my chance with a trilogy of specials—the first one was with Leslie Uggams, the second was with Petula Clark and Harry Belafonte, and the third was the Elvis Presley comeback special.

Let's talk about the second special, which made television history. Were you aware at the time in 1967 that your star pairing of Petula Clark and Harry Belafonte would turn into a racial controversy?

I was too young to really realize the impact. I had been raised to treat all people equally, and when I booked Harry on the show, he turned me down originally, saying he wasn't doing television anymore. Then he called me back and said, "Petula is that lady who's blond and blue-eyed?" I said yes, and he said he'd reconsidered and this might be a good special for him to do. So I called up Young & Rubicam, who was the ad agency for the show's sponsor, Plymouth. I phoned the agency rep, and I told him I'd just booked Harry Belafonte, and he was delighted. Then twenty minutes later he called me back and said he's just talked to Detroit and a guy from Plymouth named Doyle Lott, who was running the show, didn't want him on because, he announced off the record, Belafonte was black. I responded by saying that if he wasn't allowed on I was going to announce this "off-the-record" conversation to the press. He said he'd call me back. Twenty minutes later I got a call from Colgan Shlank who said "I'm the guy who just replaced so and so, and we've got to figure out a way to solve this problem intelligently."

They came back to me and said the contract for the show called for Petula Clark and guests and we had to find someone else to be with them. And I responded that if you can find someone else of Belafonte's caliber, I'd think about it. They began rattling off names like Milton Berle, Ray Bolger, and so forth and I wouldn't accept anybody. So the next thing that happened was that I was ordered off to Detroit to meet this Doyle Lott character and the president of Chrysler/Plymouth. I went into the meeting, surrounded by a bunch of people from Young & Rubicam, who had told me earlier they would support me if Plymouth wanted to back out of the commitment. Doyle Lott launches into his presentation that Belafonte was washed up, that he'd had no hit records in years. The guy from Plymouth turns to me and says what are your feelings and I told him that Belafonte was an icon, I'd grown up with him, and he's one of the greatest performers in the world. The reason he wasn't exposed is he didn't want to be overexposed. He asked if Petula was happy with him, and I said yes, so he turned to Doyle and said, "I'm going to override you and we're going to go ahead and do this special."

So right from the start you knew that this special was different. What was it like for you in the control room when, in an emotional moment, Petula Clark touched Belafonte's arm?

By this point everybody was at peace. At this point in time, the sponsors weren't allowed in the control room—they were off in a separate room with a monitor. It certainly wasn't like today where everybody, whether it's the studio executives, producers or the stars, tries to interfere and call the shots. Petula was performing an antiwar song called "Paths of Glory," which NBC objected to because of its theme, but which they finally allowed once I pointed out that Petula had written it herself. Harry was singing it with her, along with an ironic song written by Mason Williams which had been woven through the whole segment. We'd done three takes, but something just didn't sit right—it had been staged with Petula singing upstage of Harry and there didn't seem to be enough emotion. So

I stopped, left the control booth and went down to the stage—in fact, I now do most of my work on the stage, with a portable control booth next to me so I can spend my time working directly with the artists. I suggested that Petula walk directly down to Harry rather than stay upstage behind him. We rolled tape, and they began the duet next to each other, and all of a sudden I see a tear in Petula's eye, and then Harry's, and at the height of the chorus, she reaches out and touches Harry's forearm.

Right afterwards, a thundering herd of elephants gathered in the hallway, and an NBC executive popped his head in the control room and said the sponsor was furious and had just walked out of the building. Then I get another call from some higher ups at NBC, who'd been watching on the closed-circuit monitors, and they told me that whatever happens, they'd support me, which was great to hear. Instinctively, for whatever reason, I realized I had to get rid of those previous three takes, so I ran downstairs to the editing facility and demanded we erase the masters. The engineer was shaking and made me sign a release, but now all we had left was the take we'd just done.

It became the shot heard and seen round the world. *Newsweek* and *Time* came down to take pictures of it on the monitor, and it became an instant phenomenon. By the time it went on the air, the public had been warned to watch for "the fornication on the air of a black man and a white woman."

I didn't really grasp the impact right away, and when I got home I received an amusing call from the president of Chrysler/Plymouth, who I'd met earlier, telling me about all the humanitarian causes Chrysler had contributed to. There were all sorts of ramifications. Harry was going to go on the *The Tonight Show* and urge blacks to not buy Chrysler products. Petula had fled to Paris because she didn't want to be a part of the controversy. I also got a call from the president of Young & Rubicam who said, "Before we start talking, Steve, we must never let logic enter this conversation." To this day, it is my favorite quote, and is so applicable to my own career!

It really wasn't Chrysler's fault. It was this guy Doyle Lott. Years later when I was down south somebody handed me the official newsletter of the Ku Klux Klan, which had an article in it about how I had destroyed the reputation and the life of this solid American, and they really attacked me.

From this controversial special, you next went to a project that would be just as famous and much more important—the 1968 comeback special of Elvis Presley. What were its origins?

I've always had this approach that no matter what, I can always go back and work in my dad's gas station, so I've never really been intimidated. After the Petula special I was told by a lot of people that I would never be able to get a job in Hollywood again, which is probably why I got the call about Elvis. NBC needed to find somebody that Elvis could relate to, and there was nobody around. Bob Finkel, who was the executive producer at NBC called me and said we have this deal with Elvis for a special, but we don't ever think we'll get it made. Elvis called him "Mr. Finkel" and everyone else Mr. So-and-So, and he didn't seem to relate to anybody there. They asked if I would come and see if I could get things rolling.

At this point Elvis's career was virtually over.

Yes, he hadn't had a hit record in years and had stopped making movies. The P.R. machine was still going on, but there was really nothing happening. Bones Howe was my partner at this time, and was an established hit record producer, who I'd worked with on the audio for the Petula Clark special. Bones had worked with Elvis before, and convinced me to do the project, saying that if I'd meet him we'd really hit it off. So I arranged a meeting at my office with Bones and my writers Alan Bly and Chris Beard. Elvis and Colonel Parker and the entourage came in and right from the start it was "Hi, Elvis," "Hi, Steve," and we got along great. We didn't talk much about the program but more about life and the music business. We didn't really have a show to pitch him, but I did tell him that this program would be the third of a trilogy that our creative team (going back to *Hullabaloo*) would put together and that the show would be tailor-made to his music and his talents. He said it sounded great, and went off to Hawaii to get a tan and rest for a few weeks, and we went to work feverishly to come up with the concept. He came back, loved it all, and didn't want to change a thing. It was done like a one-camera film show, except for the mobile camera energy of the live performance segments. But the rest of the show was a book show, with the premise being Elvis's musical journey, which returned him at the end back to his roots.

We decided we would do all the rehearsing in our offices, rather than at NBC, so every day at 4 o'clock two Lincolns would pull into our garage—we were the only show business company in that building, so nobody knew what was going on. The entourage would play out in the lobby while we worked inside. When we finally did the show at NBC, Elvis decided to live out there, and we converted his big dressing room into living quarters. After rehearsals he would go there with a group of musicians and unwind. I would watch them every day having fun and thought to myself, we've got to tape this. So I went to Colonel Parker who said absolutely not, this boy is not going to be seen with his hair messed or sweaty. I kept pressuring him until he finally relented, but only if I promised him that he would be able to see it first and if he didn't like it, we wouldn't use it. He let us recreate the jam sessions on stage, which was not what I originally wanted, but it was at least a good compromise. It was the Colonel who suggested the audience be right there physically with Elvis, and I said great.

So the Colonel was now getting more involved and excited about your concept?

Not really. He was still off on the side. We had a lot of confrontations during that show, because what he had originally sold NBC was an Elvis Christmas special with no dialogue and twenty Christmas songs. I had to convince him that this would have absolutely no television impact. The Colonel was constantly on my case; when he liked me he would call me "Bindel," as sort of an internal joke, but when I was being reprimanded it was "Binder." On many occasions I would be called in to a meeting with the Colonel and Elvis, and Elvis would literally stand there with his head down. Once I was brought in and the Colonel said, "It has come to my attention that there are no Christmas songs in this show, Binder, and Elvis wants Christmas songs, don't you Elvis?" And Elvis would say, "Yes, sir." Then the Colonel said, "Is that understood?" and I said, "If that's what Elvis wants, that's what we'll do." And we would walk out of the room and Elvis would elbow me in the ribs and say "forget it, we're going to do it the way we're going to do it." We had two or three of those meetings.

Did the Colonel finally realize when the show aired that you had made the right decision?

He knew before. There were too many instances where he, I think, could have pulled the plug. Elvis loved the show; I knew that before it aired. He made me play it for him three or four times in a row after I showed him the edited version.

And NBC loved it?

NBC was incredibly concerned. They wanted guest stars on the show from the get-go. Nobody on prime-time had ever done a one-man show, but I was adamant that Elvis didn't need anybody but Elvis.

The network was also very concerned with the bordello scene, which really made me quite upset. I kept fighting them about it to the point that in order to appease me they brought someone from General Electric to make the final decision. So this guy, in suit and tie, arrives in the editing room. While they're cuing up the Elvis tape to look at the scene, he's watching Dean Martin on the next monitor performing a sketch from his show with Phil Harris and a six-foot blonde bombshell in a bikini basically doing an off-color joke without the punch line. The GE guy is laughing his head off, and I saw him and thought, this is going to be easy because our bordello scene isn't anything as risqué as that. Then he turns, watches our scene, and immediately orders it to be taken out of the show. So it was removed, but it came back in when they replayed the show and there were new people at NBC who were unaware there had even been a controversy over this thing.

NBC also didn't like the way Elvis looked in the improvisation scenes with his hair out of place and sweating.

You were one of the first TV directors to realize the importance of audio, and that sound on television needed to be approached the same way it was in the recording studio.

I knew the marriage was there, and that if I was going to be doing music on TV, the two worlds had to be merged. I had worked as an independent record producer with Bones Howe in the 1960s with Johnny Rivers' record company, working with the Fifth Dimension, and in 1973 I started my own record company, TA Records, a division of Talent Associates, which launched Seals and Croft. But I always realized at the time that TV audio engineers were nowhere near the level of engineers found in the recording world. At first I would bring in sound engineers to work as consultants—that's how I brought in Bones Howe for the Petula Clark special—and little by little, they started to slide into the seats of the audio guys on television, once it was recognized they were not the enemy and that they were there to make it better.

I found this same formula in lighting. I took rock and roll lighting directors and had them consult with TV lighting directors in order to make the look more contemporary, and it's really worked once people start recognizing they're on the same team.

During the 1970s you continued with a number of influential specials, including the 10th Anniversary of Rolling Stone *magazine, four Emmy Awards telecasts, and the first of what would be many specials with Diana Ross. Then in 1982 you worked with her again on the award-winning cablecast of her concert from Central Park. What logistical problems did that present?*

Actually, Diana and I go back all the way to *The T.A.M.I. Show* in 1965; she's a fabulous person to work with. Paramount and Showtime were the executive producers, and Diana was the producer and she'd asked me to direct. I said yes and came to New York to meet her. She'd bought a beautiful building for her offices on Sixth Avenue and when I arrived there were about 200 people there, including the NYPD, the Parks Commissioner, and the concert promoter. She'd bought a new business suit for the occasion and looked fantastic and was greeted by wild applause as she entered. She thanked us and told us how great it was to be here and how exciting this event was going to be, and then said, "If you have any questions, ask Steve Binder."

I'd been worried about how to make a two-hour concert program on one stage visually interesting, but luckily Tony Walton came up with a brilliant backdrop, which used a sailing mast so that flags could be raised and lowered to subtly change the backdrop. I'd spent some time watching most of the previous Central Park concerts, such as Barbra Streisand's and Simon and Garfunkel's, and I felt that other than the opening and closing credits, you never knew you were in New York. I wanted to make sure you could see the skyline of New York throughout the entire show in the wide shots. I also wanted to capture the intimacy of a small club, so I literally put cameras on dollies and small cranes physically on the stage with her.

I brought Diana out to see the environment the night before, because I always feel it's important to make the artist feel comfortable with their performing "turf." She walked out there on the stage, and saw the two big camera cranes staring at her in the face, and told me we've got to do something about them. I didn't think much about it, until ten minutes later she told me, "I'm serious, we've got to get rid of them." I told her they were "money" cameras, and if I could think of any way to get rid of them, I would, but they're important as a way for the worldwide audience to see her. Ten minutes later, Barry Diller, who was then the president of Paramount, came over to me and said, "Steve, I know you're really bright, and I know you can figure out a way to get rid of those cameras. It's really upsetting her." I assured him that there was nothing I wanted to do more in life at this moment than to please him and Diana, but there was no way I could get rid of those cameras.

I went back to my hotel room, and Diana comes to see me, and I could tell she was incredibly distraught. And she said, "Steve, the audience at Central Park won't be able to see me." I tried to assure her with a million people in the park, she'd never even realize they were even there and how important those cameras were for her sake, but she ordered me to get rid of them anyway. I told her that if that was true, I was leaving.

Next morning, I have to go shoot the show, and she's there, cheery, excited, kisses and hugs, as if nothing has ever happened. We go on to shoot the show, and I realized what it was—every artist, especially faced with the prospect of facing a million people, is tremendously frightened. And she needed something to focus her anxieties on. The whole show turned out to be incredible fun.

And let's not forget that this was the concert where torrential rains began falling five minutes after she began singing.

And we had to throw out my carefully prepared 300-page shooting script. Still, I knew where all the cameras were, and I knew her well enough to anticipate what she would be doing. We ended up winning a Cable Ace award for my direction of the show. Lucky for us, the rainstorm added excitement to the event and made it also an international news story!

When I came into television, the typical musical artist was told when they came on the floor that there was a mark on the floor where the back light, and the fill light and the key light is and that's where you begin. And when you get to the chorus, you can walk over there, where there's another lighting setup. My goal was to free them up from all of that. When Elvis went into the boxing ring, I said do what you want to do. I'm going to have you on camera no matter where you go. It was the same thing with the Central Park concert. Here's your stage—do whatever you want to do on it.

So your job as a director is to provide artists with a free stage for their own creativity?

Absolutely. My job is to make anybody look as great as they can look without getting in their way when they're performing live. But I can enhance their performance if they trust me, because we're not working against each other, we're working together for the best results. It's a true collaboration.

I'm supposed to be there as the objective eyes, as a sort of father figure. If artists trust you, you can do great things with them. If they don't understand why or what they're doing, my job is to help them figure it out and guide them away from what they're not supposed to do. If they don't trust you, if they make you feel insecure, you have nothing to give them.

I'm not a dictator. If anybody says to me, "I'm uncomfortable," I immediately say, "then don't do it," and I'll figure out another way to do the same thing.

As if a concert in the rain weren't enough, in 1996 you staged a Diana Ross Super Bowl halftime show with your star leaving the stage by helicopter.

Actually, that was easy, because we were operating totally on adrenaline. NBC wouldn't set up a separate control room environment for us, so we had to use the sports truck. It became like a fire drill where everyone working the Super Bowl had to get up at the halftime break and rush out while we rushed in.

The sports booth was not like the drama or variety booths I had known; there were probably 100 monitors. When I arrived in Phoenix and looked at the environment I said there was no possible way, even though I was trained as a live television director, that I would know which monitor to look for since they were all over the place and so many. So I asked the technical director to put every monitor I wasn't using to black, and then I did mock-ups on 8 x 10 sheets of paper of the control room layout, and for the next week my assistant director and my technical director and I practiced the shots in our hotel room. By the time we actually shot it, it was automatic because we'd rehearsed it so many times.

The helicopter exit was quite an event—we had to practice it about five times with Diana, and twenty-five times without her. Everybody was there to monitor us, including the NFL and the FAA. Even after we did it, I said we never should have done it, just thinking of what a disaster it would have been if anything had gone wrong. We had to tell the stadium audience in advance that it was going to happen because we didn't want them to think it was a sudden terrorist attack like the movie *Black Sunday*.

What do you see as the current state of music and variety specials?

Generally speaking, when I talk to my contemporaries and my peers, I find that nobody is ordering anything new that would give people a chance to show their talent. I think an entire generation is out there chomping at the bit to get some opportunities, but somebody is going to have to open the door again. Unfortunately directors getting started today don't get the opportunity to learn from the kind of experiences I had coming up the ranks. Now, with cameras, it's mostly point and shoot. Everybody has a place to point to, and there's very little use of dollies or cranes. The zoom lens should be blown up, and we should go back to multiple lenses and turrets, if only to know what you can do with each type of lens. I try to avoid zoom moves, and if we can dolly, we dolly, if we can track, we track, or crane.

Still, everything is cyclical, and there's got a be an innovative way to present variety. Music on TV works, I don't care what any programmer says. We live with music twenty-four hours a day, seven days a week, all of our lives. It's the way it's being packaged that's not working.

This interview took place at the Rhiga Hotel in New York in Janaury 1998. It originally appeared in Television Quarterly, Vol. XIX, No. 3, 1998.

INDEX

About the Author

Brian Rose is a professor in the Department of Communication and Media Studies at Fordham University. He is the author of *Television and the Performing Arts* and *Televising the Performing Arts*, and the editor of *TV Genres* (all published by Greenwood Press).